» ABOUT THE FORUM ON THE ENTERTAINMENT & SPORTS INDUSTRIES

The Forum's mission is to educate lawyers in the legal principles and transactional aspects of entertainment and sports law; to provide a platform for the discussion of issues affecting these fields, and to foster excellence in the practice of law in these fields. The forum is governed by a seven-member governing committee. Because of the diverse subjects covered by the forum, the governing committee created the following divisions: Interactive Media and New Technologies; Literary Publishing; Litigation; Merchandising and Licensing; Motion Pictures, Television, Cable, and Radio; Music and Personal Appearances; Sports; Theater and Performing Arts; and Visual Arts.

Kirk T Schroder	Chair
Christine Lepera	Chair-Elect
Lionel S Sobel	Immediate Past Chair
Todd Brabec	Governing Committee Member
Cynthia Sanchez	Governing Committee Member
Robert A Rosenbloum	Governing Committee Member
Deborah Lynn Spander	Governing Committee Member
Howard Jay Wiener	Budget Chair

» A NOTE FROM THE FORUM

Welcome to the new book series presented by the ABA Forum on the Entertainment & Sports Industries. This series will feature practical titles for creative artists, athletes, legal practitioners, and others working throughout the arts, entertainment and sports industries. We are delighted to launch this series with *The American Bar Association's Legal Guide to Independent Filmmaking* by Michael C. Donaldson and Lisa A. Callif. This book exemplifies the purpose of the new series—to present concise treatments of arts, entertainment and sports law topics from a "real world" business perspective. *The American Bar Association's Legal Guide to Independent Filmmaking* takes readers step-by-step through the filmmaking process from "idea" to "delivery" with proven strategies based on genuine industry standards. The book is full of realistic advice, useful forms, incisive commentary, tables and resources. Michael C. Donaldson and Lisa Callif are representative of the caliber of authors writing for this series—Donaldson is a leading Los Angeles entertainment attorney with more than 30 years experience working on films by such industry luminaries as Oliver Stone, Davis Guggenheim and Lawrence Bender; Callif's practice focuses on film financing, distribution, and clearances including work on many documentaries, such as "Daniel Ellsberg and The Pentagon Papers," nominated for an Academy Award®. On behalf of the Forum's book program Editorial Board—Lon Sobel, Eric S. Brown, and Vered N. Yakovee—I would like to thank the authors for writing such a practical and timely book.

SAN FRANCISCO
2010

ROBERT G. PIMM
Book Publishing Chair
ABA Forum on the Entertainment
and Sports Industries

ABA Forum on the Entertainment & Sports Industries
Kirk T. Schroder, Chair
http://www.abanet.org/forums/entsports/

Entertainment and Sports Lawyer
A Quarterly Publication
Vered N. Yakovee, Editor-in-Chief
http://www.abanet.org/Forums/entsports/Pages/esl.aspx

» ADVANCE PRAISE FOR *THE AMERICAN BAR ASSOCIATION'S LEGAL GUIDE TO INDEPENDENT FILMMAKING*

You need talent to make a great independent film. This book covers all the rest—none the less important. Sustaining a career is knowing all the ropes and this book will show you them all . . . including the ones that can trip you up. I love that it was laid out in a way that even a novice like me can figure it out.

—John Cooper, Director, Sundance Film Festival

Donaldson & Callif really helped me and my team get through a lot of complicated legal issues on *Countdown to Zero*. Much thanks to you!"
—Lawrence Bender, Producer (*Inglourious Basterds*, *Kill Bill*, *Inconvenient Truth*)

I love working with Donaldson & Callif. They take a really practical approach to resolving legal issues, which is reflected in this book.

—Adrian Grenier, Actor/Director

I highly recommend this book to all filmmakers. It's filled with really useful forms and negotiating tips.

—Jason Blum, Producer (*Paranormal Activity*)

This book makes clear what can be awfully daunting for any filmmaker. And—in a time when taking control of the destiny of one's film is more critical than ever—this book can be a filmmaker's lifesaver.

—Dawn Hudson, Executive Director, Film Independent

I wish I had this book when I embarked on my first film. It clearly lays out the basic legal points necessary to get a film done and ready to be delivered.

—Jeffrey Levy-Hinte, Producer (*The Kids Are All Right*,
Roman Polanski: Wanted and Desired)

This desperately needed *ABA Legal Guide* details agreements, releases, rights, and more as it clearly explains the independent filmmaking process from story acquisition to final copyright. Experienced and inexperienced filmmakers will save their sanity and money thanks to this superb resource. What problems this book will solve!

—Diane Carson, Current Past-President, University Film and Video Association

[*The American Bar Association's Legal Guide to Independent Filmmaking*] is an invaluable and authoritative resource for both professional and student movie makers. Short of hiring Donaldson and Callif, this book is a filmmaker's best way to learn all the varied legal strategies involved in making movies; as such it is a veritable road map for both the novice and the experienced professional who requires up-to-date legal facts and forms, as well as expert professional legal advice.

—Frank P. Tomasulo, Ph.D., Adjunct Full Professor, Independent Film, City College of New York, City University of New York

Donaldson & Callif helped us navigate the tricky waters of getting *I'm Still Here* made and insured so we could secure distribution. They know every corner of entertainment law, every shade of grey.

—Casey Affleck, Actor/Director

This invaluable and detailed guide is such a perennial resource, you'll want to thank the book for not charging you by the hour.

—Eddie Schmidt, President, International Documentary Association/Producer (*This Film Is Not Yet Rated*)

Every filmmaker needs a copy of this book, because it solves problems before they start. Thank you, Michael and Lisa!

—Pat Aufderheide, University Professor, School of Communication, American University

THE AMERICAN BAR ASSOCIATION'S

LEGAL GUIDE TO INDEPENDENT FILMMAKING

THE AMERICAN BAR ASSOCIATION'S

LEGAL GUIDE TO INDEPENDENT FILMMAKING

MICHAEL C. DONALDSON
AND LISA A. CALLIF

AMERICAN BAR ASSOCIATION

**Forum on the
Entertainment & Sports
Industries**

Printed in the United States of America.

18 17 16 15 14   9 8 7 6 5

Library of Congress Cataloging-in-Publication Data

Donaldson, Michael C.
  The American Bar Association's legal guide to independent filmmaking / Michael C. Donaldson and Lisa A. Callif. — 1st ed.
      p. cm.
  Includes index.
  ISBN 978-1-61632-044-7
  1. Independent filmmakers—Legal status, laws, etc.—United States.
2. Motion pictures—Law and legislation—United States. 3. Intellectual property—United States. 4. Copyright—Motion pictures—United States.
5. Motion pictures—Production and direction—United States. I. Callif, Lisa A. II. American Bar Association. III. Title.
  KF4298.D66 2010
  343.73'078791433—dc22

                                                                    2010041516

Discounts are available for books ordered in bulk. Special consideration is given to state bars, CLE programs, and other bar-related organizations. Inquire at Book Publishing, ABA Publishing, American Bar Association, 321 North Clark Street, Chicago, Illinois 60654-7598.

www.ShopABA.org

Dedication

To independent filmmakers everywhere who fight the good fight, tell their stories with integrity, and enrich our lives.

Table of Contents

Acknowledgments   *xiii*

Introduction   *xv*

Chapter 1
The Lightbulb Moment   *1*

You Have a Great Idea for a Movie   *1*

You Want to Base Your Film on an Existing Property   *2*

Form 1.01: Option and Purchase Agreement   *2*

You Want to Base Your Film on Someone's Life Story   *15*

Form 1.02: Life Story Rights Agreement   *16*

Getting the Script You Want   *27*

   Optioning a Script   *27*

Form 1.03: Option and Purchase Agreement   *27*

   Writing the Script—With or Without a Partner   *39*

Form 1.04: Collaboration Agreement   *39*

   Hiring Someone Else to Write Your Script   *46*

Form 1.05: Writer Agreement   *46*

Marketing Your Film   *58*

Chapter 2
Who Is Going to Pay for All This?   *59*

Fictitious Names   *59*
Forming a Business Entity   *60*

Form 2.01: Operating Agreement   *61*
All Papered Up and No One to Go To   *78*
Tax Incentives   *78*
Pre-sales   *78*
Bank Financing   *79*

Chapter 3
Assembling the Talent   *81*

Work-For-Hire Provisions   *82*
Union vs. Nonunion   *82*
Working Conditions   *83*
Residuals   *84*
Reuse Fees   *84*
Director   *84*

Form 3.01: Director's Agreement   *85*
Casting Director   *100*

Form 3.02: Casting Director Services Agreement   *101*
Actors Agreement (Direct Hire)   *105*

Form 3.03: Actor Services Agreement   *106*
Contracts with Minors   *115*
Composer   *115*

Form 3.04: Composer Agreement   *116*

Chapter 4
Principal Photography   *125*

Getting Through the Shoot   *125*

Form 4.01: Crew Deal Memo   *126*
Music Supervisors   *133*

Form 4.02: Music Supervisor Agreement   *133*
Locations   *140*

Form 4.03: Location Agreement   *141*
Props and Material Releases   *145*
Finding the Copyright Holder   *145*

Form 4.04: Materials Release   146

Crowds and Public Filming   148

Form 4.05: Public Filming Notice   148

Written Releases   149

Form 4.06: Interview Release   149

Form 4.07: Individual Release   151

Chapter 5
Distribution   153

Producer's Representative   154

Foreign Sales Agent   155

Domestic Distributor   156

Do You Need a Producer's Rep,
   Foreign Sales Agent, or a Distributor?   156

How to Choose with Whom to Work?   157

All-Rights Deals vs. Split Rights Deals   158

   All-Rights Deal   158

   Split Rights Deal   159

Digital Rights   161

Digital Rights Distributor/Aggregator   162

Theatrical Releases   163

   Bookers   163

   Servicing Deal   163

One-Night Events   168

Split Rights Wrap Up   171

Negotiating Tips   171

Chapter 6
Delivery   181

Chain of Title   182

E&O Insurance   182

   Title Report   183

Script Clearance Report   186

Copyright Report   189

Registering Copyright of Your Completed Film   189

   The eCO Portal   189

   Title of the Film   190

   Publication   190

   Author/Copyright Claimant   190

Limitations of Claim—Inclusions / Exclusions   *191*

Reviewing Your Submission   *191*

Submitting Copies of Your Work   *191*

Schedule of Delivery Items Required   *193*

Lab Access Letter   *196*

Completing Delivery   *192*

Index   *199*

About the Authors   *203*

Acknowledgments

First we need to thank our dedicated, hard-working associate Dean Cheley. Dean came to Donaldson & Callif as an experienced lawyer. One of his first assignments was to help prepare this book. He worked on it as hard as we did, maybe harder. If there were justice in the world, he would have some credit on the cover. Short of that, we give our huge thanks and much appreciation for lots of hard work that produced a job well done. Lisa Le Blanc, our loyal assistant, worked tirelessly—sometimes on weekends—to make sure we got the manuscript to the ABA somewhere close to the deadline. Our two outstanding summer interns, Brianna Dahlberg and Melissa Radin, read over the entire book and fine-tuned it before it was turned over to our amazingly patient editor, Erin Nevius. Of course, we have to thank our associate, Chris Perez, who helped tremendously in putting the book together, and our office support staff, Lamar Williams and Chris Lee, who took up the slack while we turned our attention to this book. We also want to thank the people who generously agreed to spend time with us to discuss their expertise about film and give us additional insight on the business aspect of making movies: Brian J. Terwilliger, Eric d'Arbeloff, Christine O'Malley, and Sam Eigen. You all helped make this book a really practical guide, rich with interesting examples. And we know there are a phalanx of designers, proofreaders, typesetters, marketers, and other folks at the American Bar Association who were essential to getting this book from our computer into your hands. They all deserve our heartiest thanks. And thanks to Marlan Willardson who worked so hard to get the word out about this book.

Like all other authors, we want to thank our families. Michael's daughters, Michelle, Amy, and Wendy, together with their families (husbands Ray and John and sons Soul, Caden, and Canyon), were cheerleaders throughout, as well as his partner, Tim Kittleson. Lisa's husband, Dustin, and son, Diggy, continually lent their support throughout this process.

Introduction

Welcome to *The American Bar Association's Legal Guide to Independent Filmmaking*.

This book has been prepared under the auspices of the American Bar Association to provide an authoritative guide through the legal morass of producing an independent film, from the moment you get the crazy idea to do such a thing, through financing, development, principal photography, distribution, and the too-often overlooked subject of delivery.

Each chapter contains a general road map for the phase of filmmaking covered by that chapter including the relevant forms and contracts for that phase of production. The contracts come with plenty of background and some selected negotiating tips. This book is NOT intended to substitute for hiring a lawyer. This book is intended to make you a better consumer of legal services. The more you know, the better you and your lawyer will get along, the further your legal dollars will stretch, and the happier everyone will be.

» WHO NEEDS TO READ THIS BOOK?

The book is written as though we were talking to a producer of an independent film. The prime audience is the production team on any picture.

Writers and directors will find this book very helpful in understanding their contracts, their place in the overall production, and how others on the film fit into the picture. Distributors will also benefit from a clear understanding of all the contracts that ought to be in place in order for a film to be ready for distribution.

All too often, books such as this assume that the reader already knows the fundamentals. This book does not assume anything. We discuss each step in the filmmaking process. If it relates to the legal or business aspect of getting an independent film made, it's in here somewhere.

The mission of this book is to help you negotiate from a position of strength and complete your film with agreements that will last.

This book is for you whether you are:

- Beginning a career and want to impress your employer and colleagues with your filmmaking know-how;
- Just looking to brush up your skills; or
- A producer, director, writer, investor, or distributor involved in making a movie or if you work for one of those folks.

» HOW TO USE THIS BOOK

Think of this book as your friend and coach, someone to go to when you have a question. Every page contains information that can help you. Work at your own pace but keep going. Even five minutes a day makes a difference.

The business of making a film goes through four distinct phases. Acquiring and developing a property is always the genesis of any film. Someone has an idea for the next great American hit. Unfortunately, that is the phase where many filmmakers think they don't need a lawyer or a contract. They will just hold hands, sing kumbaya and go into the sunset to make a film. Not always so.

Financing a film often bridges the two other phases in terms of timing, but it deserves its own chapter in any book on getting a film made. Principal photography is the most visible, notorious phase of filmmaking. Everyone likes to gather around outdoor sets and watch the action—as slow as it might be. Finally, distribution is the holy grail of filmmaking and something that you need think about right from the beginning, especially delivery obligations, to which we dedicate an entire chapter.

Chapter 1: Acquiring and Developing a Property

There are several basic ways that a project gets started: You may purchase a script; write it with someone or hire someone to write it for you; or perhaps you read a book or short story that you want to adapt for the big screen. Whether you purchase someone else's script or create your own, you may need to acquire some underlying rights, most often life-story rights or adaptation rights.

The purpose of this chapter is to get you started on solid footing. Too many folks want to move forward on the creative side of things without taking care of the fundamental agreement between or among the folks who are involved. They will "take care of that stuff later;" they think, "we're all friends;" or worse, "we are all working so well together now, I don't want to upset the apple cart." We've heard it all.

Our experience is loaded with problems that grow out of this attitude. If no one is clear about the roles, the ultimate control of a project, and the ultimate vision for the life of the project, people will almost certainly develop different expectations. When the visions finally clash, hurt feelings turn to anger and then lawsuits. Useless, needless lawsuits that would never have happened if folks had taken care of business at the beginning.

Chapter 2: Financing Your Film

Too often, no thought is given to this phase until the script is completed. It is a good idea to have a plan to finance your film even as you prepare the script. This chapter deals with the basic business decisions you will need to make before you produce your film, whether it is through a corporation, a limited partnership, or working as an individual. However, most folks end up using a single-purpose production entity in the form of a Limited Liability Company (LLC). That is what this chapter is primarily about.

This chapter also addresses raising money through equity financing in its own separate section. You would be crazy to try to do this without the aid and comfort of a good attorney to help you. Every state has its own laws and federal laws apply too. This is no game for amateurs.

Chapter 3: Putting Together the Team

You need to have a number of agreements in place before anyone says "roll film." This chapter is broken into groups of contracts that have similarities. Often the first hires are the director and a casting director. The next and most obvious grouping is for the talent agreements that you will need for actors and their union agreements.

Chapter 4: Principal Photography

This chapter covers several other contracts that are much simpler in nature: crew deal memos, the related union contracts, location agreements, and more. Various rental agreements for equipment and space are also discussed. Chapter 4 is also the chapter that covers production insurance—general liability and worker's comp.

Chapter 5: Distribution

Here we will discuss the various methods and channels of distribution both domestic and foreign. We'll define who the players are in the distribution phase of filmmaking and discuss the many ways you can exploit your film. The majority of this chapter is focused on split rights deals as that's the direction we see many of our clients heading.

Chapter 6: Delivery

This chapter covers a topic that many filmmakers do not think about or budget for: delivery of the film. Not taking this into account at the early stages can cause consternation and lots of extra expenditure at the end of the process. This chapter will discuss the technical delivery requirements in a general way and the legal requirements specifically. Chain of title, errors and omissions insurance, title reports, script clearance reports and copyright reports will all be covered in this chapter.

» OTHER GOOD STUFF IN THE BOOK

Throughout the book, you will notice little boxes with gray shading. These reference other resources, mostly books that you can use for more information on a particular subject. This book is a starter primer and overall guide. It would take ten volumes to go into every subject in detail. We would rather point you in the right direction to books we know and use.

Each chapter contains the forms and contracts you will need for the subjects covered in that chapter. Most contracts have boxes that are not part of the contracts and won't be found on the disc that comes with this book. These boxes contain either a comment or a tip. The comments are meant to expand and explain a provision. They provide you with some background. The tips are to help you negotiate the provisions common in these agreements.

» WHERE TO GO FROM HERE

Look through the book to get an overview of the process of getting a film from an idea in your head to the silver screen. Then find which part or chapter is of immediate concern to you. That is the best place to begin.

Most people won't start in the area in which they need the most help. They usually choose their favorite area—the area about which they are confident. That's okay. Even your strongest area can get stronger. Then, as you shift your focus to your weaker areas, you'll enjoy the greatest amount of progress.

The most important point to consider right now is that you're already headed toward the winner's circle. The most successful people in life are those who continue to grow. The fact that you have this book in your hand now puts you into that realm. It's not how much you know that counts, but how much you are willing to add after you "know it all."

THE LIGHTBULB MOMENT

» YOU HAVE A GREAT IDEA FOR A MOVIE

What is the first thing you should do?

Write it down.

Copyright law does not exist to protect ideas. Copyright law only protects the "expression of an idea that is fixed in a tangible form." This means that written words are protectable; the ideas behind them aren't. You can't own an idea that is in the air, but once you put pen to paper, those words are yours.

That is why you should write up your ideas for movies. You obtain legal and business protection for your idea in direct proportion to how much of your idea you write down. The more detail the better. What you do next depends on your idea. We'll discuss all the possibilities: films based on existing properties, purchasing completed scripts, writing your own or writing with someone, and hiring a writer to do all this work for you.

No matter what path you travel, the more you develop your idea on your own, without collaborators, the better off you will be to move forward. It's like the rest of life: those who work harder reap greater rewards. Try to write up a detailed treatment or synopsis – a brief summary or outline of the entire story as you see it playing out. Once you do that, it's a good idea to register your treatment or synopsis with the Writers Guild of America. You can do this online at www.wga.org. This provides you with an indisputable record of what you developed and when without making a public record of it at this early stage, which would be the case if you registered your material with the Copyright Office.

» YOU WANT TO BASE YOUR FILM ON AN EXISTING PROPERTY

Assume that your idea is to base a script for a film on a book, a play or a magazine article. Generally, the copyright owner of the book, play or magazine article controls the film rights to that property. You have to identify and contact the owner for permission, which usually involves a discussion about money. Rarely can you (or do you want to) pay the entire purchase price of those rights before you even have a script or the commitment of a financier. That is why producers option the property. An option is the exclusive right to purchase something in the future, on fixed terms and conditions.

You offer a small cash amount to the owner of the property. This guarantees that you (the filmmaker/option holder) can purchase the film rights in the future, under certain specified conditions and that no one else will be able to purchase the property. You can think of it as buying time.

No matter what kind of property you are optioning, the important thing is to always, always get it in writing. *Use this form.*

Form 1.01: Option and Purchase Agreement

OPTION AND PURCHASE AGREEMENT—UNDERLYING RIGHTS

THIS AGREEMENT, effective as of _____, ____, is made by and between _____ [name of producer] ("Producer") whose address is [PHYSICAL ADDRESS] and _____ [name of owner] ("Owner") whose address is [PHYSICAL ADDRESS] concerning the rights to a _____ [e.g., book, play, unpublished story] entitled "_____" and the materials upon which it is based. The following terms and conditions shall apply:

> **Date:** By using an effective date right at the beginning of the contract, you eliminate disputes over when a contract was signed and therefore when an option lapses. Few contracts are signed by all parties on the same day, so use any date you like as the effective date.

> **Producer:** You, as the filmmaker, are the "Producer."

> **Owner:** The author of the book or his/her publishing company is the "Owner," as in an owner of the rights you want to acquire. If there is more than one owner/author, be sure to list all of them here and have all of them sign as parties to the deal.

1. DEFINITION OF "WORK": For purposes of this Agreement, "Work" means the _____ [book/play/magazine article] entitled "_____" written by _____ and any and all other literary materials, titles, themes, formats, formulas, incidents, action, story, dialogue, ideas, plots, phrases, slogans, catchwords, art, designs, compositions, sketches, drawings, characters, characterizations, names, and trademarks now contained therein, as well as such elements as may at any time hereafter be added or incorporated therein, and all versions thereof in any form.

> **Background: Pick the best description of the property you are optioning. If there was a previous title, include that also by saying, "and previously entitled _____." If the Work has been registered with the Copyright Office, you might give that registration number by way of further identification. In the list of included items, be sure to include characters.**

2. GRANT OF OPTION: In consideration of the mutual promises contained herein, and the payment to Owner of $_____(the "Option Price"), which shall be applicable against the Purchase Price, Owner hereby grants to Producer the exclusive, irrevocable right and option (the "Option") for _____ months (the "Option Period") to acquire the exclusive motion picture, television, videocassette, and all subsidiary, allied, and ancillary rights in and to the Work pursuant to the terms set forth below.

> **HINT: You want the option price to be as low as possible. Sometimes you can even negotiate a free period. Do not be surprised if you run into someone (like me) who says: "No Free Option!" That is my mantra when representing the owner of a property, although I obtain "free" options all the time for my independent producer clients. My argument: It's not "free"! My client will be working, writing (maybe), (if not) hiring someone to write, shopping the project, and generally spending time, effort, and money on the project.**

> **HINT: Since you do not have the deep pockets of a studio, your first job is to convince the author of your passion for the work. Listen to the author's dreams and hopes. You will be the protector of those dreams and hopes. As self-serving as it may sound, it truly is not about the money at the option stage. Except in big studio deals for hot properties, the initial payment is simply not large enough to be the most important aspect of the deal. The likelihood of the film getting made is the important thing. However, the emotional hook—the sizzle that closes your negotiation—can be a simple promise from you: "If you entrust your property to me, I will be as faithful to your work as possible. I will keep you advised every step of the way, and I will do my best to protect you."**

3. EXTENSION OF OPTION:

(a)   Producer shall have the right to extend the Option Period for one (1) period of _____ months for $_____ which shall be non-applicable against the Purchase Price. For the right to the extension of the first Option Period there must be one of the following:

      (i)   letter of commitment to direct from an established director;

      (ii)   the project is set up at a company, major studio, or mini-major studio able to fund the project;

      (iii) substantial negotiations in progress for complete financing of the film;

      (iv)   letter of commitment to act in the film from one star;

or

      (v)   a full-length feature-film script has been completed.

(b)   Producer shall have the right to extend the Option Period for one (1) additional _____ month period for $_____ which shall be non-applicable against the Purchase Price. In order to have a right to a second extension, Producer must secure at least two (2) of the above five (5) items.

Background: It is standard that you have the right to extend the option. The extension period is typically the same length as the option period. This is important because it takes a very long time to get a film made. Even three years total is a short time. Inexperienced producers often think that they will get their movie made more quickly than anybody else. Based on what? Be realistic. Writers are reluctant to have their material off the market for a long period of time. Frequently, the amounts paid for the second and third years are substantially higher than the amount paid for the initial period . . . and they are non-applicable.

Background: The terms "applicable" and "non-applicable" refer to whether subsequent option payments apply or do not apply to the final purchase price, and are often a point of negotiation. The initial payment is usually applicable (i.e., deductible). More often than not, additional option payments are not deducted from the purchase price and are therefore labeled non-applicable. The money must be paid before the time elapses under the current option. This payment acts to keep the option open for the extended period of time. If you let your option expire, you no longer have any right to buy the work or to extend the option. The original owner is then free to option the work to another party.

Background: One way to soften the length of time and/or to get more time is to have your right to renew the option be a result of progress made on the film. That is the approach used above. But do not make those barriers too high. The last sentences of Subparagraph (a) and Subparagraph (b) might work for you—though you don't have to include them in your first draft. If no such demand is made, you can strike this language. (Be sure to tailor the language to your needs.) No studio ever makes this kind of deal. Studios simply pay option prices. Therefore, if you use this approach, you must provide alternatives if the project is set up at a studio. After that, the option may be renewed with a cash payment only.

4. EXERCISE OF OPTION: Producer may exercise this Option at any time during the Option Period, as it may be extended, by giving written notice of such exercise to Owner and delivery to Owner of the minimum Purchase Price as set forth below. In the event Producer does not exercise said Option during the period as it may be extended, this Agreement shall be of no further force or effect whatsoever. All rights granted hereunder become property of Owner. Upon exercise of the Option, Producer shall have the right to file the Assignment, Exhibit A, with the Copyright Office.

Background: This paragraph is what gives you the ability to purchase the rights you have optioned. It is standard.

5. PENDING EXERCISE OF OPTION: Producer shall have the right to engage in all customary development and pre-production activities during the Option Period as it may be extended.

HINT: The fact that you optioned the film rights infers this to be true. Stating the fact clearly is better. Often people add "including but not limited to" and then go on for a page or two. That's overkill.

6. GRANT OF RIGHTS: Effective upon Producer's exercise of the Option, Writer hereby exclusively sells, grants and assigns to Producer, Producer's successors, licenses and assigns all rights in and to the Work not reserved by Writer, throughout the universe, in perpetuity, in any and all media and by any means now known or hereafter devised, including, without limitation, all forms of theatrical and non-theatrical distribution and exhibition (including without limitation, free broadcast, pay television, cable, subscription, pay-per-view, video-on-demand, DVD and Internet), including without limitation the following: all motion picture rights, including the right to make remakes, new versions or adaptations of the Work or any part thereof; to make series and serials of the Work or any part thereof; the right, for advertising and publicity purposes only, to prepare, broadcast, exhibit and publish in any form or media, any synopses, excerpts, novelizations, serializations, dramatizations, summaries and stories of the Work, or any part thereof; and all rights of every kind and character whatsoever in and to the Work and all the characters and elements contained therein.

> **Background:** This is exactly what you are purchasing. This is why you are making the payments. This paragraph can also run on for pages, but the above is all-inclusive. It puts the burden on the Owner to be specific about reserved rights. Reserved rights are those rights which the owner retains. They typically include literary rights and often life story rights. See below.

> **HINT:** Some Owners want to approve the final script. The studio will not allow the author of the book to have approval over the screenplay. In fact, a studio will not allow you to have the final approval over the screenplay. Do not make this type of promise to a writer. At most, you can allow the Owner to read the final shooting script and to have a short period of consultation.

> **HINT:** If you obtain sequel rights at the same time you buy the film rights—as you always should—you can take any story character out of the film and use that character in another film. The author of the book usually retains the right to write a sequel to the book being optioned. Comic books always retain that right. Note that the language here says that you also purchased the film rights to the characters. A very sharp owner will not allow you to own the characters without a hefty additional payment.

7. PURCHASE PRICE: As consideration for all rights and property herein granted, and all warranties and covenants herein made by Owner, Producer agrees to pay Owner the following sums not later than the commencement of principal photography of a production:

(a) $_____ if the final budget for the motion picture (less contingencies, financing costs, and bank fees) based on the Work does not exceed two million dollars ($2,000,000), less any moneys paid as option exercise money and less the option payment for the initial period;

(b)   If the final budget exceeds two million dollars ($2,000,000), one percent (1%) of the final budget for the motion picture (less contingencies, financing costs, and bank fees) based on the Work less any amounts paid for option exercise; however, in no event shall the amount of such payment exceed fifty-thousand dollars ($50,000).

> **Purchase Price:** Price can be a flat fee or a percentage of the film's budget, or a combination. Most film budgets allow up to 2.5% of the budget for purchase of the underlying rights, with a floor and ceiling. The floor is the minimum price you pay, regardless of the budget. The ceiling is the maximum price you pay, regardless of the budget.

8. ADDITIONAL COMPENSATION:

(a)   **Contingent Compensation:** Producer also agrees to pay Owner ___ percent (__%) of one hundred percent (100%) of the producer's share of proceeds from any production based on the Work for which Owner receives any other payment under this Agreement. "Producer's Share of Proceeds" shall be defined, accounted for, and paid in the same manner for Owner as for Producer, whether Producer's contingent compensation is called Net Profits, Adjusted Gross Profits, or otherwise.

> **HINT:** "Net Profits" have gotten a bad name. Try using "Contingent Compensation." The language in this agreement avoids all accusations of Hollywood accounting, at least by you, because Owner gets a piece of what you get. If you are going to pay for the film yourself or through your family and friends or a company you own or control, be sure to spell out your definition of "Contingent Compensation." Be as specific as possible to avoid future conflicts. 1.5% is common. 2.5% is about as high as is ever paid.

(b)   **Bonus Compensation:** Producer shall pay Owner $_____ in addition to any other money due Owner under this agreement upon the happening of the following:

_____.

Background: Often there are bonuses if a film wins certain prizes or grosses over a certain domestic box office amount as reported in *Daily Variety* or *The Hollywood Reporter* (e.g., $10,000 if the film grosses $100 million in domestic box office). Usually such performance bonuses are advances against contingent compensation. Do not grant bonuses for things like awards or Oscar nominations. These events do not always translate into money for you as the producer which is why we caution our producer clients not to offer these types of bonuses.

Background: For books, best-seller bonuses are common. You want to be sure to put a cap on such bonuses and specify the list that qualifies. "$10,000 per week for each week on The *New York Times* Best Seller List up to 10 weeks" would be a common provision.

Background: For plays, often there are Broadway productions or Pulitzer Prize-winning or Tony Award-winning bonuses. These provisions persist in spite of the clear diminution of Broadway's importance to the national theater scene. This is due in part to the fact that there is no shorthand substitute by which to measure success. The Mark Taper Forum in Los Angeles birthed back-to-back Pulitzer Prize-winning plays, but still does not rate the mark of success that a Broadway production rates. More film rights are optioned from productions in Los Angeles than from Broadway, but this is overlooked and underrated. Broadway stoically remains the hallmark of a play's success and the trigger for bonus payments.

Background: For magazine story or song or comic book, there are rarely bonuses involved. The merchandising aspects of anything related to a comic book are very important, and may be difficult to secure for a film. They are usually reserved by or at least shared with the publisher.

Hint for merchandising: Fight this. We rarely see this for underlying material and it is not in a producer's best interest. The exception would be a graphic novel, for which the Owner would often be entitled to receive a royalty equal to ten percent (10%) of Net Merchandising Receipts attributable to the use of any character in the Work in Merchandise of any kind. Such amounts would be reducible by the aggregate amount paid on account of all royalties to others who receive a royalty. Such figure would also be less third-party sales commissions, which rarely exceed twenty-five percent (25%).

9. CREDITS:

(a)   In the event a motion picture based substantially on the Work is produced hereunder, Owner shall receive credit in the following form:

Based on the novel by _____

or if the film has a different title from the Work, then:

Based on the novel "_____" by

_____

> **HINT:** This is a standard source-material credit. A source material credit is the credit that acknowledges the original material upon which the first-draft script was based. The title of the underlying work is not listed unless it is different from the title of the film.

(b)   Such credit shall be accorded on a single card in the main titles on all positive prints of the picture and in all paid advertising in which the director has received credit, subject to Producer's and any distributor's usual and customary exclusions. All other matters regarding prominence, placement, size, style and color of said credits shall be in Producer's sole discretion. Nothing herein shall be construed to prevent so-called award or congratulatory or other similar advertising with respect to the material or Picture which omits the name of the Writer.

> **HINT:** This is a very precise description of your obligations as far as credit. It is acceptable to the studios and to any legitimate distributor.

(c)   No casual or inadvertent failure of Producer to comply with the credit provisions hereof shall be deemed a breach of this Agreement. Within a reasonable time after receipt of written notice from Owner specifying a failure to accord proper credit in accordance with this Paragraph, Producer shall use good faith efforts to cure prospectively any such failure with regard to positive prints and/or advertising materials created after the date of Producer's receipt of such notice. Producer will contractually obligate third party licensees and sub-distributors with whom Producer is in privity of contract to comply with the credit obligations set forth herein, but shall not be responsible or liable to Owner for the failure of any such third party to comply with the same.

> **HINT:** This is very important to you, since there can always be a slip-up. Often the Owner insists (and you should agree) that you take reasonable steps to correct any mistake when it is brought to your attention.

10. RESERVED RIGHTS: All publication rights are reserved to Owner for Owner's use and disposition, including but not limited to the right to publish and distribute printed versions of the Work and author-written sequels thereof (owned or controlled by Owner) in book form, whether hardcover or softcover, and in magazines or other periodicals, comics or coloring books, whether in installments or otherwise, subject to Producer's limited rights to use up to 10,000 words to promote and advertise the motion picture. Producer shall have the right of first negotiation and last refusal to enter an agreement such as this one with regard to any works created by Owner pursuant to this paragraph.

> **Background: Owners of underlying rights invariably want to reserve certain rights. The standard reserved rights for books are the rights of publication and author-written sequels that are set forth in the sample agreement. You want to get all the rights you can, but these rights are often allowed to remain with the owners of the property. Frequently, there are no reserved rights for a spec script. If you are optioning a spec script, try issuing your first contract without this paragraph. If you do that, strike the words "not reserved by Owner" from the first sentence of Paragraph 6 and eliminate the next two paragraphs as well.**

> **Background: Authors want sole publishing rights and the right to rerelease the book using film art on the cover to coincide with the release of the film. It is up to them to raise this issue. It is ultimately the studio's decision, but this is a safe item to give away.**

> **Plays: Everything having to do with the play as a play will be reserved by any author with an ounce of self-esteem. That includes publication of the play, performance of the play, and the creation of any other plays that are derivatives of the play. Some producers want to require a holdback period for the performance of the play. A holdback period is a period during which certain rights that are possessed are not used. Personally, I don't think it is necessary, but I know that many producers ask (and many playwrights give) a holdback period of 1 to 2 years from release of the film during which the playwright will not authorize the performance of the play.**

> **Magazine Story: Publication rights are the only rights normally reserved by the owners of magazine articles.**

> **Song: There probably aren't enough of these deals done to say that anything is ironclad, but I would think that everything except the right to make a film would be reserved by the songwriter.**

> **Old Movies or Documentary: The right to continue releasing and otherwise exploiting the previous film is always retained by the owner.**

11. RIGHT OF FIRST NEGOTIATION: If Owner desires to dispose of or exercise a particular right reserved to Owner herein ("Reserved Right"), then Owner shall notify Producer in writing and immediately negotiate with Producer regarding such Reserved Right. If, after the expiration of thirty (30) days following the receipt of such notice, no agreement has been reached, then Owner may negotiate with third parties regarding such Reserved Right subject to the next paragraph.

> **Background: The above and below paragraphs spell out your rights when the Owner exploits Reserved Rights. It is pretty self-explanatory. This is a strong protection from anyone making a fortune on the hard work you went through to get a film made. You can shorten some of these time periods, but do not quickly give up these rights if the Owner has Reserved Rights.**

12. RIGHT OF LAST REFUSAL: If Producer and Owner fail to reach an agreement pursuant to Producer's right of first negotiation, and Owner makes and/or receives any bona fide offer to license and/or purchase the particular Reserved Right or any interest therein in a context other than an auction ("Third Party Offer"), Owner shall notify Producer, if Owner proposes to accept such Third Party Offer, of the name of the offeror, the proposed purchase price, and other such terms of Third Party Offer. During the period of ten (10) days after Producer's receipt of such notice, Producer shall have the exclusive option to license and/or purchase said Reserved Right upon the same terms and conditions of said Third Party Offer. If Producer elects to exercise the right to purchase such Reserved Right, Producer shall notify Owner of the exercise thereof within said ten (10) day period, failing which Owner shall be free to accept such Third Party Offer. If any such proposed license and/or sale is not consummated with a third party within thirty (30) days following the expiration of the aforesaid ten- (10-) day period, Producer's Right of Last Refusal shall revive and shall apply to each and every further offer or offers at any time received by Owner relating to the particular Reserved Right or any interest therein; provided, further, that Producer's option shall continue in full force and effect, upon all of the terms and conditions of this Clause, so long as Owner retains any rights, title, or interests in or to the particular Reserved Right.

13. NO OBLIGATION TO PRODUCE: While Producer shall use best efforts to effect a production hereunder, nothing herein shall be construed to obligate Producer to produce, distribute, release, perform or exhibit a film based upon the Work, in whole or in part, or otherwise to exercise, exploit or make any use of the rights, license, privileges or property gained herein to Producer.

14. REPRESENTATIONS AND WARRANTIES:

(a)   The Work itself is original with Owner and no part of the Work is in the public domain other than the extent to which historical facts are, by their nature, in the public domain;

(b)   Owner has the right, authority and legal capacity to grant the rights granted to Producer herein;

(c)   The work is not subject to any claim, arbitration, mediation, or litigation.

(d)   The Work does not, and no use thereof will, infringe upon or violate any personal, proprietary or other right of any third party, including, without limitation, defamation, libel, slander or violation of any right of privacy or publicity or any copyright in underlying material; and

(e)   Owner shall not exploit the Work in a manner inconsistent with the terms of this Agreement, specifically, to not sell, license, exploit or transfer any rights in the Work.

15. REMEDIES: Owner recognizes and confirms that in the event of a failure or omission by Producer constituting a breach of its obligations under this Agreement, whether or not material, the damage, if any, caused Owner is not irreparable or sufficient to entitle Owner to injunctive or other equitable relief. Consequently, Owner's rights and remedies shall be limited to the right, if any, to obtain damages at law and Owner shall not have any right in such event to terminate or rescind this Agreement or any of the rights granted to Producer hereunder or to enjoin or restrain the development, production, advertising, promotion, distribution, exhibition or exploitation of the Picture and/or any of Producer's rights pursuant to this Agreement.

> **Background: No injunction clause. This clause is very important. An "injunction" is a court order that could potentially halt production of the film. This clause waives the Owner's rights to injunctive relief and limits his or her remedies to suing for money damages. The filmmaker should never risk having his film enjoined (prevented from being distributed) because of a disgruntled property owner.**

16. MISCELLANEOUS:

(a)   Arbitration. Disputes under this Agreement shall be settled pursuant to binding arbitration under the rules of the Independent Film and Television Alliance ("IFTA") in [STATE]. The prevailing party will be entitled to reasonable attorney fees and costs.

> **Background: The virtues of arbitration are many to the independent producer. Whatever you do, you want to stay out of court. Many people like to have mandatory mediation before going to arbitration. Mediation is the process by which the parties to a disagreement agree to talk through the problem with a neutral third party who is trained to bring people into agreement. Mediation is a good idea, but often involves some money, always involves some time delays and is something that many people would like to decide upon when a dispute arises. If it is appropriate, mediation is easy enough to institute.**

(b)   Indemnification. Owner shall indemnify and defend Producer from and against any and all claims and damages arising from the breach of any representation or warranty of Owner hereunder to the extent such claim or damage does not arise out of a breach by Producer hereunder. Producer shall indemnify and defend Owner from and against any and all claims and damages arising from the production, distribution, exhibition or exploitation of the Picture, or any element thereof, to the extent such claim or damage does not arise out of a breach by Owner hereunder.

(c)   Accounting. Producer agrees to keep and maintain complete and accurate books and records relating to the Picture and the proceeds derived therefrom.

> **HINT: An accounting paragraph is only necessary if the Owner is receiving any back-end compensation. Typically, a standard audit provision is included in this section: Owner or his/her representative shall have the right to examine, copy and/or cause an audit to be made of the books and records of Producer pertaining to the Picture during regular business hours at Owner's sole expense, unless the audit reveals underpayments in excess of ten percent (10%), in which case, Producer shall reimburse Owner the reasonable costs thereof. Owner shall have the right to audit Producer's books and records no more frequently than once per annum and only with respect to statements received by Owner within two (2) years prior to the commencement of the audit.**

(d)   Assignment. Owner may not assign its rights or obligations hereunder. Producer may freely assign its rights and obligations hereunder.

(e)   Choice of Law. This Agreement shall be governed by and construed in accordance with the laws of the State of [STATE].

(f)   Notices. All notices under this Agreement shall be in writing addressed to the addresses first set forth above, or at such other address as either party may designate from time to time by written notice to the other. All notices shall be served by facsimile and U.S. mail, electronic mail, recognized courier services such as Federal Express or DHL or personal delivery addressed as specified above. The date of receipt by facsimile, electronic mail or courier, as the case may be, shall be the date of service of notice.

(g)   This agreement may be signed in counterparts. Facsimile and scanned copies shall be deemed originals for all purposes.

(h)   Further Documents. Owner agrees to execute, acknowledge, and deliver to Producer and to procure the execution, acknowledgment, and delivery to Producer of any additional documents or instruments which Producer may reasonably require to effectuate fully and carry out the intent and purposes of this Agreement. If Owner shall fail to execute and deliver any such documents or other instruments, within ten (10) calendar days after such documents are delivered to Owner, Producer shall be deemed to be, and Owner irrevocably appoints Producer, the true and lawful attorney-in-fact of Owner, to execute and deliver any and all such documents and other instruments in the name of Owner, which right is coupled with an interest.

Background: Often, when a script is sold, the purchase agreement contains a provision that the writer is obligated to write one or more revisions to the script. If you are writing with someone else, it is a good idea to have that number separated out in the purchase agreement so that you do not have to get into an argument with your co-writer if you end up doing all the work on the rewrite or vice versa.

(i)   This Agreement constitutes the entire agreement between the parties hereto with respect to all of the matters herein and its execution has not been induced by, nor do any of the parties hereto rely upon or regard as material, any representations or writing whatsoever not incorporated herein and made a part hereof. No amendment or modification hereto shall be valid unless set forth in a writing signed by both parties.

IN WITNESS WHEREOF the parties hereto have caused this Agreement to be duly executed and delivered as of the day and year first above written.

PRODUCER   OWNER

_____   _____

By:_____   SSN:_____

Its: Managing Member

Most producers know instinctively that they are better off talking to the person who created the work rather than to the agent or other representative of that person. When you talk directly to the creative force, you can share visions. You can convince the work creator, who has ultimate decision-making power, that you are the best person to protect the project. You can usually find contact information for authors and other content-creators online; they usually want to be contacted by people like you and to find new formats for their work.

» YOU WANT TO BASE YOUR FILM ON SOMEONE'S LIFE STORY

What if the idea you have for a film is based on someone's life? There are a number of reasons why you might want to enter into an arrangement with the person whose life you want to portray, but you should know that you have the right to make a biographical film about someone without their permission. Think of all the books that come out about the Obamas, most without their permission or cooperation. That is permissible, not because they are public figures, but because the facts of a person's life are in the public domain. Big or small, rich or poor, your subject is fair game as long as you don't invade their privacy and you get the facts right. Problems can arise if you do not get the facts right and can end up violating a person's right not to be put in a false light.

That being said, there are several good reasons you might want to enter into a so-called Life Story Rights Agreement. First, you get increased access to your subject and to any documentation that is personal to the subject. You also gain easier access to the subject's friends and acquaintances; however, you might decrease your access to their enemies. You are also assured that no one else is creating an authorized film about your subject. The most important thing about a Life Story Rights Agreement is the waiver of the subject's right to sue you if they don't like what you did with their life story. Here is the form you will need.

Form 1.02: Life Story Rights Agreement

LIFE STORY RIGHTS AGREEMENT

THIS AGREEMENT, effective as of _____, ____, is made by and between _____ [name of producer] ("Producer") whose address is [PHYSICAL ADDRESS] and _____ [name of owner] ("Owner") whose address is [PHYSICAL ADDRESS] concerning the Owner's life story. The following terms and conditions shall apply:

> **HINT: By using an effective date right at the beginning of the contract, you eliminate disputes over when a contract was signed, which may control some of the terms. Few contracts are signed by all parties on the same day, so fill in any date you like as the effective date.**

1. DEFINITION OF LIFE STORY: For purposes of this Agreement, "Life Story" shall mean the irrevocable, exclusive, perpetual and universal rights to use Owner's name, likeness, sobriquet, voice, and biography; depict, portray, impersonate or simulate Owner in any way whatsoever, and make use of all the incidents of Owner's life preceding, surrounding, following and otherwise in any way relating to incidents about the Owner's life that the Producer deems in its sole discretion necessary or appropriate to produce one or more motion pictures, whether wholly or partially factual or fictional; and use any and all information and materials in Owner's possession or under Owner's control, which Owner shall, at Producer's request, disclose and provide to Producer freely, completely and candidly, in such forms as, without limitation, copies of any newspapers or magazine clippings, photographs, transcripts, journals, notes, recordings, home movies, videotapes or other physical materials relating to Owner's life story and all Owner's thoughts, observations, recollections, reactions and experiences surrounding, arising out of, or concerning all those events, circumstances and activities relating

---

to Owner's life story (all the aforementioned rights hereinafter collectively referred to as "Life Story").

> **Background: This paragraph defines the "Life Story" that you purchase. A living person seldom wants you to have the rights to make a picture of that portion of their lives that they have not yet lived. On the other hand, you seldom need any rights to the future. Whatever attracted you to this person's life has already happened. Therefore, feel free to narrow the above by describing that part of a person's life that you want to option. Insert the description you need in place of the second appearance of the words "the Owner's life." Use plain English and you are on safe ground. Note that personal photos, notes and journals are also pulled into this agreement. Also note that if the Owner wrote books or articles, it is important to obtain those also. Add a description of such books just before the final parenthetical statement and the books will be included in the definition of "Life Story." If you don't include such books, you may have bought the cooperation of the person and certain waivers, but someone else can buy the film rights to the book. The money you spend in this area must put you ahead of the person who relies on facts in the public domain or there is no reason to spend the money. You will want this paragraph to be as inclusive as possible. Also note "or more" in that first long sentence. Very few people will want to give you the rights to make more than one movie. If they do, they will definitely want more generous payments than the ones provided in paragraph 9b. At a minimum, they will want (and deserve) payments that are equal to the payments for the first motion picture. If you take out "or more," be sure to take it out of paragraph 5 (a) 2) also.**

2. GRANT OF OPTION: In consideration of the mutual promises contained herein, and the payment to Owner of _____ ($___), receipt and sufficiency of which is hereby acknowledged, Owner hereby grants to Producer for twelve (12) months from and after the effective date of this Agreement (the "Option Period") the exclusive, irrevocable right and option (the "Option") to acquire the exclusive rights as set forth in paragraph 5 in and to the Life Story, as defined above.

> **HINT: This is the first money you spend on the long journey of developing a screenplay and then making a movie. Even established companies try to get ninety (90) days free. This gives you a chance to set the project up with a company that can fund development activities.**

3. EXTENSION/EXERCISE OF OPTION: Producer shall have the right to extend the Option Period for one (1) period of twelve (12) months by sending notice to Owner prior to the expiration of the previous period, along with an additional payment of _____ ($____). Producer may exercise this Option at any time during the Option Period, as it may be extended, by giving written notice of such exercise to Owner. The sums paid under this Agreement, with respect to the initial and extended Option Period, shall be credited against the first sums payable as compensation under the terms of the Compensation clause below. If Producer fails to exercise this Option, then the sums paid to Owner hereunder shall be and remain the sole property of Owner.

> **HINT: Many projects based on life-story rights are for television. The range of prices for television projects is narrow. Most projects pay $35,000 to $100,000 for life-story rights whether there is one person or several persons to receive this money. Cable outlets generally pay less than broadcast networks.**

> **Background: Try to get three years if you can. It always takes longer than you think to get a movie made. Note that the first payment is generally not applicable, meaning that there is no deduction of the first payment from the purchase price, so if you are asked for this concession, you should feel comfortable in granting it.**

4. PENDING EXERCISE OF OPTION: Producer shall have the right to prepare screenplays, budgets, teleplays, treatments or other material, and engage in other customary development and pre-production activities. It is understood that if the Option is not exercised, Producer shall have no further right in and to the Life Story, but Producer shall own all rights of every kind in and to material Producer prepared.

5. RIGHTS GRANTED:

    (a)   Upon exercise of the Option by Producer, Producer shall acquire and Owner shall be deemed to have assigned, conveyed, sold and transferred to Producer all motion picture, television, home-video, allied, subsidiary and ancillary rights in and to the Life Story for use by Producer, and Producer's successors and assigns, throughout the world and in perpetuity, including, without limitation, the following rights:

        1)   the right to develop one or more scripts based on the Life Story;

        2)   the right to make one or more motion pictures based on the Life Story, any part thereof or any sequences

or characters therein (including, without limitation, theatrical productions, television series, and made-for-television movies and made-for-home-video productions);

3)   the right to distribute, exhibit and otherwise exploit any such motion pictures in any and all media and by any means now known or hereafter devised, including, without limitation, all forms of theatrical and non-theatrical distribution and exhibition (including, without limitation, free broadcast, pay television, cable, subscription and pay-per-view);

4)   the right to manufacture, distribute and otherwise exploit all forms of videocassettes, videodiscs and similar devices of any such motion pictures and to combine such motion pictures with other programs on such videocassettes, videodiscs and similar devices;

5)   the right to make changes to the Life Story, to create fictional episodes, characters and/or dialogue for dramatic purposes, and to use any portion or portions of the Life Story for any purpose of this Agreement;

6)   the right to edit and alter any motion pictures based on the Life Story and to make foreign versions thereof;

7)   the right to publicize, advertise or otherwise promote any such motion pictures and in connection therewith to prepare and use synopses (not to exceed 7,500 words each) of the Life Story;

8)   the soundtrack recording, music publishing, legitimate stage, live television, radio broadcasting and merchandising rights to the Life Story, to any such motion pictures based thereon and to any of the characters contained therein;

9)   the right to make remakes and sequels to any such motion pictures;

10) the right to copyright any such motion pictures, sound recordings, musical compositions and all other copyrightable works based on or derived from the Life Story and to secure copyright and trademark protection to all works based on or derived from the Life Story; and

11) the right to sublicense or authorize others to exercise any of the foregoing rights, subject to Producer's obligations hereunder provided.

> **Background: Well, finally, one of those long, interminable grant-of-rights paragraphs. I thought that you ought to see one, and if you are ever going to use it, you might as well use it with someone who lives outside of Hollywood and who might need a little longer rendition of what rights are being granted. Also, you need some waivers from the holder of the bundle of rights known as life-story rights. Those waivers can be very scary when you stop and think about it. Sometimes they appear less ominous when buried among all the detail that this long version of the grant-of-rights paragraph provides.**

(b) Notwithstanding anything contained in this clause to the contrary, it is Producer's intention to portray Owner's and Owner's Life Story as factually as possible with the understanding that Producer has the right to deviate from the facts of the Life Story in order to enhance the dramatic value. Owner shall be entitled to review and be consulted on the final shooting scripts of the motion pictures produced hereunder, it being understood that further changes to such final shooting scripts may be made by Producer. No approval rights are granted whatsoever in connection with any scripts created or motion pictures produced hereunder, which rights shall be held solely and exclusively by Producer and shall include, without limitation, control over all dramatic elements of said scripts and motion pictures.

> **Background: This is an important piece of reassurance for the Owner. Your obligations are minimal. Be sure you actually consult with the Owner if you promise to do so. Many producers don't offer the reassurances in subparagraph (b) until asked to do so.**

6. RESERVED RIGHTS: The Owner specifically reserves literary publishing rights to the Life Story (other than literary publishing rights of up to 10,000 words for use by Producer in advertising any motion picture based on the Life Story). However, if Producer produces a movie hereunder and if Owner writes a book, Producer owns all motion picture rights in the book without further payments.

> **Comment: This is a fairly standard reserved right. You need your 10,000 words for the synopsis you send out with your publicity packet. Most producers start by asking for 10,000 words for the synopsis. The last sentence is good to ask for, but you don't always get it.**

7. WAIVER: Owner hereby waives and relinquishes any rights or remedies at law, in equity or otherwise, and further releases Producer and Producer's employees, agents, successors, licensees and assigns from, and covenants not to sue Producer, or any of them, with respect to any claim, cause of action, liability or damages of any nature whatsoever arising out of or in connection with the exercise of any of the rights herein granted to Producer. Such liabilities include, without limitation, defamation, libel, slander, false light, false advertising, intentional or negligent infliction of mental distress or invasion or appropriation of any right of privacy or publicity in any jurisdiction. These waivers are hereby made by Owner, both on Owner's behalf and on behalf of Owner's next of kin.

> **HINT: This is at the heart of a Life Story Rights Agreement. You are obtaining the waiver of all the suits based on the personal rights held by the person whose life story you are purchasing. These rights can be violated intentionally or accidentally. There is peril in making major modifications to this paragraph.**

8. CONSULTING SERVICES: Owner shall be available to Producer as consultant in connection with the first motion picture produced hereunder at mutually convenient places, dates and times, to provide Producer with information and materials regarding the Life Story and to assist Producer in obtaining releases from any persons designated by Producer. Such consultation will involve, among other things, cooperation with Producer and any writers employed by Producer or Producer's assigns in connection with the writing of the teleplay or other forms of adaptation of the Life Story. Owner shall be entitled to compensation for the above employment in the amount of ten thousand dollars ($10,000), payable upon commencement of principal photography of said motion picture.

> **HINT: This paragraph is important in a life-story rights agreement. The only reasons to pay a person for their life-story rights are to receive their cooperation in obtaining the rich details of their story and to obtain waivers if you wander away from the literal truth to achieve dramatic impact. If you do not receive this consultation, you might as well save your money and just rely on public-domain materials. This paragraph is usually reassuring to the Owner. The payment is of course negotiable.**

9. COMPENSATION: As full consideration for all rights, licenses, privileges, waivers and property herein granted, and for all warranties, representations and covenants herein made by Owner, Producer agrees to pay Owner as follows:

(a)   Guaranteed Compensation: An amount equal to [1½%–2½%] of the final locked budget of the picture (excluding interest, book completion, bond, and contingency) with a floor of fifty thousand dollars ($50,000) and a cap of one hundred and fifty thousand dollars ($150,000), payable upon the earlier of exercise of the Option or commencement of principal photography of the first motion picture produced hereunder.

> **HINT: Obviously, this is where much of the haggling is focused. Start with 1% of the budget and try not to go over 2½ %. Equally important are the floor and the ceiling. It is hard to get a party to accept less than what we have suggested above, but in proper circumstances we have achieved less. The ceiling is less important on a low budget picture.**

(b)   Remakes and Sequels: In the event Producer, or a successor-in-interest, produces any sequel and/or remake feature motion picture based on the first motion picture produced hereunder, Owner will be paid an amount equal to fifty percent (50%) of the amounts payable to Owner pursuant to the paragraph above in connection with each such sequel and/or remake.

> **Comment: The 50% is taken from the rather standard compensation for a screenwriter when a sequel is made from a script. However, for the owner of life story rights, you should be willing to go to 100% if asked to do so.**

10. CREDITS: The Owner shall be entitled to receive the following screen credit in the main titles of any and all motion pictures produced hereunder: "Based on the life of _____". Owner shall be entitled to an end-roll screen credit in connection with consulting services performed hereunder, the form and placement of which shall be at Producer's discretion. Inadvertent failure by Producer to comply with these credit provisions shall not be deemed a breach of this Agreement. Within a reasonable time after receipt of written notice from Owner specifying a failure to accord proper credit in accordance with this Paragraph, Producer shall use good faith efforts to cure prospectively any such failure with regard to positive prints and/or advertising materials created after the date of Producer's receipt of such notice. Producer will contractually obligate third party licensees and sub-distributors with whom Producer is in privity of contract to comply with the credit obligations set forth herein, but shall not be responsible or liable to Owner for the failure of any such third party to comply with the same.

> **HINT: You may not be able to give this credit if your film disparages a living person who has not signed a release. A credit that identifies the main character serves also to identify other people portrayed in the film even if you change the names of those characters.**

> **HINT: If the Owner is not happy with the details about the words "at Producer's discretion," change these words to "subject to good-faith negotiation within customary motion picture industry parameters."**

11. REPRESENTATION AND WARRANTIES

(a)   Owner has the right, authority and legal capacity to grant the rights granted to Producer herein; and

(b)   Owner shall not exploit the Life Story in a manner inconsistent with the terms of this Agreement, specifically, to not sell, license, exploit or transfer any rights in the Life Story.

12. REMEDIES: Owner recognizes and confirms that in the event of a failure or omission by Producer constituting a breach of its obligations under this Agreement, whether or not material, the damage, if any, caused Owner is not irreparable or sufficient to entitle Owner to injunctive or other equitable relief. Consequently, Owner's rights and remedies shall be limited to the right, if any, to obtain damages at law and Owner shall not have any right in such event to terminate or rescind this Agreement or any of the rights granted to Producer hereunder or to enjoin or restrain the development, production, advertising, promotion, distribution, exhibition or exploitation of the Picture and/or any of Producer's rights pursuant to this Agreement.

> **Background: No injunction clause.** This paragraph is very important. An "injunction" is a court order that could potentially halt production of the film. This clause waives the Owner's rights to injunctive relief and limits his or her remedies to suing for money damages. The filmmaker should never risk having his film enjoined (prevented from being distributed) because of a disgruntled property owner.

13. MISCELLANEOUS:

(a)   Arbitration. Disputes under this Agreement shall be settled pursuant to binding arbitration under the rules of the Independent Film and Television Alliance ("IFTA") in [STATE]. The prevailing party will be entitled to reasonable attorney fees and costs.

> **Background: The virtues of arbitration are many to the independent producer.** Whatever you do, you want to stay out of court. Many people like to have mandatory mediation before going to arbitration. Mediation is the process by which the parties to a disagreement agree to talk through the problem with a neutral third party who is trained to bring people into agreement. Mediation is a good idea, but often involves some money, always involves some time delays and is something that many people would like to decide upon when a dispute arises. If it is appropriate, mediation is easy enough to institute.

(b)   Indemnification. Owner shall indemnify and defend Producer from and against any and all claims and damages arising from the breach of any representation or warranty of Owner hereunder to the extent such claim or damage does not arise out of a breach by Producer hereunder. Producer shall indemnify and defend Owner from and against any and all claims and damages arising from the production, distribution, exhibition or exploitation of the Picture, or any element thereof, to the extent such claim or damage does not arise out of a breach by Owner hereunder.

(c)   Accounting. Producer agrees to keep and maintain complete and accurate books and records relating to the Picture and the proceeds derived therefrom.

(d)   Assignment. Owner may not assign its rights or obligations hereunder. Producer may freely assign its rights and obligations hereunder.

> **HINT: An accounting paragraph is only necessary if the Owner is receiving any back-end compensation. Typically a standard audit provision is included in this section: Owner or his/her representative shall have the right to examine, copy and/or cause an audit to be made of the books and records of Producer pertaining to the Picture during regular business hours at Owner's sole expense, unless the audit reveals underpayments in excess of ten percent (10%), in which case, Producer shall reimburse Owner the reasonable costs thereof. Owner shall have the right to audit Producer's books and records no more frequently than once per annum and only with respect to statements received by Owner within two (2) years prior to the commencement of the audit.**

(e)   Choice of Law. This Agreement shall be governed by and construed in accordance with the laws of the State of [STATE].

(f)   Notices. All notices under this Agreement shall be in writing addressed to the addresses first set forth above, or at such other address as either party may designate from time to time by written notice to the other. All notices shall be served by facsimile and US mail, electronic mail, recognized courier services such as Federal Express or DHL or personal delivery addressed as specified above. The date of receipt by facsimile, electronic mail or courier, as the case may be, shall be the date of service of notice.

(g)   This agreement may be signed in counterparts. Facsimile and scanned copies shall be deemed originals for all purposes.

(h)   Further Documents. Owner agrees to execute, acknowledge, and deliver to Producer and to procure the execution, acknowledgment, and delivery to Producer of any additional documents or instruments that Producer may reasonably require to effectuate fully and carry out the intent and purposes of this Agreement. If Owner shall fail to execute and deliver any such documents or other instruments, within ten (10) calendar days after such documents are delivered to Owner, Producer shall be deemed to be, and Owner irrevocably appoints Producer, the true and lawful attorney-in-fact of Owner, to execute and deliver any and all such documents and other instruments in the name of Owner, which right is coupled with an interest.

> **Comment:** The last sentence of the above paragraph contains a new phrase that you might not be familiar with, "a right coupled with an interest." A right coupled with an interest refers to a legal concept concerning making someone your agent, representative or attorney-in-law or attorney-in-fact. When you appoint someone as your representative and that person has an interest in the subject, you cannot cut off that representation so easily. It is not impossible, but it certainly is not as easy as when you would normally just be able to write a letter and withdraw the power to represent you.

(i)   This Agreement constitutes the entire agreement between the parties hereto with respect to all of the matters herein and its execution has not been induced by, nor do any of the parties hereto rely upon or regard as material, any representations or writing whatsoever not incorporated herein and made a part hereof. No amendment or modification hereto shall be valid unless set forth in a writing signed by both parties.

IN WITNESS WHEREOF the parties hereto have caused this Agreement to be duly executed and delivered as of the day and year first above written.

PRODUCER   OWNER

_____   _____

By:_____   SSN:_____

Its: Managing Member

» GETTING THE SCRIPT YOU WANT

There are a few different ways that you, as a film's producer, can get the script for your movie. You can option a completed script, write your script on your own, or write the script with a writing partner.

Optioning a Script

If you've read a script that you like, you'll want to option the script. The form contract for optioning a completed script is a lot like the agreement to option an underlying work. Remember, an option is the right to purchase something at any time over the course of the term of your agreement under set terms and conditions, including the price. But there are differences; here is the form you need.

Form 1.03: Option and Purchase Agreement

OPTION AND PURCHASE AGREEMENT (COMPLETED SCRIPT)

THIS AGREEMENT, effective as of _____, ____, is made by and between _____ [name of producer] ("Producer") whose address is [PHYSICAL ADDRESS] and _____ [name of owner] (the "Writer") whose address is [PHYSICAL ADDRESS], concerning the rights to a script entitled "_____" and the materials upon which it is based. The following terms and conditions shall apply:

> **Date: By using an effective date right at the beginning of the contract, you eliminate disputes over when a contract was signed, which may control some of the terms. Few contracts are signed by all parties on the same day, so fill in whatever date fits your needs as an effective date for your agreement.**

1. DEFINITION OF "WORK": For purposes of this Agreement, "Work" means the motion picture script entitled "_____" written by _____ and any and all other literary materials, titles, themes, formats, formulas, incidents, action, story, dialogue, ideas, plots, phrases, slogans, catchwords, art, designs, compositions, sketches, drawings, characters, characterizations, names and trademarks now contained therein, as well as such elements as may at any time hereafter be added or incorporated therein, and all versions thereof in any form.

> **Background:** Pick the best description of the property you are optioning. If there was a previous title, include that also by saying, "and previously entitled _____." If the Work has been registered with the Copyright Office, you might give that registration number by way of further identification.

2. GRANT OF OPTION: In consideration of the mutual promises contained herein, and the payment to Writer of $_____ (the "Option Price"), which shall be applicable against the total Purchase Price, Writer hereby grants to Producer the exclusive, irrevocable right and option (the "Option") for _____ months (the "Option Period") to acquire the exclusive motion picture, television, DVD, Internet, and all subsidiary, allied and ancillary rights in and to the Work pursuant to the terms set forth below.

> **Option Price:** You want this to be as low as possible. Sometimes you can even negotiate a free period. Do not be surprised if you run into someone (like me) who says: "No Free Option!" That is my mantra when representing the owner of a property, although I obtain "free" options all of the time for my independent producer clients. My argument: It's not "free"! My client will be working, writing (maybe), (if not) hiring someone to write, shopping the project and generally spending time, effort and money on the project.

> **HINT:** Since you do not have the deep pockets of a studio, your first job is to convince the author of your passion for the script. Listen to the author's dreams and hopes. You will be the protector of those dreams and hopes. As self-serving as it may sound, it truly is not about the money at the option stage. Except in big studio deals for hot properties, the initial payment is simply not large enough to be the most important aspect of the deal. The likelihood of the film getting made is the important thing. However, the emotional hook—the sizzle that closes your negotiation—can be a simple promise from you: "If you entrust your property to me, I will be as honest to your work as possible. I will keep you advised every step of the way, and I will do my best to protect you."

> **Option Period:** Twelve (12) months to eighteen (18) months is standard for this first period.

3. EXTENSION OF OPTION:

(a) Producer shall have the right to extend the Option Period for one (1) period of twelve (12) months for $_____ non-applicable. For the right to the extension of the first Option Period there must be one of the following:

　　(i) letter of commitment to direct from an established director;

　　(ii) the project is set up at a company, major studio or mini-major studio able to fund the project;

　　(iii) substantial negotiations in progress for complete financing of the film; or

　　(iv) letter of commitment to act in the film from one star.

(b) Producer shall have the right to extend the Option Period for one (1) additional twelve (12) month period for $_____ non-applicable. In order to have a right to a second extension, Producer must secure at least two (2) of the above four (4) items.

> **Background: Option Extension.** It is standard that you have the right to extend the option. This is important because it takes a very long time to get a film made. Even three years total, as provided here, is a short time. Inexperienced producers often think that they will get their movie made more quickly than anybody else. Based on what? Be realistic. Writers are reluctant to have their material off the market for a long period of time. Frequently, the amounts paid for the second and third years are substantially higher than the amount paid for the initial period . . . and they are non-applicable.

> **HINT:** Whether subsequent option payments apply or do not apply to the final purchase price is often a point of negotiation. The initial payment is usually applicable (i.e., deductible). More often than not, these additional payments are not deducted from the purchase price. The money must be paid before the time elapses under the current option. This payment acts to keep the option open for the extended period of time. If you let your option expire, you no longer have any right to buy the work or to extend the option. The original owner is then free to option the work to another party.

HINT: Progress Requirements. One way to soften the length of time and/ or to get more time is to have your right to renew the option be a result of progress made on the film. That is the approach used above. But do not make those barriers too high. The last sentences of Subparagraph (a) and Subparagraph (b) might work for you—though you don't have to include them in your first draft. If no such demand is made, you can strike this language. (Be sure to tailor the language to your needs.) No studio ever makes this kind of deal. Studios simply pay option prices. Therefore, if you use this approach, you must provide alternatives if the project is set up at a studio. After that, the option may be renewed with a cash payment only.

4. EXERCISE OF OPTION: Producer may exercise this Option at any time during the Option Period, as it may be extended, by giving written notice of such exercise to Writer and delivery to Writer of the minimum Purchase Price as set forth below. In the event Producer does not exercise said Option during the period as it may be extended, this Agreement shall be of no further force or effect whatsoever. All rights granted hereunder become property of Writer. Upon exercise of the Option, the date of exercise shall be inserted in the blank space provided in the short form copyright assignment, attached hereto as Exhibit A. Exhibit A shall be and will become a binding agreement between the parties hereto without any further execution or delivery. In the event Producer does not exercise said Option within the time and in the manner herein set forth herein, Exhibit A shall be of no further force or effect whatsoever.

Comment: This paragraph is what gives you the ability to purchase the rights you have optioned. It is standard.

5. PENDING EXERCISE OF OPTION: Producer shall have the right to engage in all customary development and preproduction activities during the option period as it may be extended, including the right to revise the work.

Hint: The fact that you optioned the film rights infers this to be true. One of the things you want is to be able to change the script. That means creating a derivative work, which requires permission of the copyright owner who is the writer. This is where you obtain the writer's permission. Stating the fact clearly is better. Often people add "including but not limited to" and then go on for a page or two. That's overkill.

Comment: Many writers will want a guarantee that they will write the first revision, if any, of the script. Fair enough. If you don't think the writer is up to taking the script to the next level, look at this payment as part of the cost of the script.

6. GRANT OF RIGHTS: Effective upon Producer's exercise of the Option, Writer hereby exclusively sells, grants and assigns to Producer, Producer's successors, licenses and assigns all rights in and to the Work not reserved by Writer, throughout the universe, in perpetuity, in any and all media and by any means now known or hereafter devised, including, without limitation, all forms of theatrical and non-theatrical distribution and exhibition (including without limitation, free broadcast, pay television, cable, subscription, pay-per-view, video-on-demand, DVD and Internet), including without limitation the following: all motion picture rights, including the right to make remakes, new versions or adaptations of the Work or any part thereof; to make series and serials of the Work or any part thereof; the right, for advertising and publicity purposes only, to prepare, broadcast, exhibit and publish in any form or media, any synopses, excerpts, novelizations, serializations, dramatizations, summaries and stories of the Work, or any part thereof; and all rights of every kind and character whatsoever in and to the Work and all the characters and elements contained therein.

> **HINT: This is exactly what you are purchasing. This is why you are making the payments. This paragraph can also run on for pages, but the above is all-inclusive. It puts the burden on the Writer to be specific about reserved rights.**

7. PURCHASE PRICE: As complete consideration for all services to be performed by Writer hereunder, for all rights herein granted, and all representations and warranties made, Producer agrees to pay Writer two-and-one-half percent (2.5%) of the final locked budget for the motion picture based on the Work (less contingencies, financing, interest, and bond fees) with a floor of $_____ and a ceiling of $_____, if Writer receives sole credit; reducible to one-and-one-quarter percent (1.25%) if Writer receives shared credit, which a floor of $_____ and a ceiling of $_____. Such amount shall be paid no later than the commencement of principal photography of the production.

> **Purchase Price: Price can be a flat fee or a percentage of the film's budget, or a combination. Most film budgets allow about 2.5% or 3% of the budget for purchase of the script, with a floor and ceiling. The floor is the minimum price you pay, regardless of the budget. The ceiling is the maximum price you pay, regardless of the budget. Try to hold compensation for all writing services including the underlying rights to 5%, although I have seen those total costs sneak up above that on occasion.**

8. ADDITIONAL COMPENSATION:

(a)   Contingent Compensation: Producer also agrees to pay five percent (5%) of one hundred percent (100%) of the Producer's share of net proceeds if Writer receives sole credit; reducible to two and a half percent (2.5%) if Writer receives shared credit. "Net Proceeds" shall be defined, accounted for and paid in the same manner for Writer as for Producer, whether Producer's contingent compensation is called Net Profits, Adjusted Gross Profits or otherwise.

> **Comment: "Net Profits" have gotten a bad name. Try using "Contingent Compensation." The language in this agreement avoids all accusations of Hollywood accounting, at least by you, because Writer gets a piece of what you get. If you are going to pay for the film yourself or through your family and friends or a company you own or control, be sure to spell out your definition of "Contingent Compensation." Be as specific as possible to avoid future conflicts. The standard is 5% for sole credit, 2.5% for shared credit.**

(b)   Bonus Compensation: Producer shall pay Writer $_____ in addition to any other money due Writer under this agreement upon the happening of the following:

_____.

> **Bonus Compensation: Use this paragraph only after the Writer requests it! Often there are bonuses if a film grosses over a certain domestic box office amount as reported in *Daily Variety* or *Hollywood Reporter* (e.g., $10,000 if the film grosses $100 million in domestic box office.) Usually such performance bonuses are advances against contingent compensation. Do not grant bonuses for things like awards or Oscar nominations. These events do not always translate into money for you. Even substantial box office does not necessarily provide the producer with cash from which to pay a bonus. Be very cautious about bonuses.**

9. CREDITS:

(a)   In the event a motion picture based substantially on the Work is produced hereunder, Writer shall receive credit in the following form:

Written by _____

unless the credit guidelines of Writers Guild of America would produce another result, in which case the credit will be determined according to those guidelines.

(b)   Such credit shall be accorded on a single card in the main titles on all positive prints of the picture and in all paid advertising in which the director has received credit, subject to Producer's and any distributor's usual and customary exclusions. All other matters regarding prominence, placement, size, style and color of said credits shall be in Producer's sole discretion. Nothing herein shall be construed to prevent so-called award or congratulatory or other similar advertising with respect to the material or Picture which omits the name of the Writer.

Comment: This is a very precise description of your obligations as far as credit. It is acceptable to the studios and to any legitimate distributor. Note the reference to the Writers Guild guidelines. Even if your writer is not a member of the Writers Guild, use their guidelines when determining credits since they represent the standard in the industry. The guidelines also provide guidance on how to credit a subsequent writer who wrote enough to earn credit on the film.

(c)   No casual or inadvertent failure of Producer to comply with the credit provisions hereof shall be deemed a breach of this Agreement. Within a reasonable time after receipt of written notice from Writer specifying a failure to accord proper credit in accordance with this Paragraph, Producer shall use good faith efforts to cure prospectively any such failure with regard to positive prints and/or advertising materials created after the date of Producer's receipt of such notice. Producer will contractually obligate third party licensees and sub-distributors with whom Producer is in privity of contract to comply with the credit obligations set forth herein, but shall not be responsible or liable to Writer for the failure of any such third party to comply with the same.

HINT: This is very important to you, since there can always be a slip-up. Often the Writer insists (and you should agree) that you take reasonable steps to correct any mistake when it is brought to your attention. If asked, you should agree to add, "provided Producer takes reasonable steps to prospectively cure upon written notice from Writer."

10. REMEDIES: Writer recognizes and confirms that in the event of a failure or omission by Producer constituting a breach of its obligations under this Agreement, whether or not material, the damage, if any, caused Writer is not irreparable or sufficient to entitle Writer to injunctive or other equitable relief. Consequently, Writer's rights and remedies shall be limited to the right, if any, to obtain damages at law and Writer shall not have any right in such event to terminate or rescind this Agreement or any of the rights granted to Producer hereunder or to enjoin or restrain the development, production, advertising, promotion, distribution, exhibition or exploitation of the Picture and/or any of Producer's rights pursuant to this Agreement.

> **Background: No injunction clause. This is very important. An "injunction" is a court order that could potentially halt production of the film. This clause waives the Writer's rights to injunctive relief and limits his or her remedies to suing for money damages. The filmmaker should never risk having his film enjoined (prevented from being distributed) because of a disgruntled property owner.**

11. REPRESENTATIONS AND WARRANTIES:

(a)   The Work itself is original with Owner and no part of the Work is in the public domain other than the extent to which historical facts are, by their nature, in the public domain;

(b)   Owner has the right, authority and legal capacity to grant the rights granted to Producer herein;

(c)   The work is not subject to any claim, arbitration, mediation, or litigation.

(d)   The Work does not, and no use thereof will, infringe upon or violate any personal, proprietary or other right of any third party, including, without limitation, defamation, libel, slander or violation of any right of privacy or publicity or any copyright in underlying material; and

(e)   Owner shall not exploit the Work in a manner inconsistent with the terms of this Agreement, specifically, to not sell, license, exploit or transfer any rights in the Work.

12. MISCELLANEOUS:

(a)   Arbitration. Disputes under this Agreement shall be settled pursuant to binding arbitration under the rules of the Independent Film and Television Alliance ("IFTA") in [STATE]. The prevailing party will be entitled to reasonable attorney fees and costs.

> **Background: The virtues of arbitration are many to the independent producer. Whatever you do, you want to stay out of court. Many people like to have mandatory mediation before going to arbitration. Mediation is the process by which the parties to a disagreement agree to talk through the problem with a neutral third party who is trained to bring people into agreement. Mediation is a good idea, but often involves some money, always involves some time delays and is something that many people would like to decide upon when a dispute arises. If it is appropriate, mediation is easy enough to institute.**

(b)   Indemnification. Writer shall indemnify and defend Producer from and against any and all claims and damages arising from the breach of any representation or warranty of Writer hereunder to the extent such claim or damage does not arise out of a breach by Producer hereunder. Producer shall indemnify and defend Writer from and against any and all claims and damages arising from the production, distribution, exhibition or exploitation of the Picture, or any element thereof, to the extent such claim or damage does not arise out of a breach by Writer hereunder.

(c)   Accounting. Producer agrees to keep and maintain complete and accurate books and records relating to the Picture and the proceeds derived therefrom.

> **HINT: Only use the Accounting paragraph if the Owner is receiving back-end compensation. If so, you should also include a standard audit provision in this section: Owner or his/her representative shall have the right to examine, copy and/or cause an audit to be made of the books and records of Producer pertaining to the Picture during regular business hours at Owner's sole expense, unless the audit reveals underpayments in excess of ten percent (10%), in which case, Producer shall reimburse Owner the reasonable costs thereof. Owner shall have the right to audit Producer's books and records no more frequently than once per annum and only with respect to statements received by Writer within two (2) years prior to the commencement of the audit.**

(d)   Assignment. Writer may not assign its rights or obligations hereunder. Producer may freely assign its rights and obligations hereunder.

(e)   Choice of Law. This Agreement shall be governed by and construed in accordance with the laws of the State of [STATE].

(f)   Notices. All notices under this Agreement shall be in writing addressed to the addresses first set forth above, or at such other address as either party may designate from time to time by written notice to the other. All notices shall be served by facsimile and U.S. mail, electronic mail, recognized courier services such as Federal Express or DHL or personal delivery addressed as specified above. The date of receipt by facsimile, electronic mail or courier, as the case may be, shall be the date of service of notice.

(g)   Employment Eligibility. In accordance with the Immigration Reform and Control Act of 1986, any offer of employment contained herein is conditioned upon satisfactory proof of Writer's identity and United States employment eligibility. Writer must present required documentation within ten (10) days of acceptance of this offer. Failure to comply will result in termination of employment.

(h)   This agreement may be signed in counterparts. Facsimile and scanned copies shall be deemed originals for all purposes.

(i)   Further Documents. Writer agrees to execute, acknowledge, and deliver to Producer and to procure the execution, acknowledgment, and delivery to Producer of any additional documents or instruments which Producer may reasonably require to effectuate fully and carry out the intent and purposes of this Agreement. If Writer shall fail to execute and deliver any such documents or other instruments, within ten (10) calendar days after such documents are delivered to Writer, Producer shall be deemed to be, and Writer irrevocably appoints Producer, the true and lawful attorney-in-fact of Writer, to execute and deliver any and all such documents and other instruments in the name of Writer, which right is coupled with an interest.

> **Comment:** The last sentence of the above paragraph contains a new phrase that you might not be familiar with, "a right coupled with an interest." A right coupled with an interest refers to a legal concept concerning making someone your agent, representative or attorney-in-law or attorney-in-fact. When you appoint someone as your representative and that person has an interest in the subject, you cannot cut off that representation so easily. It is not impossible, but it certainly is not as easy as when you would normally just be able to write a letter and withdraw the power to represent you.

(j)   This Agreement constitutes the entire agreement between the parties hereto with respect to all of the matters herein and its execution has not been induced by, nor do any of the parties hereto rely upon or regard as material, any representations or writing whatsoever not incorporated herein and made a part hereof. No amendment or modification hereto shall be valid unless set forth in a writing signed by both parties.

IN WITNESS WHEREOF the parties hereto have caused this Agreement to be duly executed and delivered as of the day and year first above written.

PRODUCER   WRITER

_____   _____

By:_____   SSN:_____

Its: Managing Member

EXHIBIT A

ASSIGNMENT (Short Form)

FOR good and valuable consideration, receipt of which is hereby acknowledged, the undersigned Writer does hereby sell, grant, assign and set over unto _____ (hereinafter referred to as "Producer"), and Producer's heirs, successors, licensees and assigns, forever, the sole and exclusive motion picture rights, television motion picture and other television rights, DVD and Internet rights and all subsidiary, allied and ancillary rights, including merchandising rights and limited publication rights, for advertising and exploitation purposes only, throughout the universe in perpetuity, in and to the script (e.g., original literary/musical) described as follows:

Title: "_____"

By: _____

including all contents thereof, all present and future adaptations and versions thereof, and the theme, title and characters thereof. The undersigned and Producer have entered into a formal option and purchase agreement dated _____, 20__, relating to the transfer and assignment of the foregoing rights in and to said Work, which rights are more fully described in said Option and Purchase Agreement. This Assignment is expressly made subject to all of the terms and conditions of said Agreement.

IN WITNESS WHEREOF, the undersigned has executed this assignment on _____, 20__.

WRITER: _____

> **HINT:** This document is signed along with the main agreement so that you don't have to obtain it later. You do not use it until you actually exercise the option agreement and own the film rights to the script. When you exercise the option and own the script, one of the first things you do is to file the assignment with the Copyright Office for all the reasons stated in the Chain of Title section of the Delivery chapter (Chapter 6).

> **Background:** "Consideration" is legalese shorthand for whatever is of value that you give up for what you get. Money is the "consideration" that most people think of. Your promises can also be consideration. It is okay to reference the fact of consideration without spelling out details, especially in a document like this that will be open to the public.

Writing the Script—With or Without a Partner

If you are bold of heart and have the time and inclination to do so, writing the first draft of your screenplay can be a rewarding, frustrating, exhilarating, discouraging, uplifting, depressing experience . . . in other words, a real roller coaster. But it can be incredibly rewarding: even if you have someone else help you along the way, you will be providing the shape and direction of the film you want to produce.

If you want to write with a partner, lay not one word on paper until you have reached an agreement on some very fundamental questions. The survival rate for writing partnerships is somewhere near the survival rate for new restaurants in America. If you are friends with the person you plan to write with, it is even more important to have an agreement on the important points. Every month, someone comes into our law office with a story that starts "we were friends so we didn't need a written agreement." Before we listen to the rest of the story, we always get them to correct the intro: "We didn't THINK we needed an agreement, but now I KNOW that we really, really should have had one."

Most disputes we see involve who gets final say when there is a creative disagreement; if one party bails out after the first draft, what rights do they have; who gets to shop the project; and what happens when one person decides that the effort of the other party is not equal to their effort. All these unhappy topics should be discussed in advance. It might get awkward, but it is so much better to decide these things when you are still friends and wanting to work together than deciding them when one party or the other is feeling hurt, betrayed, scared, or just plain angry. The form below is a sample of an agreement you can use.

Form 1.04: Collaboration Agreement

COLLABORATION AGREEMENT

THIS AGREEMENT, effective as of _____, ____, is made by and between _____ ("Writer A") whose address is [PHYSICAL ADDRESS] and _____ ("Writer B") whose address is [PHYSICAL ADDRESS] with respect to the parties' services on the feature-length motion picture currently entitled, "_____" (the "Picture").

> **Date: By using an effective date right at the beginning of the contract, you eliminate disputes over when a contract was signed, which may control some of the terms. Few contracts are signed by all parties on the same day, so fill in a date that works for you as the effective date.**

> **Background:** Fill in the names in the agreement in the same order as you want them to appear in the credit. The credit paragraph is on the next page, but you will want to start off the agreement in the same way. Fill in the most permanent address available for each writer, which is often not his or her current residence.

> **HINT:** This agreement will be more user-friendly if you use the writers' last names rather than Writer A and Writer B.

1. Each Writer will provide the other with access to all material prepared to date on the Work. The Writers agree to be available to each other at convenient times to supply additional information and for consultations, conferences and story meetings.

2. Writer A will write the script of the Work. In writing the Work, Writer A agrees to adhere to material supplied to Writer A by Writer B or by others to whom Writer B introduces Writer A and not introduce any extraneous incidents or anecdotes without first obtaining Writer B's personal approval. Notwithstanding anything to the contrary contained herein, Writer B shall have personal approval over the contents of the script. Writer A shall deliver the first draft screenplay on or before _____, _____.

> **HINT:** Both these paragraphs assume that you are clearly the producer on this project and you have entered into this collaboration agreement because you have a great idea, but no money; these paragraphs also assume that you will be helping and performing some writing service, especially with regard to the idea and developing the story, but that "Writer A" will be doing most of the work at the computer. If you are two friends starting out to write a script together, you can describe your working relationship in the above paragraph stating clearly that you are working on a joint idea and anticipate spending about the same amount of time on the project. This is a true collaboration situation. You would also need to modify the next paragraph to cover the situation if one of you wants to quit or, worse, starts slacking off on the work.

3. Should Writer A be unable to deliver a complete and satisfactory script because of Writer B's failure to cooperate with Writer A, Writer A shall have the right to terminate this Agreement, but Writer A may retain any moneys already paid to him or his designee for his work and Writer B retains all rights in and to the material created. Should Writer A deliver a script that is unacceptable for any reason directly relating to the quality of Writer A's work, Writer B may terminate this Agreement and Writer A shall have the obligation to return any moneys paid to Writer A under this Agreement. If this Agreement is terminated for any of the aforementioned reasons, it is specifically understood that Writer B shall have the unencumbered right to enter into an agreement with regard to the Work with another writer.

4. If either party shall be unavailable for the purposes of collaborating on such revision or screenplay, then the party who is available shall be permitted to do such revision or screenplay and shall be entitled to the full amount of compensation in connection therewith, provided, however, that in such a case wherein there shall be a revision in the original selling price; the party not available for the revision or screenplay shall receive from the other party _____% of the total selling price.

> **Background: Often, when a script is sold, the purchase agreement contains a provision that the writer is obligated to write one or more revisions to the script. If you are writing with someone else, it is a good idea to have that number separated out in the purchase agreement so that you do not have to get into an argument with your co-writer if you end up doing all the work on the rewrite or vice versa.**

5. Upon completion of the Work, it shall be registered with the Writers Guild of America, West, Inc. ("WGA") as the joint work of the parties. If the work shall be in the form such as to qualify it for copyright protection under the Copyright Act, it shall be registered for such copyright protection with the United States Copyright Office in the names of each of the parties, and each party hereby designates the other party or parties as such party's true and lawful attorney-in-fact to so register such Work on behalf of the other party or parties, which right is coupled with an interest.

> **Comment: The last sentence of the above paragraph contains a new phrase that you might not be familiar with, "a right coupled with an interest." A right coupled with an interest refers to a legal concept concerning making someone your agent, representative or attorney-in-law or attorney-in-fact. When you appoint someone as your representative and that person has an interest in the subject, you cannot cut off that representation so easily. It is not impossible, but it certainly is not as easy as when you would normally just be able to write a letter and withdraw the power to represent you.**

6. The credit on the Work where credit appears, and in any and all forms and in any and all media in which the Work is used or licensed, will be the same size, color and boldness and shall read as follows:

Written by [A] _____ & [B] _____

Background: Note the ampersand instead of the word "and". There is a big difference when it comes to writing credits on films. The ampersand indicates that two writers wrote as a team. The word "and" indicates that the second writer was hired to rewrite the first writer and made enough of a contribution to warrant on-screen credit. Be sure that you use the correct form. Note that this writer is not a member of the Writers Guild. If your writer is a member of the guild, go to Chapter 3 and be sure you understand all the implications on compensation and working conditions. Also, you are hiring this writer directly.

7. Writer A and Writer B represent and warrant that each is free to enter into this Agreement, and that insofar as material created by each is concerned, the work is original, it does not contain any libelous or other unlawful matter; and it does not invade any right of privacy or publicity nor infringe any statutory or common-law copyright. Each writer agrees to hold the other harmless from and against any and all claims of libel or of copyright infringement or of invasion of privacy or similar rights arising out of material created by each writer in the Work.

8. The parties agree that all income received from the worldwide sale or disposition of any and all rights in and to the Work (including but not limited to print publication rights, dramatic motion picture, television and allied rights) shall be divided between the parties as follows: __% to Writer A and __% to Writer B. Neither party shall enter into any other agreement or dispose of rights in or to the Work unless it is done so under this Agreement. The parties will each be paid directly by any third party.

Background: Without an agreement to the contrary, the law imposes an even split, no matter how uneven the contributions are. The last sentence benefits everybody by eliminating future accounting disputes.

9. Neither party may enter into any agreement for any of the rights in and to the Work without the written consent of the other party. Co-signature of agreements for the disposition of any such rights shall constitute written consent by both parties.

Background: This language reflects the law without an agreement. As a producer, you will probably want to replace this language with the following, which shifts control to you: "Writer B has the right to market, develop and exploit the work so long as Writer A is kept fully informed and all receipts are divided as provided herein."

10. If the parties cannot agree on how to exploit the Work after one or both of them have completed the Work or cannot agree on how to complete the Work, then Writer A will take over the project for two years to complete and market the property and may enter any agreement with a bona fide third party, so long as A keeps B advised of all significant activities, advises B before entering into an agreement transferring rights of any kind in the property and provides in the agreement of transfer for direct payment to B of B's share of the proceeds as provided in this Agreement. After the two-year period elapses, A's rights pursuant to this paragraph will shift to B, subject to all the same conditions for the next two years. The right to complete, market and exploit the work will continue to switch back and forth until the work is sold.

> **HINT: This is a scheme that prevents the script from being the victim of a disagreement between two collaborators. The project can still move forward. It is not ideal, but then the situation is not ideal either. This paragraph creates a workable solution where none else might be available. Feel free to craft your own solution to this problem.**

11. If any disposition is made for any rights in or to the Work, this Agreement shall be in force and effect and continue for the life of the copyright therein.

12. The parties agree that Writer B shall be responsible for all expenses incurred in the preparation of the Work until such time as funds are received from any source, at which time expenses shall be reimbursed after payment of commissions and before the agreement to split between Writer A and Writer B.

> **Background: This is the standard agreement when Writer B is a producer. If you two are writers who will be looking for a producer once the script is completed, you should each bear your own expenses. If the script requires a research trip somewhere or some other substantial expenditure, the party making the expense should be reimbursed off the top. "Off the top" means that the reimbursement is made before the agreed split of proceeds.**

13. REMEDIES: Each party recognizes and confirms that in the event of a failure or omission by the other writer constituting a breach under this Agreement, whether or not material, the damage, if any, is not irreparable or sufficient for injunctive or other equitable relief. Consequently, the parties' rights and remedies shall be limited to the right, if any, to obtain damages at law and neither party shall have any right in such event to terminate or rescind this Agreement or any of the rights granted hereunder or to enjoin or restrain the development, production, advertising, promotion, distribution, exhibition or exploitation of the Picture.

Background: No injunction clause. This is very important. An "injunction" is a court order that could potentially halt production of the film. This clause waives Writer A's rights to injunctive relief and limits his or her remedies to suing for money damages. The filmmaker should never risk having his film enjoined (prevented from being distributed) because of a disgruntled employee.

14. MISCELLANEOUS:

(a) Arbitration. Disputes under this Agreement shall be settled pursuant to binding arbitration under the rules of the Independent Film and Television Alliance ("IFTA") in [STATE]. The prevailing party will be entitled to reasonable attorney fees and costs.

Background: The virtues of arbitration are many to the independent producer. Whatever you do, you want to stay out of court. Many people like to have mandatory mediation before going to arbitration. Mediation is the process by which the parties to a disagreement agree to talk through the problem with a neutral third party who is trained to bring people into agreement. Mediation is a good idea, but often involves some money, always involves some time delays and is something that many people would like to decide upon when a dispute arises. If it is appropriate, mediation is easy enough to institute.

HINT: If Writer A is receiving any back-end compensation, then a standard audit provision is typically included in this section: Writer A or his/her representative shall have the right to examine, copy and/or cause an audit to be made of the books and records of Writer B pertaining to the Picture during regular business hours at Writer A's sole expense, unless the audit reveals underpayments in excess of ten percent (10%), in which case, Writer B shall reimburse Writer A the reasonable costs thereof. Writer A shall have the right to audit Writer B's books and records no more frequently than once per annum and only with respect to statements received by Writer A within two (2) years prior to the commencement of the audit.

(b) Assignment. Neither party may assign his rights or obligations hereunder.

(c) Choice of Law. This Agreement shall be governed by and construed in accordance with the laws of the State of [STATE].

(d)   Notices. All notices under this Agreement shall be in writing addressed to the addresses first set forth above, or at such other address as either party may designate from time to time by written notice to the other. All notices shall be served by U.S. mail and electronic mail, recognized courier services such as Federal Express or DHL, or personal delivery addressed as specified above. The date of receipt by electronic mail or courier, as the case may be, shall be the date of service of notice.

(e)   This Agreement constitutes the entire agreement between the parties hereto with respect to all of the matters herein and its execution has not been induced by, nor do any of the parties hereto rely upon or regard as material, any representations or writing whatsoever not incorporated herein and made a part hereof. No amendment or modification hereto shall be valid unless set forth in a writing signed by both parties.

IN WITNESS WHEREOF the parties hereto have caused this Agreement to be duly executed and delivered as of the day and year first above written.

WRITER A   WRITER B

_____   _____

Hiring Someone Else to Write Your Script

You have an idea for a script. You may even have an option on an underlying property. But you don't want to write the script yourself. You will need some money to hire a writer, and you want to take great care in deciding which writer to hire. Look at several scripts that the writer wrote alone. When you have the perfect writer in your sights, here is the form that you will want to use.

Form 1.05: Writer Agreement

WRITER AGREEMENT—WORK FOR HIRE

THIS AGREEMENT, effective as of _____, ____, is made by and between _____ [name of producer] ("Producer") whose address is [PHYSICAL ADDRESS] and _____ [name of writer] ("Writer") whose address is [PHYSICAL ADDRESS] with respect to Writer's services on the feature-length motion picture currently entitled, "_____" (the "Picture").

> **Date: By using an effective date right at the beginning of the contract, you eliminate disputes over when a contract was signed, which may control some of the terms. Few contracts are signed by all parties on the same day, so fill in any date you like as the effective date.**

> **Producer: You, as the filmmaker, are the "Producer."**

1. ENGAGEMENT:

    (a)   Writer shall render all services customarily rendered by writers in the motion picture industry and at all times promptly comply with Producer's reasonable instructions with respect to writing the screenplay for the Picture ("Screenplay").

    (b)   First-Draft Screenplay: Writer shall write the first-draft screenplay ("First Draft") based upon material supplied to Writer by Producer (the "Assigned Material"). Writer shall commence writing services upon execution hereof and shall deliver the First Draft to Producer within ten (10) weeks thereafter.

Background: This paragraph and the ones that follow present a carefully thought-out model that tracks the writing schedules set forth in the Writers Guild of America Minimum Basic Agreement (MBA). You can modify the schedule according to your discussions with the writer you hire, but keep a schedule in your contract. Many of the problems that come up between a writer and a producer are a function of different expectations and attitudes about time. You have a much better chance at a good, working relationship with the writer you hire when you start out with a written schedule.

HINT: Many contracts concerning writing services refer to the minimum payments or other minimum rights set forth in the MBA, even though the producer is a non-signatory to the MBA. This a common way to shorthand such things as wages, credits, and creative rights even when the writer is not a member of the guild. For instance, in the above paragraph, you could replace the last sentence with "Writer shall perform services according to the minimum schedule of payments contained in the MBA of the WGA." If the contract is to be pursuant to the WGA, state that clearly and ensure the Writer is or will become a member in good standing.

(c)   Option For Rewrite and Polish: Producer shall have an irrevocable and exclusive option ("Option"), for a period of three (3) weeks after delivery of the First Draft, to engage Writer to write and deliver to Producer a rewrite of the First Draft ("Rewrite") and a polish ("Polish") thereof. Producer may exercise said Option by written notice to Writer at any time during the Option period. Writer shall commence Writer's services with respect to the Rewrite upon exercise of the Option, and shall deliver the Rewrite to Producer, incorporating such changes to the First Draft that Producer may require, no later than four (4) weeks after commencement of services.

Producer shall have a period of three (3) weeks from the date of Producer's actual receipt of the Rewrite (the "Reading Period") to study the Rewrite and to confer with Writer regarding any changes to the Rewrite that Producer may require. Writer shall commence Writer's services with respect to the Polish on or before the expiration of the Reading Period, and Writer shall deliver the Polish to Producer, incorporating such changes to the Rewrite that Producer may require, no later than two (2) weeks after commencement of services.

HINT: By stating that this is an option, you have the right, but not the obligation, to obtain additional services from this writer.

(d)   Postponement of Services: Producer may require Writer to postpone writing either the Rewrite or Polish for a maximum period of six (6) months, provided that Producer pay Writer the applicable fixed compensation for such services as if the services had been timely performed. Writer shall render such postponed services when required by Producer, subject only to Writer's professional availability.

> **Background: This is a fair balancing of interests of the producer to pace progress during development and of the writer not to be hassled by a producer who can't decide what to do.**

(e)   Time of the Essence: Time of delivery is of the essence to Producer.

2. EXCLUSIVITY: At all times during the writing periods hereunder, Writer's services shall be furnished by Writer to Producer on an exclusive basis. At all other times, Writer's services shall be furnished on a non-exclusive, but first-priority, basis with no other services to materially interfere.

> **HINT: This paragraph does not add much in most situations, since writers work at home, but it does give you certain rights in case of a flagrant violation. Writers have to avoid contractual conflicts, but as a practical matter most writers don't work exclusively on a single script. They are always noodling about multiple projects.**

3. COMPENSATION: Upon condition that Writer shall fully perform all material services required to be performed by Writer and that Writer is not in default of this Agreement, Producer agrees to pay to Writer, as full consideration for all services to be performed by Writer hereunder, and for all rights herein granted, and all representations and warranties made, the following sums in the following manner:

(a)   Fixed Compensation:

       (1)   First Draft. $_____, payable one half (1/2) upon execution of this Agreement and one half (1/2) upon delivery to Producer of the completed First Draft.

       (2)   Rewrite. In the event Producer exercises Producer's Option hereunder, Producer shall pay to Writer $_____, payable one half (1/2) upon

commencement of Writer's services and one half (1/2) upon Writer's delivery to Producer of the completed Rewrite.

(3)   Polish. In the event Producer exercises Producer's Option hereunder, Producer shall pay to Writer $_____ in connection with the Polish, payable upon commencement of Writer's services in connection therewith.

(b)   Additional Compensation: If the Picture is produced, Writer shall receive two and one-half percent (2.5%) of the final locked budget of the Picture (less insurance, bond, financing charges, and contingency) with a ceiling of $_____ and a floor of $_____, less any amount previously paid to Writer, payable on or before the first day of principal photography.

> **HINT:** For experienced writers, there are quotes that are used as a basis for payment. A quote is the price that a writer received for a past assignment. Such quotes tend to establish a floor for the price that the writer accepts in the future. If one of those past scripts was produced and did very well at the box office, that fact usually increases the price. If the film made from the script was a bomb, that fact can soften the price from the past quote. Be sure to verify that the quote given to you was legitimate.

> **HINT:** If you don't have much money up front, be prepared to pay more when principal photography begins. However, there are limits. Every film has its own economics. No matter how much money there is to spend on a production, there is a limit to the amount of the film's budget that goes to the script. That is why this paragraph is structured as a percentage of the budget. The real test of a script is whether it is made into a movie. You don't want to pay up front for the full value of the script if the picture isn't actually made (this is why options are recommended). Even studios do not throw around the big bucks unless they are sure that the film is going to be made. Instead, there is a standard paragraph calling for additional payments to the writer in the event that the film is made. If you are on a real shoestring, even these will be deferred until money comes in as in the next paragraph. If the writer is a member of WGA, minimum upfront compensation is 10% of WGA minimum.

(c)   Contingent Compensation: An amount equal to five percent (5%) of one hundred percent (100%) of the Producer's share of Net Proceeds, if any, from the Picture, if Writer receives sole "screenplay by" credit in connection with the Picture, or an amount equal to two and one-half percent (2.5%) of the Producer's share of Net Proceeds, if any, from the Picture, if Writer receives shared "screenplay by" credit in connection with the Picture. "Net Proceeds" shall be defined, accounted for, and paid in the same manner for Writer as for Producer whether Producer's contingent compensation is called Net Profits, Adjusted Gross Profits, or otherwise.

> **Background:** The word "profit" in the film industry has become a joke due to some ingenious studio accounting practices. "Contingent compensation" avoids much of the negative reaction triggered by the word "profit."

> **HINT:** More for reasons of history than logic, the contingent participation that goes to writers has settled in at 5% for sole writing credit, reducible to 2.5% for shared writing credit. That is the standard in the industry in spite of the fact that the contingent compensation is not mentioned in the MBA of the WGA. So, if a writer asks for such participation, it is hard to argue against it. In a situation where a screenwriter is also your partner, you might go above that, but you would be doing so as a function of the role that the screenwriter plays as a partner, not for the screenwriter's role as a screenwriter. The key is the definition of "net proceeds." The language above leaves everything to be negotiated in the future. The most generous language you can possibly agree to is a definition that links the writer's definition to the producer's. For example: "Net Proceeds shall be defined, calculated, and paid on the same basis as Producer's contingent compensation, whether such compensation is designated Net Profits, Adjusted Gross Profits, or otherwise." This is a generous provision because all of the various categories of profit participation are treated as one.

4. CREDIT:

(a) In the event the Picture is produced and Writer has performed all services required of Writer hereunder, Writer shall be entitled to "screenplay by" credit in connection with the Picture as determined pursuant to Exhibit A. All other matters regarding prominence, placement, form, size, style, and color of Writer's credits shall be in Producer's sole discretion. Any paid ad credit to which Writer is entitled hereunder shall be subject to Producer's and any distributor's usual and customary exclusions. Nothing herein shall be construed to prevent so-called award or congratulatory or other similar advertising with respect to the material or Picture that omits the name of the Writer.

> **HINT:** Note the deferment to Exhibit A. Read it carefully to understand the process being proposed. Do not commit irrevocably to the writer's credit unless you are absolutely sure there will not be another writer and you are planning to finance the movie yourself, or you have the financial commitment well in hand. The WGA requires producers who sign their agreement to follow the guidelines they have adopted. Even if you are not a signatory, it is best to use their guidelines. The WGA provides a well thought-out, detailed guideline to determining credits, which ought to hold down disputes. It is difficult for a writer to argue against the use of the WGA credit guidelines. Exhibit A was prepared by one of the oldest and largest law firms based in Los Angeles and avoids the pitfalls of merely referencing the WGA agreement, which carries with it certain procedural requirements not available to you unless you sign the WGA agreement.

    (b)   No casual or inadvertent failure of Producer to comply with the credit provisions hereof shall be deemed a breach of this Agreement. Within a reasonable time after receipt of written notice from Writer specifying a failure to accord proper credit in accordance with this Paragraph, Producer shall use good faith efforts to cure prospectively any such failure with regard to positive prints and/or advertising materials created after the date of Producer's receipt of such notice. Producer will contractually obligate third party licensees and sub-distributors with whom Producer is in privity of contract to comply with the credit obligations set forth herein, but shall not be responsible or liable to Writer for the failure of any such third party to comply with the same.

> **HINT:** This is very important to you, since there can always be a slip-up. Often the Writer insists (and you should agree) that you take reasonable steps to correct any mistake when it is brought to your attention.

5. WORK-MADE-FOR-HIRE:

    (a)   Writer hereby acknowledges that all of the results and proceeds of Writer's services produced for the Picture hereunder shall constitute a "work-made-for-hire" specially commissioned by Producer and Producer or Producer's assignee shall own all such results and proceeds. Producer shall have the right to use Writer's name and approved likeness with respect to distribution and exploitation of the Picture. Producer may make such use of the Picture and distribution of the Picture as Producer, in its sole discretion, shall deem appropriate.

(b)   If Writer's services are not recognized as a "work-made-for-hire," Writer hereby irrevocably grants, sells, and assigns to Producer, its successors and assigns, all of Writer's rights, title, and interest of any kind and nature, in and to the Picture, including, without limitation, all copyrights in connection therewith and all tangible and intangible properties with respect to the Picture, in perpetuity, whether in existence now or as may come into existence in the future.

(c)   Writer waives the exercise of any "moral rights" and "droit moral" and any analogous rights however denominated now or hereafter recognized. All rights granted and agreed to be granted to Producer hereunder are irrevocable and shall vest and remain perpetually vested in Producer, its successors and assigns, whether this Agreement expires in normal course or is sooner terminated, and shall not be subject to rescission by Writer for any cause whatsoever.

> **HINT: This paragraph is at the heart of a writer's agreement. It says that you own everything that the writer writes. As a Work for Hire, you (or your production company) will be listed as the Author for copyright purposes.**

(d)   Certificate of Authorship: Writer will execute and deliver to Producer in connection with all such material the Certificate of Authorship attached hereto as Exhibit B.

> **HINT: See comments on that form.**

6. WRITER'S INCAPACITY: If, by reason of mental or physical disability, Writer shall be incapacitated from performing or complying with any of the terms or conditions of this Agreement ("Writer's Incapacity") for a consecutive period in excess of five (5) days or an aggregate period in excess of seven (7) days during the performance of Writer's services, then one of the following will result:

(a)   Suspension: Producer shall have the right to suspend Writer's services hereunder so long as Writer's Incapacity shall continue, but in no event shall any suspension hereunder exceed sixty (60) days.

(b) Termination: Producer shall have the right to terminate this Agreement and all of Producer's obligations and liabilities hereunder upon written notice to Writer; except, however, said termination shall not terminate Producer's obligations and liabilities hereunder with respect to any drafts of the Screenplay delivered by Writer to Producer in conformance with the terms and conditions hereof (including, without limitation, any obligations and liabilities that may have accrued relating to the payment of Additional Compensation and the according of credit hereunder).

> **Background:** The above paragraph and the next four paragraphs all deal with your rights when you believe the writer is in default. Some independent producers think this all looks too ominous and leave these provisions out. Because the money involved is so much less than that involved in studio deals, it is usually okay just to "cut your losses" and go to another writer. You have the right to terminate even if it is not spelled out in the contract, unless other terms prevent termination.

7. WRITER'S DEFAULT: If Writer fails or refuses to write, complete, and deliver to Producer any material herein provided for within the respective periods herein specified, or if Writer otherwise fails or refuses to perform or comply with any of the material terms or conditions hereof other than by reason of Writer's Incapacity ("Writer's Default"), then one of the following will result:

(a) Suspension: Producer shall have the right to suspend Writer's services hereunder so long as Writer's Default shall continue, but in no event shall any suspension hereunder exceed a duration of thirty (30) days.

(b) Termination: Producer shall have the right to terminate this Agreement and all of Producer's obligations and liabilities hereunder upon written notice to Writer; except, however, said termination shall not terminate Producer's obligations and liabilities hereunder with respect to any drafts of the Screenplay delivered by Writer to Producer prior to Termination in conformance with the terms and conditions hereof (including, without limitation, any obligations and liabilities that may have accrued relating to the payment of Additional Compensation and the according of credit hereunder).

(c) Anticipatory Default: Any refusal or statement by Writer implying that Writer will refuse to keep or perform Writer's obligations and/or agreements hereunder shall constitute a failure to keep and perform such obligations and/or agreements from the date of such refusal or indication of refusal and shall be a Writer's Default hereunder.

8. TERMINATION RIGHTS: Termination of this Agreement, for any reason whatsoever, shall result in the following:

(a) Compensation: Terminate Producer's obligation to pay Writer any further compensation; except, however, said termination shall not terminate Producer's obligation to compensate Writer as provided hereunder with respect to any drafts of the Screenplay theretofore delivered by Writer to Producer in conformance with the terms and conditions hereof (including, without limitation, any obligation that may have accrued relating to the payment of Additional Compensation hereunder).

(b) Refund or Delivery: If termination occurs prior to Writer's delivery to Producer of the material on which Writer is then currently working, then Writer shall either immediately refund to Producer the compensation which may have been paid to Writer as of that time for such material, or immediately deliver to Producer all of the material then completed or in progress, to be decided in Producer's sole discretion.

9. SUSPENSION RIGHTS: No compensation shall accrue or become payable to Writer during the period of any suspension. If Producer shall have paid compensation to Writer during any period of Writer's Incapacity or Writer's Default, then Producer shall have the right (exercisable at any time) to require Writer to render services hereunder without compensation for a period equal to the period for which Producer shall have paid compensation to Writer during such Writer's Incapacity of Writer's Default; unless Writer immediately refunds to Producer said compensation paid to Writer, upon receipt of notice from Producer to commence such services hereunder.

10. WRITER'S RIGHT TO CURE: If any Writer's Default is inadvertent and reasonably curable, Writer shall have a period of three (3) calendar days from the date of notice of default to cure (one time only) such Writer's Default; provided that if such Writer's Default occurs during principal photography of the Picture, Writer's cure period shall be reduced to twenty-four (24) hours. Any such cure by Writer shall not preclude Producer from exercising any rights or remedies Producer may have hereunder or at law or in equity by reason of Writer's Default.

11. REMEDIES: Writer recognizes and confirms that in the event of a failure or omission by Producer constituting a breach of its obligations under this Agreement, whether or not material, the damage, if any, caused Writer is not irreparable or sufficient to entitle Writer to injunctive or other equitable relief. Consequently, Writer's rights and remedies shall be limited to the right, if any, to obtain damages at law and Writer shall not have any right in such event to terminate or rescind this Agreement or any of the rights granted to Producer hereunder or to enjoin or restrain the development, production, advertising, promotion, distribution, exhibition or exploitation of the Picture and/or any of Producer's rights pursuant to this Agreement.

> **Background: No injunction clause. This is very important. An "injunction" is a court order that could potentially halt production of the film. This clause waives the Writer's rights to injunctive relief and limits his or her remedies to suing for money damages. The filmmaker should never risk having his film enjoined (prevented from being distributed) because of a disgruntled employee.**

12. MISCELLANEOUS:

(a)   Arbitration. If not subject to WGA arbitration provisions, disputes under this Agreement shall be settled pursuant to binding arbitration under the rules of the Independent Film and Television Alliance ("IFTA") in [STATE]. The prevailing party will be entitled to reasonable attorney fees and costs.

> **Background: The virtues of arbitration are many to the independent producer. Whatever you do, you want to stay out of court. Many people like to have mandatory mediation before going to arbitration. Mediation is the process by which the parties to a disagreement agree to talk through the problem with a neutral third party who is trained to bring people into agreement. Mediation is a good idea, but often involves some money, always involves some time delays and is something that many people would like to decide upon when a dispute arises. If it is appropriate, mediation is easy enough to institute.**

(b)   Indemnification: Writer shall indemnify and defend Producer from and against any and all claims and damages arising from the breach of any representation or warranty of Writer hereunder to the extent such claim or damage does not arise out of a breach by Producer hereunder. Producer shall indemnify and defend Writer from and against any and all claims and damages arising from the production, distribution, exhibition or exploitation of the Picture, or any element thereof, to the extent such claim or damage does not arise out of a breach by Writer hereunder.

(c)   Accounting. Producer agrees to keep and maintain complete and accurate books and records relating to the Picture and the proceeds derived therefrom.

> **HINT: Like almost all writer agreements, this deal includes contingent compensation for the writer. Strike subparagraph (c) if, for some reason, the writer won't receive contingent compensation. A standard audit provision is typically included in this section: Writer or his/her representative shall have the right to examine, copy and/or cause an audit to be made of the books and records of Producer pertaining to the Picture during regular business hours at Writer's sole expense, unless the audit reveals underpayments in excess of ten percent (10%), in which case, Producer shall reimburse Writer the reasonable costs thereof. Writer shall have the right to audit Producer's books and records no more frequently than once per annum and only with respect to statements received by Writer within two (2) years prior to the commencement of the audit.**

(d)   Assignment. Writer may not assign its rights or obligations hereunder. Producer may freely assign its rights and obligations hereunder.

(e)   Choice of Law. This Agreement shall be governed by and construed in accordance with the laws of the State of [STATE].

(f)   Notices. All notices under this Agreement shall be in writing addressed to the addresses first set forth above, or at such other address as either party may designate from time to time by written notice to the other. All notices shall be served by facsimile and U.S. mail, electronic mail, recognized courier services such as Federal Express or DHL or personal delivery addressed as specified above. The date of receipt by facsimile, electronic mail or courier, as the case may be, shall be the date of service of notice.

(g) Employment Eligibility. In accordance with the Immigration Reform and Control Act of 1986, any offer of employment contained herein is conditioned upon satisfactory proof of Writer's identity and United States employment eligibility. Writer must present required documentation within ten (10) days of acceptance of this offer. Failure to comply will result in termination of employment.

(h) This agreement may be signed in counterparts. Facsimile and scanned copies shall be deemed originals for all purposes.

(i) Further Documents. Writer agrees to execute, acknowledge, and deliver to Producer and to procure the execution, acknowledgment, and delivery to Producer of any additional documents or instruments that Producer may reasonably require to effectuate fully and carry out the intent and purposes of this Agreement. If Writer shall fail to execute and deliver any such documents or other instruments, within ten (10) calendar days after such documents are delivered to Writer, Producer shall be deemed to be, and Writer irrevocably appoints Producer, the true and lawful attorney-in-fact of Writer, to execute and deliver any and all such documents and other instruments in the name of Writer, which right is coupled with an interest.

Comment: The last sentence of the above paragraph contains a new phrase that you might not be familiar with, "a right coupled with an interest." A right coupled with an interest refers to a legal concept concerning making someone your agent, representative or attorney-in-law or attorney-in-fact. When you appoint someone as your representative and that person has an interest in the subject, you cannot cut off that representation so easily. It is not impossible, but it certainly is not as easy as when you would normally just be able to write a letter and withdraw the power to represent you.

(j) This Agreement constitutes the entire agreement between the parties hereto with respect to all of the matters herein and its execution has not been induced by, nor do any of the parties hereto rely upon or regard as material, any representations or writing whatsoever not incorporated herein and made a part hereof. No amendment or modification hereto shall be valid unless set forth in a writing signed by both parties.

IN WITNESS WHEREOF the parties hereto have caused this Agreement to be duly executed and delivered as of the day and year first above written.

PRODUCER   WRITER

_____   _____

By:_____   SSN:_____

Its: Managing Member

» MARKETING YOUR FILM

Many independent filmmakers do not give one thought to this aspect of their film's life until *after* the film is complete. We suspect you want to be a successful filmmaker; you want the film to be seen. To achieve your dream you will need to answer this question: "Who will want to watch this film?" Stated another way, "Who is the audience for this film?" If you want the film to be successful, describe with a good deal of specificity who is a typical member of your core audience. You count on those people to tell their friends and their friends to tell more folks.

This is a surprisingly disciplined question that no one asks you as you work alone to wrangle the story from your brain to the page. Once you have the typical member of your core audience well in mind, be sure the script speaks to that person. You can put a picture of your imaginary friend somewhere near your writing desk. It will influence the settings you select, the words your characters speak, the humor, the pathos, and every aspect of your script. If someone else is writing the script with you or for you, make sure that person has the same vision as you do.

We will discuss marketing in greater depth in the chapter on distribution and getting your film out in the world, but for now, answer the basic question concerning your core audience and you will be well ahead of the competition.

2

WHO IS GOING TO PAY FOR ALL THIS?

Not too much time goes by before you will face the harsh realities of financing your film. You can do this in a number of ways, but distributors, at home and abroad, are the primary funders of films. Sometimes, you will cover the early expenses out of your pocket. Be smart about it. Set up a separate bank account and begin handling this venture like the business that it is. You may set it up in your own name, but the better practice would be to use a fictitious name. A fictitious name is just that: a name you use instead of your real name in order to keep things separate, to look more professional, or just for the fun of it.

» FICTITIOUS NAMES

It is easy to obtain a fictitious name or DBA (doing business as) name in every state in the union. Just pick a name, any name (except an existing business) and contact your county clerk's office. They will provide you with the necessary forms and assist with publishing it in the local paper. You can contact the paper directly and most newspapers have an online form for submitting a classified ad, charge a fairly low fee, and will be happy to help you (Lord knows they need the money). In Los Angeles, the common place to publish fictitious names is the *Daily Journal*. After publication, the newspaper sends you a proof of publication and armed with that, you can open a bank account using the fictitious name.

Hint: A DBA is not a corporate entity and will not shield you from liability in the event something goes wrong. It is merely an inexpensive convenient way to keep one's personal records distinct from the film's records.

Once you have an account, you might think about getting a credit card in the name of your new business. That's not hard to do either, if your personal credit is good.

Now keep things separate from here on in. Even if you are completely self-financing these early efforts, you should keep separate records. If the film is made, these early expenses can be recovered. Even if you don't recover them, they can be used as an advantage at tax time. You don't want to be caught with messy accounting records that are mingled with your personal finances.

» FORMING A BUSINESS ENTITY

If you've decided to create your own business entity to support the early expenses of your film, first you have to decide whether to form a corporation or an LLC (Limited Liability Company). Both these entities protect you from liability, and both can go on forever even though the folks involved with them might change. These are good qualities when your business is creating a film for which the copyright will last until you die, plus 70 years (or if it is a work made for hire, 95 years). You don't want to form a general partnership because that does not give you protection from liability and the partners are each liable for everything that the other partners do and say. It's just not worth it.

Both an LLC and a corporation require some formal documents to be filed with the state in which your business is located (generally the same as your residence). Some will elect to form their corporation in another state in which taxes are minimized or in the state they will be shooting. The pros and cons of filing out of state should be discussed with your lawyer and CPA. In most states, there is an annual minimum tax that a business has to pay. And always, such entities have to file an income tax return, even if there is no income.

Today, most films are produced by a single film production company (often called a single purpose vehicle or single purpose entity) using an LLC. The reason to set up a new and separate entity for each film is that each film is a different business. Even studios tend to set up such single-purpose companies. Check out the copyright notice on the next studio film you watch. The most common name for these LLCs is the name of the film followed immediately by the letters "LLC." Lenders and insurance companies like a new entity because it reduces the risk of a surprise claim from another project. Investors like a new entity because they know that their money will not be going for any other project than the one they are investing in.

Since our law firm always recommends an LLC, that is what we are going to discuss in depth. The LLC forms to be filed vary from state to state, so just go online to your state government's Web site, download the form, fill it out and submit it. The form you are looking for will be entitled something like "Articles of Organization." It

WORKING WITH YOUR LAWYER
If you really, really want a corporation instead of an LLC, you should discuss the matter with your local attorney and CPA. The advantages and disadvantages vary from state to state.

will ask for your name and address, the name of the LLC, the address of the LLC (which can be the same as your address if you like), and some other basic questions about your new company. The state will require you to designate someone who can accept service of process in case you are sued or subpoenaed in connection with another lawsuit. This person is known as an agent for service of process. It must be someone who lives in that state, is older than 18 years old, and should be someone who does not move around a lot, someone other than yourself who can be reached (and served) if someone wants to sue you or otherwise get in touch with you even after your film has been shot and released. Many people use their lawyer for this function.

The more difficult document is the agreement among the members of your LLC as to how it will be managed, how money will be distributed, and what happens if things come to a halt—either happily or unhappily. This document is called an Operating Agreement. It can be long or short. Some lawyers load them up with a lot of references to the corporation and tax code. We strongly favor a rather straightforward, plain English document that contains everything that you need, but avoids the extraneous gobblety gook that puts your investor to sleep and is simply a repetition of the law. We are including a form of an operating agreement that is a good starting point, but will not work for anyone without a good deal of tweaking. We are including it so that you can read through it and see what to expect when you receive your own version from your lawyer. Particularly focus on the background and hints or negotiating tips that are included in this form. Your investors will often have lawyers or CPAs or someone who wants something changed, no matter who wrote the agreement. The hints sprinkled throughout the agreement will help you negotiate with those folks.

Form 2.01: Operating Agreement

OPERATING AGREEMENT

OPERATING AGREEMENT for _____**, LLC**

THE SECURITIES REPRESENTED BY THIS AGREEMENT HAVE NOT BEEN REGISTERED UNDER THE SECURITIES ACT OF 1933, AS AMENDED ("SECURITIES ACT") NOR REGISTERED NOR QUALIFIED UNDER ANY STATE SECURITIES LAWS. SUCH SECURITIES MAY NOT BE OFFERED FOR SALE, SOLD, DELIVERED AFTER SALE, TRANSFERRED, PLEDGED OR HYPOTHECATED UNLESS QUALIFIED AND REGISTERED UNDER APPLICABLE STATE AND FEDERAL SECURITIES LAWS OR UNLESS, IN THE OPINION OF COUNSEL SATISFACTORY TO THE COMPANY, SUCH QUALIFICATION AND

REGISTRATION IS NOT REQUIRED. ANY TRANSFER OF THE SECU-RITIES REPRESENTED BY THIS AGREEMENT IS FURTHER SUBJECT TO OTHER RESTRICTIONS, TERMS AND CONDITIONS WHICH ARE SET FORTH HEREIN.

A. This Operating Agreement is entered into as of [date] by and among the "Managing Members" and the "Investment Members" (whom hereinafter may be referred to individually as a "Member" or collectively as "Members") as further defined below.

B. The Members desire to form a [insert the name of the state in which your company is located]_____ limited liability company (the "Company") for the purposes set forth in Paragraph 2.5.

C. The Members enter into this Agreement to form and to provide for the governance of the Company and the conduct of its business, and to specify their relative rights and obligations.

NOW, THEREFORE, the Parties agree as follows:

ARTICLE I: DEFINITIONS

Capitalized terms used in this Agreement have the meanings specified in this Article or elsewhere in this Agreement; and, when not so defined, shall have the meanings set forth in the Act.

1.1 "Agreement" means this Operating Agreement, as originally executed and as amended from time to time.

1.2 "Capital Contribution" means, with respect to any Member, the amount of money or the Fair Market Value of any property (other than money) contributed to the Company. A Capital Contribution shall not be deemed a loan.

1.3 "Investment Members" means all members of the Company making monetary Capital Contributions to the Company, aside from the Managing Members.

1.4 "Managing Members" mean __[This will be you as the producer of the film and organizer of this venture] _____ ("_____") and _____ [this would be your partner or associate, although you may be happier if you don't have to share management with anyone] _____

("____"), or the entity(ies) or person(s) who from time to time succeed said Managing Member and who, in either case, are serving at the relevant time as Managing Member. The Managing Members may be referred to herein as "Managers."

1.5   "Picture" means the feature length motion picture currently titled, "XXXXX" produced by [Your LLC] and directed by [XXXXX], to which Company intends to produce and control all rights, including appurtenant and ancillary thereto. A copy of the business plan for the Picture is attached hereto as EXHIBIT A.

> **HINT: If the picture is really low budget or the investors are all family friends or old school pals, you may not need a business plan. Most low-budget producers try to avoid that and many of them succeed.**

1.6   "Revenue" means all monies actually received by the Company for the exploitation of the Picture.

ARTICLE II: ORGANIZATIONAL MATTERS

2.1   The Managers have caused organizing documents in the form of the ARTICLES OF ORGANIZATION attached to this Agreement as EXHIBIT B, to be filed with the Secretary of State.

2.2   The name of the Company shall be _____, LLC.

2.3   The principal executive office of the Company shall be _____, or such other place or places as may be determined by the Manager from time to time.

2.4   The registered agent for service of process on the Company shall be _____, whose address is _____. Managers from time to time may change the Company's agent for service of process.

> **HINT: This is a requirement in all states. You would normally name your lawyer.**

2.5   The business of the Company shall be to produce and control the rights to the Picture and to perform and conduct any other activity necessary or incidental to the foregoing or in the opinion of the Managers in furtherance of the objects of the business of the Company.

2.6   The Members intend the Company to be a limited liability company under the Act. Neither the Managers nor any Member shall take any action inconsistent with the law and the express intent of the parties to this Agreement.

2.7   The "Term of Existence" of the Company shall commence on the effective date of filing of the Articles of Organization with the _____ Secretary of State, which was _____, and shall continue until the last expiration of copyright on the Picture unless sooner terminated by the provisions of this Agreement, or as provided by law.

2.8   The name and address of the Managing Members are as follows:

[Name of Managing Member]

[Address]

[Name of Managing Member]

[Address]

2.9   The name and address of the Investment Members are attached hereto as EXHIBIT C.

ARTICLE III: CAPITAL AND CAPITAL CONTRIBUTIONS

3.1   Capital Contribution. Members shall contribute the funds, property and other such benefits as necessary to produce the Picture and cover other expenses as reasonably necessary.

3.2   The Company will comply with all applicable laws and regulations concerning securing financing hereunder.

3.3   The Managers shall contribute as their Capital Contribution services to the Company, including, but not limited to, producing and directing the Picture and other such services.

3.4   Investment Members' Capital Contribution shall be as outlined on EXHIBIT C.

3.5   No Member shall be required to make any additional Capital Contributions. No Investment Member may voluntarily make any additional Capital Contribution, without the prior written consent of the Managers.

3.6   Except as set forth herein, no Member may sell, donate or pass over his, her or its Economic Interest in Company to any third party without the express written consent of the Managers.

3.7   Except as outlined herein, no Investment Member shall have priority over any other Member with respect to the return of a Capital Contribution or distributions or allocations of income, gain, losses, deductions, credits, or items thereof.

3.8   No interest shall be paid on Capital Contributions.

3.9   The Company's total capitalization will not exceed $_____.00 The current budget for the Picture is attached hereto as EXHIBIT D.

> **HINT: Investors want to know that the value of their investment will not be reduced lower than a given percentage and this provision provides that protection.**

ARTICLE IV: ALLOCATIONS

4.1   The allocation of Revenue shall be as follows:

4.1.1   First, a reasonable amount of the Company's income shall be used for operating and production expenses, including salaries;

4.1.2   Then, the Company shall satisfy any outstanding obligations of the Company in connection with the Picture, including deferred payments incurred in connection with the Picture;

4.1.3   Then, each Member shall recoup 120% of his/her Capital Contribution on a pro rata basis;

> **HINT: Investors typically expect to recoup their investment and receive a premium between 10–20%. The position on the revenue allocation is an important negotiation. Investors may expect recoupment prior to any deferrals paid out. Work with your lawyer to discuss the best structure for your project.**

4.1.4   Next:

    4.1.4.1 50% shall be paid out to Investment Members on a pro rata basis determined by the amount of each Investment Members' Capital Contribution;

> **Background: *Pro rata* means that all the investment members will be paid at the same time in proportion to the amount of money they invested.**

    4.1.4.2 Simultaneously, 50% shall be paid out equally to the Managers (i.e, 50/50);

4.1.5   Any losses of the Company shall be allocated 100% to all Members on a pro rata basis.

ARTICLE V: MANAGEMENT

5.1   The Company shall be managed by the Managers.

5.2   The Managers shall have the powers and duties set forth in this Agreement.

5.3   All decisions about, regarding or otherwise pertaining to the creative and business aspects of the Picture, including, but not limited to, the production, distribution and exploitation of the Picture shall be made mutually by the Managers. The Managers agree not to use this process to prevent the production or development of any project or to frustrate the purpose of the Company. However, after good faith discussions, if the Managers cannot agree with respect to an aspect of the Picture or the business of the Company, the Managers agree to present such disagreement to _____ who shall act as a neutral mediator.

5.4   Investment Members shall not have say over any aspects regarding the Picture, including but not limited to all, artistic production elements in connection with the production of the Picture, and all commitments and contracts relative to any of the foregoing.

5.5   All credits accorded the Company and Managers shall be in the sole discretion of the Managers and shall be mutually approved upon, except to
the extent such credit is controlled by a third party (e.g., financier, studio,
union or guild requirements). The Managers have agreed that _____ shall
receive a "Producer" credit and _____ shall receive a "Director" credit.
All other aspects of the credits, including but not limited to size, prominence and placement shall be mutually determined by the Managers.

> **HINT: Many investors ask for credit. We feel producer credits should only be
> given to folks who do producer work. Any investor who puts in half the
> budget certainly deserves an Executive Producer credit.**

5.6   The Managers may have other business interests to which they each
devote a portion of their time. Managers shall devote such time to the
conduct of the business of the Company as Managers, in their own
good faith and discretion, deem necessary. Managers may engage in
other activities reasonably related to or competitive with the Picture.

ARTICLE VI: RISK FACTORS

6.1   Investment in the film industry is highly speculative and inherently
risky. There can be no assurance of the economic success of any
motion picture since the revenues derived from the production and
distribution of a motion picture depend primarily upon its acceptance
by the public, which cannot be predicted. The commercial success
of a motion picture also depends upon the quality and acceptance of
other competing films released into the marketplace at or near the
same time, general economic factors and other tangible and intangible
factors, all of which can change and cannot be predicted with certainty.

6.2   The entertainment industry in general, and the motion picture industry
in particular, are continuing to undergo significant changes, primarily
due to technological developments. Although these developments have
resulted in the availability of alternative and competing forms of leisure
time entertainment, such technological developments have also resulted
in the creation of additional revenue sources through licensing of rights
to such new media, and potentially could lead to future reductions in
costs of producing and distributing motion pictures. In addition, the theatrical success of a motion picture remains a crucial factor in generating
revenues in other media such as videocassettes and television. Due to

the rapid growth of technology, shifting consumer tastes, and the popularity and availability of other forms of entertainment, it is impossible to predict the overall effect these factors will have on the potential revenue from and profitability of feature-length motion pictures.

6.3   The Company itself is in its organizational stage and is subject to all the risks incident to the creation and development of a new business, including the absence of a history of operations and minimal net worth. In order to prosper, the success of the Picture will depend partly upon the ability of the Manager to produce a film of exceptional quality at a lower cost which can compete in appeal with higher-budgeted films of the same genre. In order to minimize this risk, the Manager plans to participate as much as possible throughout the process and will aim to mitigate financial risks where possible. Fulfilling this goal depends on the timing of investor financing, the ability to obtain distribution contracts with satisfactory terms, and the continued participation of the current management.

WORKING WITH YOUR LAWYER
Different lawyers have a different view on the above language. Many leave it out all together. We like it because it assures you that your investor knows they are investing in a high risk venture when they invest in an independent film.

ARTICLE VII: ACCOUNTS AND ACCOUNTING

7.1   Complete books of account of the Company's business, in which each Company transaction shall be fully and accurately entered, shall be kept at the principal business office, or at such other locations as the Manager may determine from time to time, and shall be open to inspection and copying on reasonable Notice by any Member or the Member's authorized representatives during normal business hours, but no more than once per calendar year. The costs of such inspection and copying shall be borne solely by the Member individually and in no way shall be considered to increase Members' Capital Contribution.

7.2   Financial books and records of the Company shall be kept on the cash or accrual method of accounting, which shall be the method of accounting followed by the Company for federal income tax purposes. The financial statements of the Company shall be prepared in accordance with generally accepted accounting principles and shall be appropriate and adequate for the Company's business and for carrying out the provisions of this Agreement. The fiscal year of the Company shall be January 1 to December 31.

ARTICLE VIII: MEMBERSHIP MEETINGS, VOTING, INDEMNITY

8.1 There shall be two classes of membership, Investment Members and Managing Members. No Investment Member shall have any rights or preferences in addition to or different from those possessed by any other Investment Member.

8.2 The Managing Members shall maintain controlling interest in the Company and make all decisions regarding the Company and the Picture, except Investment Members shall have the right to vote on those minimum items as required by the Act.

8.3 The Company may, but shall not be required, to issue certificates evidencing membership interests to Members of the Company.

8.4 Members may participate in a meeting through use of conference telephone or similar communications equipment, provided that all Members participating in such meeting can hear one another. Such participation shall be deemed attendance at the meeting.

8.5 No Member acting solely in the capacity of a Member is an agent of the Company, nor can any Member acting solely in the capacity of a Member bind the Company or execute any instrument on behalf of the Company. Accordingly, each Member shall indemnify, defend, and save harmless each other Member and the Company from and against any and all loss, cost, expense, liability or damage arising from or out of any claim based upon any action by such Member in contravention of the first sentence of this Section 8.5.

ARTICLE IX: INDEMNIFICATION

9.1 The Company shall have the power to indemnify any Person who was or is a party, or who is threatened to be made a party, to any Proceeding by reason of the fact that such Person was or is a Member, Manager, officer, employee, or other agent of the Company, or was or is serving at the request of the Company as a director, officer, employee or other Agent of another limited liability company, corporation, partnership, joint venture, trust, or other enterprise, against expenses, judgments, fines, settlements, and other amounts actually and reasonably incurred by such Person in connection with such proceeding, if such Person acted in good faith and in a manner that such Person reasonably believed to be in the best interests of the Company, and, in the case of a criminal proceeding, such Person had no reasonable cause to believe that the Person's conduct was unlawful. The termination of any proceeding by judgment, order, settlement, conviction, or upon a plea of *nolo contendere* or its equivalent, shall not, of itself, create a presumption that the Person did not act in good faith and in a manner that such Person reasonably believed to be in the best interests of the Company, or that the Person had reasonable cause to believe that the Person's conduct was unlawful.

ARTICLE X: DISSOLUTION AND WINDING UP

10.1   The Company shall be dissolved upon the first to occur of the following events:

10.1.1   The expiration or termination of the Company's rights and interest to the Picture;

10.1.2   The expiration of the Term of Existence of the Company;

10.1.3   The sale of all or substantially all of the assets of Company;

10.1.4   Upon the vote of Members holding the majority of the interest in the Company;

10.1.5   The happening of any event that makes it unlawful or impossible to carry on the business of the Company; or

10.1.6   Entry of a decree of judicial dissolution.

10.2.   On the dissolution of the Company, the Company shall engage in no further business other than that necessary to wind up the business and affairs of the Company. The Managers shall wind up the affairs of the Company.

10.3.   Each Investment Member shall look solely to the assets of the Company for the return of the Investment Member's investment, and if the Company property remaining after the payment or discharge of the debts and liabilities of the Company is insufficient to return the investment of each Investment Member, such Investment Member shall have no recourse against any other Member for indemnification, contribution, or reimbursement, except as specifically provided in this Agreement.

ARTICLE XI

GENERAL PROVISIONS

11.1   PARTNERSHIP: NO THIRD PARTY BENEFICIARIES. No Member shall hold itself out to others contrary to the provisions hereof. This Agreement is not for the benefit of any third party and shall not be deemed to give any right or remedy contrary to the terms of this Agreement and neither party shall become liable or responsible for any representation, act or omission of such party whether referred to herein or not.

11.2   WAIVER: No waiver by any party hereto of the breach of any term or condition of this Agreement shall be deemed or construed to be a waiver of the breach of such term or condition in the future, or of any preceding or subsequent breach of the same or any other term or condition of this or any other agreement.

11.3   REMEDIES CUMULATIVE: All remedies, rights, undertakings, obligations and agreements contained in this Agreement shall be cumulative, and none of them shall be in limitation of any other remedy, right, undertaking, obligation or agreement of either party.

11.4   ASSIGNMENT: No Member may assign its rights or obligations hereunder without prior written consent of the Managers, which they may exercise at their sole discretion.

11.5   ADDITIONAL DOCUMENTS: Each member shall execute, acknowledge and deliver to the managers, promptly upon the request of the managers, any other instruments or documents necessary or desirable to evidence, effectuate, or confirm this Agreement or any of the terms and conditions hereof.

11.6   MODIFICATIONS: This Agreement, together with its exhibits, cannot be amended, modified or changed in any way whatsoever except by written instrument duly executed by the party being charged.

11.7   SEVERABILITY: In the event that any term, condition, covenant, agreement, requirement or provision herein contained shall be held by any Court or arbitration tribunal having jurisdiction to be unenforceable, illegal, void or contrary to public policy, such term, condition, covenant agreement, requirement or provision shall be of no effect whatsoever upon the binding force or effectiveness of any of the others hereof, it being the intention and declaration of the parties hereto that had they or either of them, known of such unenforceability, illegality, invalidity or contrariety to public policy, they would have entered in to a contract each with the other, containing all of the other terms, conditions, covenants, agreements, requirements, and provisions hereof.

11.8   NOTICES: All notices under this Agreement shall be in writing addressed to the addresses first set forth above, or at such other address as either party may designate from time to time by written notice to the other. All notices shall be served by facsimile and U.S. mail, electronic mail, recognized courier services such as Federal Express or DHL or personal delivery addressed as specified above. The date of receipt by facsimile, electronic mail or courier, as the case may be, shall be the date of service of notice.

11.9   ARBITRATION: All disputes arising out of this Agreement shall be submitted to arbitration in accordance with the rules of the Independent Film and Television Alliance before a single arbitrator. The prevailing party shall be entitled to reasonable attorneys' fees and costs. The arbitrator's award shall be final, and judgment may be entered upon it by any court having jurisdiction thereof.

> **Background: The virtues of arbitration are many to the independent producer. Whatever you do, you want to stay out of court. Many people like to have mandatory mediation before going to arbitration. Mediation is the process by which the parties to a disagreement agree to talk through the problem with a neutral third party who is trained to bring people into agreement. Mediation is a good idea, but often involves some money, always involves some time delays and is something that many people would like to decide upon when a dispute arises. If it is appropriate, mediation is easy enough to institute.**

11.10   CHOICE OF LAW: This Agreement shall be governed by and construed in accordance with the laws of the State of [STATE].

11.11   ENTIRE AGREEMENT: This Agreement constitutes the entire agreement between the parties hereto with respect to all of the matters herein and its execution has not been induced by, nor do any of the parties hereto rely upon or regard as material, any representations or writing whatsoever not incorporated herein and made a part hereof. No amendment or modification hereto shall be valid unless set forth in a writing signed by both parties.

IN WITNESS WHEREOF, the parties have executed or caused to be executed this Agreement on the day and year first above written.

MANAGING MEMBERS: **INVESTMENT MEMBERS:**

_____   _____

_____   _____

By:

_____

By:

_____

EXHIBIT A

BUSINESS PLAN

Comment: A business plan is rarely used for small amounts or films financed by friends and family; it's just too much trouble. But substitute a business plan with any written material you gave your friends and family to get them to part with their cash. If you need a full-blown business plan, there are several books. The best is *Filmmakers and Financing: Business Plans for Independents* by Louise Levison. It contains sample forms to get you started.

EXHIBIT B

ARTICLES OF ORGANIZATION

EXHIBIT C

INVESTMENT MEMBERS

Name and Address	Capital Contribution	Percentage Interest

Comment: You will not be able to fill in the right-hand column until you have raised all the money you need and have closed your fundraising efforts.

EXHIBIT D

BUDGET

» ALL PAPERED UP AND NO ONE TO GO TO

"Where do I find investors?" is a common question among first time filmmakers. Honestly, if you don't have a clue as to who might be a potential investor in your film, this may not be the best route for you to follow. We know that doesn't sound very encouraging or supportive, but it does you no favor to push down a path that will lead to nowhere. Even folks with a lot of targets for potential investors find it difficult to separate folks from their money . . . no matter how much money they might have.

If you do have some idea of whom you can go to for investing in your film, you will need to give them written information about the film. What that information needs to be varies from state to state, but wherever you live, you should include a synopsis of the film, bios of the key members on your team, a suggested poster for the film, the top sheet of a budget, and something about your distribution plans. What you must not include—no matter where you live—is over-selling the project, over-stating commitments or interest from the industry, or using examples of extraordinary successes without pointing out the long, long odds of any indie film making money. Thousands of independent films are completed each year. Only a fraction get into the better festivals and only a fraction of those receive distribution. There are still ways to monetize your film, but never, ever exaggerate the potential or minimize the challenge.

Tax Incentives

One major factor in your financial planning will be the location of your principal photography. You will want to decide the two or three places that will be the most beneficial to shoot. Various states have tax incentives that can be very beneficial. Unfortunately, these incentives change on a regular basis. The best single resource for the latest status of tax incentives around the country is *Incentive Guide,* published by The Incentive Office. Don't be shy about exploring unlikely places for your shoot. When you find a state that interests you because of the tax incentives, contact the film commission and ask for help in finding locations within that state that can serve your purposes. We are constantly amazed how one area can masquerade as another area that is far, far away on the map.

Pre-sales

This used to be a popular and effective way of financing many independent films. Here is how it would work. You would have a script, a director attached, and maybe two leads attached to your picture. You would then create a poster and—if you are really lucky—a sizzle reel with a taste of what the film will be about, hopefully featuring your stars. A foreign sales agent would take all of this to a film market abroad. Foreign sales agents and the markets where they ply their trade are discussed in Chapter 5. In this situation, they would not be selling a completed film. They are selling the promise of a completed film—a film that never turns out exactly as anyone expects, especially the buyer. Therefore, the buyer pays less for the privilege of locking the film up early. It is a bet that can pay off well or can turn out profoundly sad. That is why the possibility of pre-sales has diminished.

But pre-sales are not completely dead. There are still deals to be made on films that are still a twinkle in the producer's eye. Today, you need solid elements, more specific plans, and that sizzle reel is more important than ever. Your sizzle reel will contain as strong a taste as possible of what the finished film will look like. Exactly what that would be must necessarily change from picture to picture. Work closely with your sales agent, who is in the best position to advise you what it is about your film that will appeal to sales agents' clients around the world. Remember, this is not your strong suit. You may be very helpful in marketing your film at home, but foreign territories are, well, foreign to you. Every culture is different and the sales effort needs to be molded by your sales agent. Trust him or her even if you would hate to see the poster used here in the USA.

Bank Financing

Banks do not loan money on scripts, on completed films, or on dreams. Banks loan money on a contract or, better yet, on a series of contracts. We have discussed bank financing in the above section. The same approach could be used on a contract for domestic distribution, although that is not as common because you can usually work out a cash flow solution with domestic distributors.

Another way of approaching a bank is to take out a standard loan if you can find some wealthy person to guarantee the payment. Basically, you would be looking for a sugar daddy who wants to defer his loss, so he sets it up knowing that he will probably have to pay up eventually.

chapter **3**

ASSEMBLING THE TALENT

You have obtained the rights to make your film, have your business entity created, and have your financing lined up. It's time to assemble your team. These folks are divided into above-the-line and below-the-line personnel. The line that is being referred to is an arbitrary line that appears in all film budgeting programs. The line divides the expensive folks who are likely to demand a piece of the income from the film and who are generally represented by agents from the more predictable crew expenses. Typically, the above-the-line personnel include the writer, director, cast, and producers, and the below-the-line personnel is your crew. Since hiring a casting director is typically done before hiring actors, we have included a form contract in this chapter as well.

If it's your first film, you may feel under the gun to hire a good crew. The best way to find a crew is to work on other productions and discover the key personnel that you enjoy working with and whose skills you like. You'll also get a better idea of the different types of directors, producers, and other key staff you like to work with and those you don't. So when it comes time for you to assemble your team, you'll know the personality and skills to look for or you may have met individuals whom you trust to bring onboard. If you live in a region where film production is popular, there may also be groups, trade organizations, and community-oriented events where you can go to network. The good news is that once you've found a good crew, you will most likely want to work with them time and time again.

You will need service agreements that clearly define the rights and obligations of each member of this creative team. These agreements should identify each person's duties, compensation, term of service, and film credit. The terms of these contracts will control the relationship between you and your employees, unless they are trumped by a union or guild agreement, which we discuss below.

» WORK-FOR-HIRE PROVISIONS

If you are like many filmmakers, you may go into this portion of the project's development thinking something along these lines: "These guys are cool. We're all friends and have worked together on other projects before. They're not going to hassle me. We shook on it. Isn't that enough?"

No. While oral contracts are enforceable in many instances, there are consequences to not having an agreement in writing. Perhaps more importantly, without a written agreement in place, you may run into problems during production when someone's expectations or understanding of their duties and responsibilities differ from yours. In case of an argument, it's best to have agreements in place that clearly state who has the final say when conflicts arise. Without a written agreement, you may also run into chain-of-title issues (see Delivery chapter), since many crew members create things that are copyrightable and without a written agreement in place, those folks own the copyright to their contributions. For instance, prop makers, set designers, costume designers, and cinematographers routinely create items that could be registered for copyright protection in their own name. Under current copyright law, even choreography is protected by copyright. Many producers fail to take this into account and, accordingly, their agreements may not be sufficient.

To ensure that you own all the rights to your film, every agreement must contain standard work-for-hire language, which is included in the following model agreements. Another important item that should be addressed in your crew and talent agreements is the right to use their names and likenesses in the publicity and the advertising of your film. It would seem that most people involved in a film would want to be included in publicity, but without specific permission, distributors won't allow it. Related to publicity is formal credit—on screen and in paid ads. How much credit, or credit for what, becomes an issue. Size, placement, and relative position are all hotly negotiated items for the cast and crew.

» UNION VS. NONUNION

Directors, writers, and actors have their own unions, which are called guilds, even though they are not guilds; they are unions. In fact, actors have three unions: Screen Actors Guild, or SAG, for movies and TV shows shot on film, American Federation of Television and Radio Artists, or AFTRA, for things shot on tape (tape?, yes, tape), and/or for performances in a stage play. You don't have to worry about the last one.

Most actors who have any experience at all will be in a union, so it is probably not very productive to think about shooting a motion picture using non-union actors. However, you have two decisions to make: which union (i.e., SAG or AFTRA) and which contract of the several each offers to filmmakers. Since film or tape were the choices when these unions were formed and things change slowly in union land, that is still the division, although increasingly movies are shot on digital equipment so you get to pick. Far be it for us to get in the middle of that jurisdictional squabble. But we do advise that you look at both contracts and decide after doing a lot of math.

Some of that math will vary widely depending on the contract you choose. SAG has a low-budget contract, an experimental film contract, and the SAG Basic Agreement contract, all of which were developed in the last few years in order to keep them competitive with AFTRA and current with the market place. The various contracts are discussed in greater depth in the section on actors.

The Director's Guild and the Writer's Guild contracts are more straight forward. When working with a member of the union, you will sign a contract with the union as a production company. These contracts are not negotiable by the time it is your turn to sign them. Union contracts are negotiated by the unions and management of the studios as they come up for renewal. The trade papers cover these negotiations in depth. As an independent producer, you don't have a seat at the table. You just sign whatever union agreement is in place at the time you make your picture.

When you sign a contract with someone who is a member of a union, you need to think of it as a three-way contract. You sign with the actor or director or writer, but that contract is subject to the contract you signed with the union.

Nothing in the personal contract can lower or reduce what you agreed to with the union. If you put a provision in your contract with the artist that is less than the provision in the union contract, the union contract controls. The union contract is called a Minimum Basic Agreement. Nothing you negotiate or write into your agreement with the artist that is less than the Minimum Basic Agreement will have any effect.

» WORKING CONDITIONS

The most important things that will not show up in your contract, but that you need to be keenly aware of, are the working conditions. The actors' contracts have a lot of rules about meal times, turn-around time (the time between the close of one day of filming and the next), and such. Violate these working rules and you are subject to a fine, which you agreed to pay when you signed your agreement with the union. The Directors Guild has rules about the amount of personnel you have to provide when you hire a union director. The Writers Guild has specific periods of time you have to read and give notes on a script.

Residuals

One of the items that will not be in your personal services contract with the artist is residuals. Residuals are payments that will be due the artist, above and beyond anything that you agree to pay. They cannot be waived. They can be a big headache. How big a headache? Check out the residual chart that shows you exactly what you will owe as your film goes out into the world. It's at http://riskybusiness.hollywoodreporter.com.

Reuse Fees

This is another item that won't show up in the contract with the artist. It will not cause you any heartburn, however. These are the fees that you will have to pay if you reuse some footage you shot for another film, other than the film which you hired the person for. Today, the issue arises almost exclusively in two contexts: looking-back shows for television and the licensing of clips from one film to use in another film.

The television shows in which they have everybody sitting around talking about a series and what happened in various episodes are classified as new films that use a lot of clips from previous shows, so reuse fees have to be paid. If someone wants to license a clip from your film for use in another film, then you just charge them what you want and put the onus on them to pay the reuse fees as a condition to having the right to use the footage. The reason we mention reuse fees here is that many people use the words "reuse fees" and "residuals" interchangeably. They are very different payments for very different purposes.

» DIRECTOR

The primary person—besides the writer—who contributes creative efforts to the film is the director. The Director's Agreement is similar to other above-the-line agreements like the Actor or Writer's Agreement; however, there are a number of clauses which specify the director's creative control and how approvals are managed. The Director's Agreement should also identify the director's delivery requirements for the film. These may include approving a budget, finalizing a production schedule, reshoots, delivering a director's cut and other post production tasks.

High-earning, above-the-line personnel such as actors and directors, often use what is called a "Loan-Out company." A loan-out company is a company formed by the artist to employ his or her services to a production company. The production company makes all payments for the Artist's services directly to the loan-out company. Typically, loan-out companies are limited liability companies or a corporation. These companies offer several advantages to artists, including sheltering the Artist from personal liability for debts and offering tax benefits available to companies.

An agreement with a loan-out company must be drafted so that the contracting party is the loan out-company. For example, "Producer agrees to employ Loan-Out Company, LLC ("Lender") f/s/o Director, Frankie Filmmaker." The loan-out company is typically called the "lender." The term f/s/o stands or "for the services of." The following Director's agreement shows how a producer would contract with a Director's loan-out company.

Form 3.01: Director's Agreement

DIRECTOR'S AGREEMENT

THIS AGREEMENT, effective as of _____, 20__ is made by and between [YOUR NAME/COMPANY] ("Producer") whose address is [PHYSICAL ADDRESS] and [DIRECTOR'S LOAN-OUT CORPORATION] ("Lender") f/s/o [DIRECTOR] ("Director") whose address is [PHYSICAL ADDRESS] with respect to Director's services on the feature-length motion picture currently entitled, "_____" (the "Picture").

> **HINT: You must be aware of whether you are contracting with an individual or loan-out company. Notice the loan-out language in this agreement. When contracting with a loan-out company, the agreement must also include inducement language that states that the Director has read the agreement and agrees to perform the applicable service, as you will see at the end of this agreement.**

> **Date: By using an effective date right at the beginning of the contract, you eliminate disputes over when a contract was signed, which may control some of the terms. Few contracts are signed by all parties on the same day. You can select any date as your effective date.**

1. CONDITIONS PRECEDENT:

(a) **Execution of Agreement**. Producer's receipt of fully-executed copies of this Agreement by Lender and Director;

(b) **Employment Eligibility**. In accordance with the Immigration Reform and Control Act of 1986, any offer of employment contained herein is conditioned upon satisfactory proof of Director's identity and United States employment eligibility. Lender must present required documentation within ten

---

(10) days of acceptance of this offer. Failure to comply with this section will result in termination of employment;

(c) **Insurance**. Director's ability to qualify for all insurance Producer deems necessary for the Picture (e.g., life, health, accident and/or cast insurance) at customary rates and subject only to customary exclusions and deductible amounts (if any);

(d) **Completion Guarantor Approval**. The completion guarantor of the Picture ("Guarantor") having approved the terms and conditions of Director's services as director of the Picture, and execution by Director of an inducement letter and/or side letter with Guarantor as Guarantor may require ("Guarantor Inducement Letter");

(e) **Budget, Screenplay, Schedule, Cast**. Approval by Producer and the Completion Guarantor of the following: (i) an "all-in" budget for the Picture including without limitation bond fee, contingency, interest, premiums and financing charges ("Approved Budget"), (ii) the screenplay, (iii) the production schedule and post production schedules for the Picture; and (iv) the principal cast;

(f) **Setting Picture for Production**. Producer electing to set the Picture for production. For purposes of the foregoing, Producer shall be deemed to have set the Picture for production when all of the Conditions Precedent in this paragraph have been satisfied and additionally, (i) when the Picture is fully financed, (ii) Producer has set a firm start date for the commencement of principal photography of the Picture, (iii) the long form actor agreements for lead actors have been signed and approved of by Producer and each of such actors;

(g) **Approval of Shooting Schedule for Picture**. Director and Lender's approval of the shooting schedule in writing for the Picture—it being agreed by Lender and Producer that Producer shall have final control of the shooting schedule of the Picture if Director and Producer cannot agree on the shooting schedule for the Picture.

HINT: Engaging a director's services is often contingent upon a number of factors that must be considered at the time you formalize the agreement. These may include the film acquiring full financing, engagement of principal actors, approval of the production schedule and budget, and the completion guarantor of the film having approved the terms and conditions of the Director's services. If the Conditions Precedent are not met, then neither party is obligated to fulfill any other provisions of the agreement. This is especially important if the director is pay-or-play. DGA members must be pay-or-pay for the minimum guaranteed weeks.

2. SERVICES:

(a)   **Development Services.** Lender shall cause Director to render such development services in connection with the Picture as are customarily rendered by directors of first-class feature length motion pictures and as Producer may require, including without limitation the supervision of the development of the screenplay for the Picture. Such development services shall be rendered by Director on a non-exclusive, first priority basis.

(b)   **Production Services.** Lender shall cause Director to render all such services in connection with the pre-production, photography and post-production of the Picture as are required by the Producer and customarily rendered by directors of first-class feature length motion pictures, and Director shall comply with all reasonable directions and requests of Producer in connection therewith, whether or not the same involve matters of artistic taste or judgment. Such production services shall be rendered by Director on an exclusive basis.

HINT: Your Director's Agreement should have language that sets the standard under which the Director will perform such services ("as are customarily rendered by directors of first-class feature length motion pictures") and include other services common of director's including "pre-production, photography and post-production." Your director may also have a hand working with the writer to prepare the script for production, casting, location scouts, and other pre-production activities that you may want to include in this section.

(c)   **Schedule/Term**. Director shall commence directing services hereunder on a date to be designated by Producer, which date may be eight (8) weeks prior to the scheduled start date for principal photography of the Picture, and Director shall continue to render such services on an exclusive basis until the delivery of the "Director's Cut" (as defined in paragraph 14(b) below) of the Picture to Producer and thereafter, on a non-exclusive, first priority basis until delivery of completed answer print to Producer, unless terminated earlier pursuant to the terms of this Agreement.

> **HINT: A director wears many hats from writing and development to post-production, and those duties and obligations that require a director on an exclusive basis should be clearly defined. You will want the director on an exclusive basis for principal photography, and ideally for a period of time prior to principal photography and during post-production. For other periods of time, the Director's services should be on a "first priority" basis, meaning he can work on other projects, but your project is the one he has to work on if there is a time crunch.**

3. COMPENSATION: Subject to: (i) the Conditions Precedent being fulfilled to the satisfaction of Producer, (ii) the Picture being produced, (iii) Lender nor Director being in material breach of any representation, warranty or agreement of this Agreement, and (iv) the lead actors being engaged to render acting services, Producer shall pay to Lender the following compensation ("Fixed Compensation"):

    (a)   **Fixed Compensation**. A total fixed compensation of __ percent of the Approved Budget (excluding overhead, contingency, executive producing fees, bond, legal, interest and financing) payable as follows:

        (i)   Twenty percent (20%) thereof in consecutive equal weekly installments over the schedule period of pre-production of the Picture.

        (ii)   Sixty percent (60%) thereof in consecutive equal weekly installments over the scheduled period of principal photography of the Picture.

        (iii)   Ten percent (10%) thereof upon Director's completion and delivery to Producer of the Director's Cut of the Picture.

(iv)   Ten percent (10%) thereof upon completion and delivery to Producer of the answer print of the Picture.

HINT: The Director's agreement details the amount of fixed compensation and the method and timing of payment. There are other variations on the theme of fixed compensation, including deferred payments (different from contingent compensation) which comes out of the gross revenue received by the production company from the film. It is in the best interest of the production company to stagger payments based on deliverables which provides the Director with continued incentive to deliver services on time and within budget. Here, we include weekly payments starting over pre-production and during principal photography. A payment is made once the director's cut is delivered, and a final payment is made when the answer print is completed. You may consider other payment milestones depending on the production. These may include sizzle reels, an approved budget, storyboards, etc.

Background: An Answer Print as mentioned above is the first composite print which includes sound, music, floor, title and fades, color and sound balance. It "answers" the question affirmatively that a print is potentially ready for commercial presentation. However, the Answer Print typically needs additional fine-tuning before the final print for mass release, which is called the "Release Print."

(b)   **Contingent Compensation.** Lender shall be paid an amount equal to: (i) five percent (5%) of one-hundred percent (100%) of Producer's Net Proceeds (collectively, "Director's Participation"). Director's Participation shall be applied against any residuals due Director pursuant to the terms of the DGA Basic Agreement and vice versa. "Net Proceeds" as used herein shall mean all money received or credited to Producer from the exploitation of the Picture less (i) Producer's out-of-pocket distribution expenses in connection with the Picture, including without limitation all third party participations and residuals and (ii) the Approved Budget of the Picture.

Background: A director may receive a portion of the net proceeds of the picture, typically 5–10% of the Producer's Share of net proceeds. On independent films that percentage may be higher, depending upon whether the Director has any salary deferred and whether the director contributes any additional services.

(c)   **Box Office Bonuses**. Lender shall be entitled to receive the following box office bonuses payable to Lender within ninety (90) days following the initial publication of such worldwide theatrical box office gross receipts level and DVD sales combined as reported in *Daily Variety* ("Sales"):

    (i)   _____ dollars ($_____) when the Picture reaches Sales in an amount equal to two and a half (2.5) times the Approved Budget;

    (ii)   _____ dollars ($_____) when the Picture reaches Sales in an amount equal to three and a half times (3.5) times the Approved Budget; and

    (iii)   _____ dollars ($_____) when the Picture reaches Sales in an amount equal to four (4) times the Approved Budget.

> **HINT: If you can avoid box office bonuses, do so. The trouble with box office bonuses is that the indie filmmaker ends up paying so many fees and has to allow the distributors to recoup all of their costs before the filmmaker sees a dime. Often what happens is that the box office numbers seem good, but the producer hasn't seen a penny. The box office numbers above are designed to help ensure that the producer actually has the money to pay the bonuses, but are certainly no guarantee. We propose bonuses based on monies actually received.**

4. CREDIT: Provided that neither Lender nor Director are in material, uncured breach of this Agreement, Director shall receive a credit on a single card in the main title credits (whether at the beginning or end of the Picture). Such credit shall be in accordance with and subject to the requirements contained in the DGA Basic Agreement, substantially as follows:

"Directed by [DIRECTOR]"

    (a)   Director's credit shall appear in all positive prints of the Picture and all paid advertisements (subject to standard exclusions), with size, color, boldness and duration comparable to that of the writer's credit.

    (b)   All other aspects of credit and all other credits shall be at the sole discretion of Producer.

(c)   No casual or inadvertent failure of Producer to comply with the credit provisions hereof shall constitute a breach of this Agreement. Within a reasonable time after receipt of written notice from Lender specifying a failure to accord proper credit in accordance with this Paragraph, Producer shall use good faith efforts to cure prospectively any such failure with regard to positive prints and/or advertising materials created after the date of Producer's receipt of such notice. Producer will contractually obligate third party licensees and sub-distributors with whom Producer is in privity of contract to comply with the credit obligations set forth herein, but shall not be responsible or liable to Lender or Director for the failure of any such third party to comply with the same.

> **Background: The position in the credits is negotiable. Directors will almost always receive credit in the main titles on a separate card. If the director belongs to the Directors Guild of America, the production will necessarily be a signatory to the Directors Guild of America Minimum Basic Agreement and the credits will be governed by that agreement. For all credit provisions, you should always include the language on "inadvertent failure" as included above because you don't want to be on the hook for someone else's screw up.**

5. TRANSPORTATION/ACCOMMODATIONS: Producer shall provide all necessary transportation and accommodations for Director in connection with the Picture as needed throughout pre-production, production and post-production. Specifically, Producer shall provide Director with _____.

6. FESTIVALS/PREMIERES: Producer shall invite Director and a guest to all premieres and film festivals in connection with the Picture. Director and his guest's transportation and accommodations for such premieres and festivals shall be on a most-favored nations basis with any individual Producer. Additionally, Lender shall be reimbursed for all reasonable documented expenses upon receipt of such documentation.

> **HINT: Directors are typically encouraged to attend premieres and festivals to help promote the film. Depending on the budget of the film, you may want to specify travel (i.e. coach air fare), limit the reimbursement amount, or require the production company's prior written approval. You don't want to be stuck with unexpected expenses.**

Background: A "favored nations" clause means that the terms granted to one party are at least as favorable as the best terms being granted to anyone else. For example, in the above festival/premiere section, if a producer gets business class air travel and accommodations at a five star hotel, then the director's travel arrangements has to be as good or better than any other producer. You will see most-favored nations clauses on many independent film contracts, where talent will waive their usual demands to accommodate a low-budget film.

7. APPROVALS AND CONTROLS:

(a) Producer shall solely have all approvals and controls of all kinds and nature, with respect to the Picture, including, but not limited to, all decisions involving artistic taste and judgment. Notwithstanding, Producer shall meaningfully consult with Director on all material creative elements of the Picture, including the hiring of talent and key crew members.

(b) **Director's Cut**. Director shall be entitled to make one (1) cut of the Picture (the "Director's Cut") as required pursuant to the DGA Basic Agreement. Director's right to prepare the Director's Cut shall be conditioned upon (a) Director not being in material default of the Agreement; and (b) Director preparing and delivering the Director's Cut in conformance with the requirements set forth in this Paragraph.

HINT: To avert conflicts regarding creative control, it is best to expressly state who has final say over the creative decisions of the film. Depending on the leverage of the producer or director, you may negotiate several options. Here, we follow the DGA basic agreement and allow the Director a director's cut. Notice, however, that while the Director has "meaningful consultation" rights, it is the Producer who has final say over any particular creative decision. It is also beneficial to provide a postproduction schedule which to deliver a director's cut, in order to stay on time and within budget. Here, we have provided eight weeks. If following the DGA Basic Agreement, then you must provide a minimum of ten weeks from the time the editor has assembled and delivered the picture.

(i) The choice of editing location shall be at Producer's sole discretion.

(ii) Director shall deliver to Producer the Director's Cut of the Picture no later than eight (8) weeks after the completion of principal photography. The Picture, as delivered, shall (i) strictly adhere to the final approved shooting script (subject to such minor changes required by the exigencies of production and as approved by Producer), (ii) be no less than ninety (90) minutes and no more than one hundred twenty (120) minutes in length (including main and end titles), (iii) be in color in a standard thirty-five millimeter (35mm) format, and (iv) qualify with the Motion Picture Association of America ("MPAA") for a rating no more restrictive than "R," unless Producer agrees in writing to a more restrictive rating.

(iii)   Nothing in the foregoing or elsewhere in this Agreement shall in any way limit Producer's absolute and final cutting authority with respect to the Picture or to otherwise modify, edit, add to and delete from the Picture at any time as Producer may determine in its sole discretion.

8. REPRESENTATIONS AND WARRANTIES:

(a)   **Free to Enter into Agreement**. Lender and Director represent and warrant that Director is free to enter into this Agreement and will not do or permit any act which will interfere with or derogate from the full performance of Director's services or Producer's exercise of the rights herein granted.

(b)   **Director's Material**. Lender and Director represent and warrant that with respect to any material supplied by Director hereunder, such material shall be wholly original and shall not infringe upon or violate the copyright, literary, dramatic or photoplay rights, the right of privacy or publicity of any person or entity, nor defame any person or entity, nor shall it be based in whole or in part on the life of any real person except as approved in writing by Producer, nor be the subject of any litigation or any claim that might give rise to litigation.

(c)   **Guild**. Director represents that he is currently a member of the Director's Guild of America ("DGA") and Producer is a signatory thereto.

9. WORK-MADE-FOR-HIRE:

(a)   Lender and Director hereby acknowledge that all of the results and proceeds of Director's services produced for the Picture hereunder shall constitute a "work-made-for-hire" specially commissioned by Producer, and Producer or Producer's assignee shall own all such results and proceeds. Producer may make such use of the Picture and distribution of the Picture as Producer, in its sole discretion, shall deem appropriate.

(b)   If Director's services are not recognized as a "work-made-for-hire," Lender and Director hereby irrevocably grant, sell and assign to Producer, its successors and assigns, all of Director's rights, title and interest of any kind and nature, in and to the Picture, including, without limitation, all copyrights in connection therewith and all tangible and intangible properties with respect to the Picture, in perpetuity, whether in existence now or as may come into existence in the future.

(c)   Director waives the exercise of any "moral rights" and "droit moral" and any analogous rights however denominated now or hereafter recognized. All rights granted and agreed to be granted to Producer hereunder are irrevocable and shall vest and remain perpetually vested in Producer, its successors and assigns, whether this Agreement expires in normal course or is sooner terminated, and shall not be subject to rescission by Director for any cause whatsoever.

> **Background: Work-for-Hire clause:** All agreements with cast and crew, including artists, actors, writers, directors, other employees and independent contractors should include a work-for-hire provision, which gives copyright ownership of the film to the production company. Work-for-Hire is defined in U.S. Copyright Law as either (1) a work prepared by an employee within the scope of employment; or (2) a work specially ordered or commissioned for use as one of a very limited number of specified works. A Work-for-Hire provision is critical because without one, the director could claim copyright ownership of the film, as discussed earlier.

> **Background: Moral Rights or Droit Moral clause:** Note how the waiver of moral rights is at the end of the paragraph. It is customary for agreements to also include a waiver of moral rights, or as referred to by the French name "droit moral." Moral rights are primarily recognized in Europe. These rights entitle a filmmaker to have a say in how his or her film is used and may limit a producer's ability to modify the film or create remakes and sequels. All of your contracts with writers, directors, actors, and other artists should waive their moral rights in the film. However, under the law of many countries, the "author" of a work of art cannot waive moral rights. For added protection, an assignment clause is included that transfers the ownership of the copyright, if any, to the production company.

10. **NAME AND LIKENESS**. Lender hereby grants Producer the right to use Director's name, likeness and/or biography in connection with the production, distribution, exhibition, advertising, promotion and other exploitation of the Picture and all subsidiary and ancillary rights therein, including without limitation, soundtrack albums, publications, merchandising and commercial tie-ups (but not as an endorsement of any product or service); provided that in no event will Director be depicted as using or endorsing any product, commodity or service without Director's prior consent. Promptly following the execution hereof, Lender shall furnish Producer with a short-form biography and a long-form biography of Director, which Producer may reasonably edit.

> **HINT: The production company should also include publicity restrictions that give the company complete control of publicity, and restrain the creative team from issuing public statements about the picture without the production company's prior written consent. With social networking sites such as Facebook and Twitter, we have found it increasingly necessary to include such limitations.**

11. **CONTINGENCIES**: Producer shall have the right to suspend or delay the Term during all periods in which Lender or Director is in breach of this Agreement; Lender or Director is prevented from or fails, refuses or neglects to fully perform Director's Services; or the development, production or distribution of the Picture is prevented by a "Force Majeure" event, by the death, illness, disability or incapacity of a principal cast member, producer or director of photography of the Picture.

    (a)   Director's services shall only be suspended or delayed due to a Force Majeure event if the services of all others working on the Picture are also suspended or delayed. Producer shall have no right to engage in selective suspension.

    (b)   In the event Director's services are suspended or delayed due to a Force Majeure event, Director shall have the right to work for third parties during such period so long as any such services do not interfere with production of the Picture and Director shall be available to recommence his services immediately upon written notice of reinstatement.

    (c)   Producer shall be entitled to suspend or delay production no more often than once per each Force Majeure event.

12. **TERMINATION**: Producer shall have the right to terminate this Agreement, effective immediately, if one of the following occurs:

(a)   Director fails to fully perform Director's Services or fails to cure a material breach of this Agreement within forty-eight (48) hours of receipt of written notice of same;

(b)   Death, illness, disability or incapacity of a principal cast member, Director, producer or director of photography of the Picture, which exceeds ten (10) days; or

(c)   A Force Majeure event which exceeds six (6) weeks, reduced to three (3) weeks during principal photography, in which event, Director shall also have the right to terminate this Agreement.

13. MATERIAL BREACH: The parties acknowledge and agree that in addition to other material terms of this Agreement, delivery of the Picture on time and on budget (according to the schedule and Approved Budget that will be provided to Director prior to commencement of official pre-production) are material elements of this Agreement and failure to deliver the Picture on time and on budget, except to the extent such delay or overage is caused or approved in writing by Producer, is the result of a Force Majeure event, third party breach or lab delays, unless any of the previously listed events are caused by Director, shall constitute a material breach hereof.

14. INSURANCE: Producer shall add Director to Producer's Errors and Omissions and General Liability insurance policies as an insured in connection with the Picture, as necessary. Producer shall cover Director under worker's compensation policies during the period of Director's services. Director acknowledges that his, his successors' and his heirs', sole remedy for injuries occurring while working on the Picture shall be limited to making a claim under Producer's worker's compensation insurance policy.

15. UNIQUE SERVICES: Except as specifically provided to the contrary hereinabove, Director's services shall be rendered exclusively to Producer, or Producer's assignee, until expiration of this Agreement, it being mutually understood and agreed that Director's services are extraordinary, unique and not replaceable, and that there is no adequate remedy at law for any breach of this Agreement by Director, and that Producer, in the event of breach by Director, shall be entitled to seek equitable relief by way of injunction or otherwise.

16. REMEDIES: Director recognizes and confirms that in the event of a failure or omission by Producer constituting a breach of its obligations under this Agreement, whether or not material, the damage, if any, caused Director is not irreparable or sufficient to entitle Director to injunctive or other equitable relief. Consequently, Director's rights and remedies shall be limited to the right, if any, to obtain damages at law and

Director shall not have any right in such event to terminate or rescind this Agreement or any of the rights granted to Producer hereunder or to enjoin or restrain the development, production, advertising, promotion, distribution, exhibition or exploitation of the Picture and/or any of Producer's rights pursuant to this Agreement.

> **Background: No injunction clause. This is very important. An "injunction" is a court order that could potentially halt production of the film. This clause waives the Director's rights to injunctive relief and limits his or her remedies to suing for money damages. The filmmaker should never risk having his film enjoined (prevented from being distributed) because of a disgruntled employee.**

17. NO OBLIGATION TO PROCEED. Nothing herein contained shall in any way obligate Producer to use Director's services hereunder or to include the results and proceeds of Director's services in the Picture or to produce, exhibit, advertise or distribute the Picture; provided that, upon the condition that neither Lender nor Director is in material default of the terms and conditions hereof, nothing contained in this Paragraph shall relieve Producer of its obligations to Lender or Director hereunder, which shall be deemed fully performed by payment to Lender of the foregoing amounts. All of the foregoing shall be subject to the other terms and conditions of this Agreement (including, without limitation, force majeure, disability and default).

> **Background: No-obligation-to-produce clause. This language makes clear that although you may have been granted the right to hire and utilize the Director, you are not obligated to use his or her service or to release the film.**

18. MISCELLANEOUS:

    (a)   **Arbitration.** To the extent not subject to DGA arbitration, all disputes under this Agreement shall be settled pursuant to binding arbitration under the rules of the Independent Film and Television Alliance ("IFTA") in _____ before a single arbitrator. The prevailing party will be entitled to reasonable attorneys' fees and costs.

> **Background: The virtues of arbitration are many to the independent producer. Whatever you do, you want to stay out of court. Many people like to have mandatory mediation before going to arbitration. Mediation is the process by which the parties to a disagreement agree to talk through the problem with a neutral third party who is trained to bring people into agreement. Mediation is a good idea, but often involves some money, always involves some time delays and is something that many people would like to decide upon when a dispute arises. If it is appropriate, mediation is easy enough to institute.**

(b)   **Indemnification**. Lender and Director shall indemnify and defend Producer from and against any and all claims and damages arising from the breach of any representation or warranty of Lender or Director hereunder to the extent such claim or damage does not arise out of a breach by Producer hereunder. Producer shall indemnify and defend Lender and Director from and against any and all claims and damages arising from the production, distribution, exhibition or exploitation of the Picture, or any element thereof, to the extent such claim or damage does not arise out of a breach by Lender or Director hereunder.

(c)   **Accounting**. Producer agrees to keep and maintain complete and accurate books and records relating to the Picture and the proceeds derived therefrom.

> **HINT:** The accounting paragraph is only used if the Director is receiving back-end compensation. If so, a standard audit provision is included in this section: Lender or his/her representative shall have the right to examine, copy and/or cause an audit to be made of the books and records of Producer pertaining to the Picture during regular business hours at Lender's sole expense, unless the audit reveals underpayments in excess of ten percent (10%), in which case, Producer shall reimburse Lender the reasonable costs thereof. Lender shall have the right to audit Producer's books and records no more frequently than once per annum and only with respect to statements received by Lender within two (2) years prior to the commencement of the audit.

(d)   **Assignment**. Lender nor Director may assign its rights or obligations hereunder except to the extent Lender wishes to assign its right to receive its compensation to another party or entity. Producer may assign its rights and obligations hereunder, provided, however, that if this Agreement is assigned to a person or entity other than a bona fide distributor, financier, major or mini-major studio that assumes Producer's obligations in writing, Producer shall remain secondarily liable to Lender and Director.

(e)   **Choice of Law**. This Agreement shall be governed by and construed in accordance with the laws of the State of [STATE].

(f)   **Notices.** All notices under this Agreement shall be in writing addressed to the addresses first set forth above, or at such other address as either party may designate from time to time by written notice to the other. All notices shall be served by facsimile and U.S. mail, electronic mail, recognized courier services such as Federal Express or DHL or personal delivery addressed as specified above. The date of receipt by facsimile, electronic mail or courier, as the case may be, shall be the date of service of notice.

(g) **Employment Eligibility.** In accordance with the Immigration Reform and Control Act of 1986, any offer of employment contained herein is conditioned upon satisfactory proof of Artist's identity and United States employment eligibility. Artist must present required documentation within ten (10) days of acceptance of this offer. Failure to comply will result in termination of employment.

(h) This agreement may be signed in counterparts. Facsimile and scanned copies shall be deemed originals for all purposes.

(i) **Further Documents.** Lender and Director agree to execute, acknowledge, and deliver to Producer and to procure the execution, acknowledgment, and delivery to Producer of any additional documents or instruments which Producer may reasonably require to effectuate fully and carry out the intent and purposes of this Agreement. If Lender or Director shall fail to execute and deliver any such documents or other instruments, within ten (10) calendar days after such documents are delivered to Lender or Director, Producer shall be deemed to be, and Lender and Director irrevocably appoints Producer, the true and lawful attorney-in-fact of Lender and Director, to execute and deliver any and all such documents and other instruments in the name of Lender and Director, which right is coupled with an interest.

> **Comment:** The last sentence of the above paragraph contains a new phrase that you might not be familiar with, "a right coupled with an interest." A right coupled with an interest refers to a legal concept concerning making someone your agent, representative or attorney-in-law or attorney-in-fact. When you appoint someone as your representative and that person has an interest in the subject, you cannot cut off that representation so easily. It is not impossible, but it certainly is not as easy as when you would normally just be able to write a letter and withdraw the power to represent you.

(j) This Agreement constitutes the entire agreement between the parties hereto with respect to all of the matters herein and its execution has not been induced by, nor do any of the parties hereto rely upon or regard as material, any representations or writing whatsoever not incorporated herein and made a part hereof. No amendment or modification hereto shall be valid unless set forth in a writing signed by both parties.

IN WITNESS WHEREOF the parties hereto have caused this Agreement to be duly executed and delivered as of the day and year first above written.

PRODUCER   LENDER

_____   _____

By: By:

_____   _____

Its: EIN:

_____   _____

INDUCEMENT CLAUSE

I have read the foregoing terms of the Agreement dated _____ between Producer and Lender, and to the extent such terms apply to me as an individual, I agree to be bound as if I had personally signed such Agreement.

BY: _____

> **Inducement Clause: This clause must be included in any contract between you and a loan-out company. Because you are contracting with the loan-out company, and not the artist directly, you will need some assurance by the artist that they will be bound by the terms and conditions of the contract. This is a very brief inducement clause. Others may be at least a page long.**

» CASTING DIRECTOR

Another key, early hire is the casting director. A good casting director will have ideas that go beyond the director and producer. He or she knows actors of all types and talents. He or she must also be an excellent negotiator. They are usually on the front line to "sell" your film to the director and to the actors, so make sure their love of you and your script is genuine.

Form 3.02: Casting Director Services Agreement

CASTING SERVICES AGREEMENT

THIS AGREEMENT, effective as of _____ ("Effective Date") is made by and between _____("Producer") whose address is [PHYSICAL ADDRESS] and _____ ("Casting Director") whose address is [PHYSICAL ADDRESS] with respect to casting services in connection with the feature-length motion picture currently entitled, "_____" ("Picture").

> **Date: By using an effective date right at the beginning of the contract, you eliminate disputes over when a contract was signed, which may control some of the terms. Few contracts are signed by all parties on the same day, so put in whatever date you want as an effective date.**

1. **SERVICES**: Casting Director shall render all services customarily rendered by casting directors in the feature-length motion picture industry and at all times promptly comply with Producer's reasonable instructions. Casting Director's services shall include, but not be limited to, compiling cast lists, conducting casting sessions and interviews, and preparation (through to execution) of all cast deal memos as may be required by Producer in connection with the Picture.

2. **TERM**: Casting services shall begin upon signing and shall continue until all roles are cast. If casting services are required after the Term, due to the need to replace a role, Casting Director shall continue working on the Picture. Casting Director shall ensure that at least one of the individuals comprising Casting Director shall be available for any such additional services.

3. **EXCLUSIVITY**: Casting Director's services shall be non-exclusive, but on a first priority, non-material interference basis so that no other activities materially interfere with Casting Director's performance.

4. **COMPENSATION**: For the Term of this Agreement, Producer shall pay the Casting Director a flat fee of $_____, which shall be paid as follows:

        (i)   One-half (1/2) upon full execution of this Agreement; and

(ii)   One-half (1/2) upon commencement of principal photography.

5. **CONTRACT CONSULTATION**: Any and all deals that fall within any of the following four (4) categories must have prior approval by the Producer before the deal may be finalized: Deals in which an actor receives (1) over scale or more; (2) main title credit; (3) inclusion in paid ads; (4) any bonus, deferred or contingent compensation.

6. **OWNERSHIP**: Producer is not obligated to actually utilize Casting Director's services or the results and proceeds thereof. However, the Producer shall own exclusively and perpetually throughout the universe all rights in and to the results and proceeds of such services as such services relate to the Picture and the exclusive perpetual right to use all or any part thereof as the Producer may desire throughout the universe in connection with the Picture or otherwise. This includes but is not limited to all rights under copyright.

7. **TRAVEL**: If any travel is required in connection with the casting of the Picture, Producer shall provide travel accommodations and airfare equal to that offered to the individual producers.

8. **SCREEN CREDIT**:

a.   If Casting Director is not in material, uncured breach of this Agreement, Casting Director shall receive a credit in the main titles of the Picture on a separate card in substantially the following form: Casting by _____; or, if there are no main titles, equivalent placement in the end titles.

b.   Casting Director's credit shall appear in all positive prints of the Picture and all paid advertisements (subject to standard exclusions). All other aspects of Casting Director's credit and all other credits shall be at the sole discretion of Producer.

9. **UNION BENEFITS**: Producer will pay four (4) weeks of union benefits for Casting Director at the rate of Two Hundred Eighteen Dollars Twenty-Five Cents ($218.25) per week.

10. **STATUS OF PARTIES**: It is expressly acknowledged by the parties hereto that Casting Director is an independent casting director and nothing in this Agreement is intended or shall be construed to create with Producer a joint

venture relationship, employer/employee relationship or to allow Producer to exercise control or direction over the manner or method by which Casting Director performs the services which are the subject matter of this Agreement; provided always that the services to be provided hereunder by Casting Director shall be provided in a manner consistent with professional standards governing such services and the provisions of this Agreement.

11. **PREMIERE TICKETS**: Producer will provide Casting Director invitations to any Los Angeles premiere or festival screening. Such invitations shall be for each person composing Casting Director plus one (1) guest.

12. **EXPENSES/OFFICE**: The compensation paid to Casting Director is considered an all-inclusive flat fee and shall include expenses and office space.

13. **CONTINGENCIES**: Producer shall have the right to terminate, suspend or delay the Term during all periods in which Artist is in breach of this Agreement; Artist is prevented from or fails, refuses or neglects to fully perform Artist's services; or the development, production or distribution of the Picture is prevented by a "force majeure" event, by the death, illness, disability or incapacity of a principal cast member, director, producer or director of photography of the Picture, or for any other reason whatsoever.

14. **MISCELLANEOUS.**

    (a)   *Indemnification*: Casting Director shall indemnify and defend Producer from and against any and all claims and damages arising from the breach of any representation or warranty of Casting Director hereunder to the extent such claim or damage does not arise out of a breach by Producer hereunder. Producer shall indemnify and defend Casting Director from and against any and all claims and damages arising from the production, distribution, exhibition or exploitation of the Picture, or any element thereof, to the extent such claim or damage does not arise out of a breach by Casting Director hereunder.

    (b)   *Arbitration.* All disputes under this Agreement shall be settled pursuant to binding arbitration under the rules of the Independent Film and Television Alliance ("IFTA") before a single arbitrator in [STATE]. The prevailing party will be entitled to collect reasonable attorneys' fees and costs.

Background: The virtues of arbitration are many to the independent producer. Whatever you do, you want to stay out of court. Many people like to have mandatory mediation before going to arbitration. Mediation is the process by which the parties to a disagreement agree to talk through the problem with a neutral third party who is trained to bring people into agreement. Mediation is a good idea, but often involves some money, always involves some time delays and is something that many people would like to decide upon when a dispute arises. If it is appropriate, mediation is easy enough to institute.

(c)   *Assignment.* Casting Director may not assign its rights or obligations hereunder. Producer may freely assign its rights and obligations hereunder.

(d)   *Choice of Law.* This Agreement shall be governed by and construed in accordance with the laws of the State of [STATE].

(e)   *Notices.* All notices under this Agreement shall be in writing addressed to the addresses first set forth above, or at such other address as either party may designate from time to time by written notice to the other. All notices shall be served by facsimile and U.S. mail, electronic mail, recognized courier services such as Federal Express or DHL or personal delivery addressed as specified above. The date of receipt by facsimile, electronic mail or courier, as the case may be, shall be the date of service of notice.

(f)   This agreement may be signed in counterparts. Facsimile and scanned copies shall be deemed originals for all purposes.

(g)   This Agreement constitutes the entire agreement between the parties hereto with respect to all of the matters herein and its execution has not been induced by, nor do any of the parties hereto rely upon or regard as material, any representations or writing whatsoever not incorporated herein and made a part hereof. No amendment or modification hereto shall be valid unless set forth in a writing signed by both parties.

IN WITNESS WHEREOF the parties hereto have caused this Agreement to be duly executed and delivered as of the day and year first above written.

PRODUCER   CASTING DIRECTOR

By:_____   By: _____

» ACTORS AGREEMENT (DIRECT HIRE)

The first talent contracts you will enter will be the actors or the director. Often you will approach these people before you have enough financial backing to actually sign a contract for their services, while simultaneously, the backers you are talking to want them under contract before they commit to giving you their money. It's a real catch-22. The compromise is to obtain a so-called letter of intent or attachment from the major talent. A letter of intent or attachment may simply state that the actor agrees to participate in the film subject to approved financing. While not typically a binding contract, it may serve the filmmaker's need of securing financing by showing that the talent is committed to the project. Once you have this letter of intent or attachment, you can use it to help secure your financial backing; once that is in place, you can proceed in preparing a deal memo or more formal agreement with the talent. A letter of intent or attachment may simply state:

- That the actor has read the script and wants to participate in the project
- The actor is interested in playing the role subject to the actor's availability
- Any agreement will be subject to the actor and the producer agreeing to the terms of employment.

When you are ready to sign on an actor, you want to start by asking whether the actor has a loan-out company. We discussed loan-out companies on page 84. If your actor has a loan-out, you better read up on that first before going forward. The following contract is for an actor without a loan-out company; this will have to be adjusted to take an actor's loan-out into account.

The Actor's Agreement typically contains a detailed description of the services they will be fulfilling, such as his or her role, start date, duration of the production, compensation and credit. If you use a Screen Actors Guild (SAG) actor, the Standard Day-Player and Standard Weekly contracts have a clause that incorporates the SAG Basic Agreement into each deal. SAG is a labor union for professional actors in film and television. Their Basic Agreement clause includes ownership by the production company of the performances rendered by the actors.

If the filmmaker wants to work with actors who are members of SAG, he must become a signatory to the SAG Codified Basic Agreement. This means that the filmmaker must sign a contract with SAG in which he agrees to follow SAG's rules and regulations with respect to any SAG actors in his film. The Basic Agreement will regulate the minimum requirements for terms such as the actor's compensation, the hours they are required to work, pension and health contributions, overtime (if any), and work conditions. Becoming a signatory can be technically challenging, but it's a straightforward process and a guild representative will typically help walk you through the necessary paperwork. The screen actor's guild Web site also has information available for beginning actors, member and industry services, FAQs, and contracts, at http://www.sag.org.

Form 3.03: Actor Services Agreement

ACTOR SERVICES AGREEMENT (Short-form Agreement)

THIS AGREEMENT, effective as of _____, ____, is made by and between [YOUR NAME/COMPANY] ("Producer") whose address is [PHYSICAL ADDRESS] and [ARTIST] ("Artist") whose address is [PHYSICAL ADDRESS] with respect to Artist's portrayal of the role "_____" in the production of the feature-length motion picture currently entitled "_____" (the "Picture").

> **Date: By using an effective date right at the beginning of the contract, you eliminate disputes over when a contract was signed, which may control some of the terms. Few contracts are signed, by all parties on the same day, so fill in any date you want as the effective date.**

1. ARTIST'S SERVICES: Artist shall render all services customarily rendered by actors in first-class feature-length theatrical motion pictures in the motion picture industry and at all times promptly comply with Producer's reasonable instructions. The Start Date for principal photography is on or about _____. Artist will be available for rehearsals and other pre-production services for approximately _____ (#) weeks before the Start Date. Artist's services during principal photography shall be exclusive and rendered consecutively until the completion thereof. After the completion of principal photography, Artist shall be available for customary post-production services, subject to his/her then-existing prior professional commitments.

2. TERM: The term of Artist's services pursuant to this Section shall commence _____, and shall continue until the full and satisfactory completion of all services to be rendered by Artist hereunder or the earlier termination of this Agreement.

3. FIXED COMPENSATION: Provided Artist is not in material breach of this Agreement, in consideration of Artist's services hereunder, Producer shall pay to Artist and Artist hereby accepts as complete consideration the following compensation:

    (a)   GUARANTEED COMPENSATION _____ Dollars, payable in equal _____ (weekly/bi-weekly/monthly) installments on Producer's regular payday. SAG-mandated fringes and residuals, including but not limited to pension and health and welfare, will be paid by Producer in addition to the Guaranteed Compensation. The Guaranteed Compensation buys out all overtime, holidays and other like terms to the maximum extent permissible under the applicable SAG Agreement.

> **Background:** Generally, the production company will pay the actor's salary on a weekly basis, starting with the commencement of services and ending at the conclusion of the term. Actors are not always needed for the entire shooting period, so their pay schedules will differ. However, if the salary is above the SAG-minimum, it's a good idea to retain a portion of the fee through the release of the film, as an incentive for the actor to provide post-production and promotion services, if needed. If the actor is a member of SAG, such rates are defined under the applicable SAG Agreement.

> **HINT:** Some actors or other artists may demand a "pay-or-play" clause, which obligates you to pay the artist a certain sum of money regardless of whether their services are actually used. We recommend making a pay-or-pay option dependent on certain "conditions precedent," such as obtaining full financing, securing entire cast, or on the condition of the artist arriving to the place of the shoot. Other times, a producer may want to use a "pay-or-play" offer as a strategy to obtain attachments of a particular star actor on the project. You will only want to use such a strategy if you are certain that the star actor will ensure full financing from investors because of his or her appeal, and that such payment is within your budget.

(b)   DEFERRED COMPENSATION, IF ANY

(c)   CONTINGENT COMPENSATION: Performer shall also receive ___percent (___%) of the Net Proceeds of the Picture. "Net Proceeds" as used herein shall mean Gross Receipts actually received by or credited to Producer from the exploitation of the Picture less all costs of production, plus all financing costs including without limitation, investor premiums and interest payments. Net Proceeds shall be calculated and accounted for on terms not less favorable than terms to any other individual participants of Net Proceeds of the Picture.

Background: When someone refers to "back-end points" or "contingent compensation," they are referring to a film's net profits. In a nutshell, "net profits" is the money which remains after producing the film. Depending on the scope of your definition, this may be the amount remaining after the costs of making, marketing, advertising, financing, and distributing the film have been repaid, which typically includes recoupment to all investors plus a premium. In the independent film market, the investor premium varies widely, but we most often see a range between 10–25%. Any artist that has been promised a deferred salary must also be paid before declaring net profit. The key is that you want everyone to be whole before giving out any profit participation.

4. CREDIT: Provided Artist is not in material breach of this Agreement, Artist shall receive a credit, in substantially the following form:

(a) [CREDIT]

(b) [Artist's credit will be in the end titles of the Picture.] OR [Artist's credit will be in the main titles of the Picture on a [single/shared] card and shall appear in all positive prints of the Picture and all paid advertisements (subject to standard exclusions).

(c) *Paid Advertisements*: Artist's credit shall be included in any paid advertisements for the film, other than an award, nomination or congratulatory-type advertising crediting only another individual.

HINT: Paid advertisement credits should only be reserved for actors in the main title credits.

(d) All other aspects of credit and all other credits shall be at the sole discretion of Producer.

(e) No casual or inadvertent failure of Producer to comply with the credit provisions hereof shall constitute a breach of this Agreement. Within a reasonable time after receipt of written notice from Artist specifying a failure to accord proper credit in accordance with this Paragraph, Producer shall use good faith efforts to cure prospectively any such failure with regard to positive prints and/or advertising materials created after the date of Producer's receipt of such notice. Producer will contractually obligate third party licensees and sub-distributors with whom Producer is in privity of contract to comply with the credit obligations set forth herein, but shall not be responsible or liable to Artist for the failure of any such third party to comply with the same.

> **HINT: This is very important to you, since there can always be a slip-up. Often the Artist insists (and you should agree) that you take reasonable steps to correct any mistake when it is brought to your attention.**

5. PUBLICITY AND PROMOTION: Producer has the unlimited right to use the name, voice and likeness of Artist to promote and advertise the Picture, and to include the name, voice and likeness of Artist in DVD extra or bonus materials, such as "behind the scenes" and "making of." No product endorsement may be implied.

> **Background: A main title artist may request that only "approved" likeness of Artist to promote the picture and/or "making of" clips. Such approvals may be granted, however, a clause should be added that "such approvals herein shall not be unreasonably withheld.**

> **HINT: The production company may also want to include publicity restrictions that give the company complete control of publicity, and restrain the actor from issuing publicity statements about the motion picture without the production company's prior written consent. With social networking sites such as Facebook and Twitter, we have found this increasingly necessary.**

6. REPRESENTATIONS AND WARRANTIES: Artist represents and warrants that he is a member of the Screen Actors Guild, is free to enter into this Agreement and will not do or permit any act which will interfere with or derogate from the full performance of Artist's services or Producer's exercise of the rights herein granted.

7. WORK-MADE-FOR-HIRE:

(a)   Artist hereby acknowledges that all of the results and proceeds of Artist's services produced for the Picture hereunder shall constitute a "work-made-for-hire" specially commissioned by Producer and Producer or Producer's assignee shall own all such results and proceeds. Producer shall have the right to use Artist's name and likeness with respect to distribution and exploitation of the Picture. Producer may make such use of the Picture as Producer, in its sole discretion, shall deem appropriate.

(b)   If Artist's services are not recognized as a "work-made-for-hire," Artist hereby irrevocably grants, sells and assigns to Producer, its successors and assigns, all of Artist's rights, title and interest of any kind and nature, in and to the Picture, including, without limitation, all copyrights in connection therewith and all tangible and intangible properties with respect to the Picture, in perpetuity, whether in existence now or as may come into existence in the future.

(c)   Artist waives the exercise of any "moral rights" and "droit moral" and any analogous rights however denominated now or hereafter recognized. All rights granted and agreed to be granted to Producer hereunder are irrevocable and shall vest and remain perpetually vested in Producer, its successors and assigns, whether this Agreement expires in normal course or is sooner terminated, and shall not be subject to rescission by Artist for any cause whatsoever.

> **Background: Work-for-Hire clause:** All agreements with cast and crew, including artists, actors, writers, directors, other employees and independent contractors should include a work-for-hire provision, which gives copyright ownership of the film to the production company. Work-for-Hire is defined in U.S. Copyright Law as either (1) a work prepared by an employee within the scope of employment; or (2) a work specially ordered or commissioned for use as one of a very limited number of specified works. A Work-for-Hire provision is critical because without one, the director could claim copyright ownership of the film, as discussed earlier.

8. CONTINGENCIES: Producer shall have the right to terminate, suspend or delay the Term during all periods in which Artist is in breach of this Agreement; Artist is prevented from or fails, refuses or neglects to fully perform Artist's services; or the development, production or distribution of the Picture is prevented by a "force majeure" event, by the death, illness, disability or incapacity of a principal cast member, director, producer or director of photography of the Picture, or for any other reason whatsoever.

9. REMEDIES: Artist recognizes and confirms that in the event of a failure or omission by Producer constituting a breach of its obligations under this Agreement, whether or not material, the damage, if any, caused Artist is not irreparable or sufficient to entitle Artist to injunctive or other equitable relief. Consequently, Artist's rights and remedies shall be limited to the right, if any, to obtain damages at law and Artist shall not have any right in such event to terminate or rescind this Agreement or any of the rights granted to Producer hereunder or to enjoin or restrain the development, production, advertising, promotion, distribution, exhibition or exploitation of the Picture and/or any of Producer's rights pursuant to this Agreement.

> **Background: No injunction clause. This is very important. An "injunction" is a court order that could potentially halt production of the film. This clause waives the Director's rights to injunctive relief and limits his or her remedies to suing for money damages. The filmmaker should never risk having his film enjoined (prevented from being distributed) because of a disgruntled employee.**

10. INSURANCE: Producer has the right, but not the obligation, to secure life, health, accident and/or other insurance covering Artist hereunder and Artist shall not have any rights, titles or interests to such insurance. Artist shall fully cooperate with Producer regarding the securing of such insurance, including, but not limited to, submitting to usual and customary medical exams. Notwithstanding the foregoing, as between Artist and Producer, Artist is solely responsible for obtaining and maintaining any and all types of insurance desired by or required of Artist regarding Artist's services under this Agreement, including, but not limited to, worker's compensation insurance, health/medical insurance, and liability insurance.

> **Insurance Issues: Productions generally require several types of insurance, including general liability, worker's compensation, errors and omissions insurance (discussed later) and a production insurance package that may cover talent, equipment, film damage and car insurance. An insurance provision is common in many talent agreements and may require an actor to submit to a physical exam for insurance purposes. The exam is typically carried out by a doctor from the production's insurance carrier. Talent insurance would compensate you for losses incurred as a result of an actor's injury or illness.**

11. APPROVALS AND CONTROLS: Producer shall solely have all approvals and controls of all kinds and nature, with respect to the Picture, including, but not limited to, all decisions involving artistic taste and judgment.

12. MISCELLANEOUS:

(a) *Arbitration.* If not subject to the SAG arbitration provisions, disputes under this Agreement shall be settled pursuant to binding arbitration under the rules of the Independent Film and Television Alliance ("IFTA") in [STATE]. The prevailing party will be entitled to reasonable attorneys' fees and costs.

> **Background: The virtues of arbitration are many to the independent producer. Whatever you do, you want to stay out of court. Many people like to have mandatory mediation before going to arbitration. Mediation is the process by which the parties to a disagreement agree to talk through the problem with a neutral third party who is trained to bring people into agreement. Mediation is a good idea, but often involves some money, always involves some time delays and is something that many people would like to decide upon when a dispute arises. If it is appropriate, mediation is easy enough to institute.**

(b) *Indemnification.* Artist shall indemnify and defend Producer from and against any and all claims and damages arising from the breach of any representation or warranty of Artist hereunder to the extent such claim or damage does not arise out of a breach by Producer hereunder. Producer shall indemnify and defend Artist from and against any and all claims and damages arising from the production, distribution, exhibition or exploitation of the Picture, or any element thereof, to the extent such claim or damage does not arise out of a breach by Artist hereunder.

(c) *Accounting.* Producer agrees to keep and maintain complete and accurate books and records relating to the Picture and the proceeds derived therefrom.

> **HINT: The accounting paragraph is only used if the Actor is receiving back-end compensation. If there is an accounting provision, a standard audit provision is included in this section: Artist or his/her representative shall have the right to examine, copy and/or cause an audit to be made of the books and records of Producer pertaining to the Picture during regular business hours at Artist's sole expense, unless the audit reveals underpayments in excess of ten percent (10%), in which case, Producer shall reimburse Artist the reasonable costs thereof. Artist shall have the right to audit Producer's books and records no more frequently than once per annum and only with respect to statements received by Artist within two (2) years prior to the commencement of the audit.**

(d)   *Assignment*. Artist may not assign its rights or obligations hereunder. Producer may freely assign its rights and obligations hereunder.

(e)   *Choice of Law*. This Agreement shall be governed by and construed in accordance with the laws of the State of [STATE].

(f)   Notices. All notices under this Agreement shall be in writing addressed to the addresses first set forth above, or at such other address as either party may designate from time to time by written notice to the other. All notices shall be served by facsimile and U.S. mail, electronic mail, recognized courier services such as Federal Express or DHL or personal delivery addressed as specified above. The date of receipt by facsimile, electronic mail or courier, as the case may be, shall be the date of service of notice.

(g)   *Employment Eligibility*. In accordance with the Immigration Reform and Control Act of 1986, any offer of employment contained herein is conditioned upon satisfactory proof of Artist's identity and United States employment eligibility. Artist must present required documentation within ten (10) days of acceptance of this offer. Failure to comply will result in termination of employment.

(h)   This agreement may be signed in counterparts. Facsimile and scanned copies shall be deemed originals for all purposes.

(i)   Further Documents. Artist agrees to execute, acknowledge, and deliver to Producer and to procure the execution, acknowledgment, and delivery to Producer of any additional documents or instruments which Producer may reasonably require to effectuate fully and carry out the intent and purposes of this Agreement. If Artist shall fail to execute and deliver any such documents or other instruments, within ten (10) calendar days after such documents are delivered to Artist, Producer shall be deemed to be, and Artist irrevocably appoints Producer, the true and lawful attorney-in-fact of Artist, to execute and deliver any and all such documents and other instruments in the name of Artist, which right is coupled with an interest.

> **Comment:** The last sentence of the above paragraph contains a new phrase that you might not be familiar with, "a right coupled with an interest." A right coupled with an interest refers to a legal concept concerning making someone your agent, representative or attorney-in-law or attorney-in-fact. When you appoint someone as your representative and that person has an interest in the subject, you cannot cut off that representation so easily. It is not impossible, but it certainly is not as easy as when you would normally just be able to write a letter and withdraw the power to represent you.

(j)   This Agreement constitutes the entire agreement between the parties hereto with respect to all of the matters herein and its execution has not been induced by, nor do any of the parties hereto rely upon or regard as material, any representations or writing whatsoever not incorporated herein and made a part hereof. No amendment or modification hereto shall be valid unless set forth in a writing signed by both parties.

IN WITNESS WHEREOF the parties hereto have caused this Agreement to be duly executed and delivered as of the day and year first above written.

PRODUCER   ARTIST

_____   _____

Contracts with Minors

Contracts for the services of minors present unique issues and challenges. With little exception, a minor does not have the capacity to bind himself to a contract, even where a parent or guardian has approved the contract. In order to make the contract binding on the minor, you'll need to get court approval of the contract. In California, this means that you need to file a petition with the superior court in the county where the minor resides or is employed (or where any party to the contract has its principal office) in order to "confirm" the contract and make it binding on the minor. You'll also include a "Proposed Order" approving the minor's contract for the judge to sign. The forms for these documents vary, but you can contact the court's filing clerk to figure out exactly what you'll need to include. In any event, make sure to attach a copy of the minor's contract to the petition.

You should also be aware that California requires that 15 percent of a minor's gross earnings from his contract be set aside by the minor's employer in a court-monitored trust (a "Coogan Account") to be preserved for the benefit of the minor until he reaches the age of 18 (or is declared emancipated). As the employer, you need to deposit that 15 percent within 15 days of employment.

California is quite strict when it comes to regulating minors' work conditions in the entertainment industry, addressing the employer's responsibility for providing teachers, the presence of parents or guardians on location, working hours, meal periods and so on. In addition, several unions (including SAG) have adopted additional work rules for minors. As laws vary state by state, it's important to contact your local SAG office or state labor department for information about the specific regulations that apply.

» COMPOSER

Composer contracts are a bit different than the other cast and crew agreements in that the composer of the film's soundtrack often retains a financial interest in the copyright for the music composed for the film. Sometimes composers retain actual ownership of the copyright. The only reason to make this sharp departure from the comprehensive grant of rights discussed here for everybody else is to pick up music for your film at a good price. Do not lightly give up ownership of the music in your film if you can avoid doing so. If you do, make sure you have a license in perpetuity throughout the universe to use the music in your film.

Form 3.04: Composer Agreement

COMPOSER AGREEMENT

THIS AGREEMENT, effective as of _____, 20__, is made by and between [YOUR NAME/COMPANY] ("Producer") whose address is [PHYSICAL ADDRESS] and [COMPOSER] ("Composer") whose address is [PHYSICAL ADDRESS].

> **Date: By using an effective date right at the beginning of the contract, you eliminate disputes over when a contract was signed, which may control some of the terms. Few contracts are signed by all parties on the same day, so fill in any date you want as the effective date.**

1. SERVICES:

(a)   Producer hereby engages Composer to render certain services and to compose, write and arrange music (collectively the "Work") for use in the soundtrack of the feature-length documentary motion picture "_____" (the "Picture").

(b)   **Composer Services**. Composer shall compose, write and arrange music for use in the Picture. Composer shall deliver all music in accordance with the reasonable instructions and technical requirements of Producer; and a fully produced final mix of all music composed in accordance with the reasonable instructions and technical requirements of Producer. Thereafter, Composer shall render reasonable services in revising and/or adding additional music. Composer's services hereunder shall include the "spotting" of the Picture for the placement of music, and consulting on an ongoing basis with Producer and other persons designated by Producer.

(c)   Composer's services shall be non-exclusive with no other services to materially interfere, until delivery of the final mix of all music. Producer anticipates the Picture to be completed by _____ 20__.

2. COMPENSATION:

(a)   **Guaranteed Compensation**. Provided Composer is not in material breach of this Agreement, in consideration of Composer's services hereunder, Producer shall pay to Composer and Composer hereby accepts as complete consideration Two Thousand Five Hundred Dollars ($2,500), payable 50% on signing and 50% on delivery of final mix of music.

> **HINT: Composers receive royalities when your film is distributed outside the U.S. and when played on television within the U.S. For that reason, you may be able to obtain composer services for free! It's worth a try.**

(b) **Publishing Rights**. With respect to the exercise of publishing rights in the Work, Composer shall be entitled to fifty percent (50%) ownership of the "Publisher's share," for the Work, the other fifty percent (50%) of which shall belong to Producer. Additionally, Producer and Publisher shall administer their respective shares, as in this case, fifty/fifty (50%/50%).

(c) **Other Royalties**. If the master recordings of the Work are exploited in any manner other than in the soundtrack of the Film, such as, included in phonorecords or published as sheet music, Producer shall pay, or will cause the record company distributing the phonorecord to pay to the Composer, an appropriate royalty, which will be negotiated in good faith and based on industry standards.

> **HINT: Many composer agreements set forth all possible royalty situations, especially if songs have been written that can be exploited independently as a single or if the soundtrack is likely to be exploited apart from the film.**

3. TERM: The term of this Agreement, and the time during which the Producer shall be entitled to the services of the Composer, commence on _____ and shall continue until completion of all services required by the Producer hereunder, including any services required in connection with changes or modifications during the recording and dubbing of the Work. Producer shall have the right and option to terminate this Agreement forthwith and thereafter shall be under no obligation to Composer of any nature whatsoever if, in the absence of delay caused by the Producer, Composer fails to: (1) complete and deliver any element of the Work on a date later than the agreed date for delivery of such element; or (2) render services in connection with any added scenes, changes, additional sound recordings or any retakes of any portion of the Picture, upon Producer's request, at such times and places as Producer shall designate without any additional compensation, unless Composer is unable to do so because of a then-existing exclusive services agreement with another person.

4. COMPOSER ENGAGING OTHERS:

(a) To the extent that Composer engages the services of other individuals (e.g., lyricists, orchestrators, singers and musicians) in connection with creation of the Work in connection with the Picture, Composer represents and warrants that it will be solely responsible for obtaining grants of rights, releases and representations and warranties from those individuals as broad and inclusive as Composer's own, throughout the world, in perpetuity and in all media, in order to enable Producer to exploit the Work free and clear of any claims relating to (i) use of any material and/or equipment utilized by Composer in connection with the Work (other than the material supplied by Producer) and (ii) the performances of any persons rendering services in connection with the Work (other than persons engaged by Producer). Such persons will be creating works made for hire for Producer. Composer agrees to indemnify Producer from any and all claims arising out of Composer's failure to obtain sufficient grants of rights, releases and representations and warranties under this paragraph. When requested, Composer will provide Producer with full and complete documentation of such grants, releases and representations and warranties. If union residuals are required to be paid, Composer will be responsible for such payments.

(b) Composer shall be solely responsible for and shall pay any and all costs and expenses incurred in the production and delivery of the Work including without limitation all costs and expenses relating to (i) all material and equipment utilized by Composer in connection with the Work (except for the material supplied by Producer) and (ii) all compensation, fees, royalties, and any other sums payable to all persons rendering services in connection with the Work (other than persons engaged by Producer); all tape and copywork; any fees payable to any guild or union as a result of the rehearsal, performance and recording of the Work and (iii) any other costs and expenses incurred in connection with the production of the Work. Producer shall not be required to make any payments of any nature for, or in connection with, the Work, except under union contracts growing out of the exploitation of the Picture.

> **HINT: This is very important because you don't want to be hit with extra payments beyond the flat fee you have agreed to. Before you sign this agreement, be sure to go over the budget that specifies the number of musicians to be used in recording the music. A lot of misunderstandings arise out of unshared visions of what the music will sound like.**

5. RIGHTS: Composer hereby grants Producer rights to synchronize the Work in the Picture and thereafter to exploit the Picture, including the Work in all media whether now known or hereafter created in perpetuity throughout the universe, including in connection with advertising and promotion of the Picture. Composer further grants Producer the right to produce a soundtrack album based on the Picture, which may include the Work, in Producer's sole discretion.

6. WORK-MADE-FOR-HIRE:

(a)   Composer hereby acknowledges that all of the results and proceeds of Composer's services produced for the Picture hereunder shall constitute a "work-made-for-hire" specially commissioned by Producer and Producer or Producer's assignee shall own all such results and proceeds. Producer may make such use of the Picture and distribution of the Picture as Producer, in its sole discretion, shall deem appropriate.

(b)   If Composer's services are not recognized as a "work-made-for-hire," Composer hereby irrevocably grants, sells and assigns to Producer, its successors and assigns, all of Composer's rights, title and interest of any kind and nature, in and to the Picture, including, without limitation, all copyrights in connection therewith and all tangible and intangible properties with respect to the Picture, in perpetuity, whether in existence now or as may come into existence in the future.

(c)   Composer waives the exercise of any "moral rights" and "droit moral" and any analogous rights however denominated now or hereafter recognized. All rights granted and agreed to be granted to Producer hereunder are irrevocable and shall vest and remain perpetually vested in Producer, its successors and assigns, whether this Agreement expires in normal course or is sooner terminated, and shall not be subject to rescission by Composer for any cause whatsoever.

> **Rights:** This provision is standard in all crew member, talent and artist agreements. The composer must agree that all rights and proceeds of his or her services on the film are treated as a "work-made-for-hire" and belong to the production company. Since "moral rights" laws, which primarily exist in Europe, may not be captured by the work-made-for-hire clause, then they are assigned to the production company.

7. CREDITS: Provided that Composer's Work comprises more than fifty percent (50%) of the original musical underscore of the Picture as released, Composer shall receive credit on screen in the main titles of the Picture (whether at the beginning or end of the Picture) in substantially the following form:

"Music by _____"

8. NAME AND LIKENESS: Composer hereby grants to Producer the perpetual right to issue and authorize publicity concerning Composer, and to use Composer's name and likeness and biographical material in connection with the exhibition, advertising and exploitation of the Picture. Composer hereby covenants and agrees not to make any claim or bring any suit or action which will or might interfere with or derogate from Producer's rights under this Agreement.

9. NO OBLIGATION TO PRODUCE: Nothing contained in this Agreement shall be deemed to require Producer or its assignees to publish, record, reproduce or otherwise use the Work or any part thereof, whether in connection with the Picture or otherwise; and Composer hereby releases the Producer from any liability for any loss or damage Composer may suffer by reason of Producer's failure to utilize the Work. Payment of the Compensation at the time set forth shall fully discharge Producer of all its obligations hereunder. Producer may not use the Work except in connection with the Picture, the exploitation thereof (including a soundtrack of the Picture) and all advertising and promotion relating to the Picture.

10. REPRESENTATIONS AND WARRANTIES: Composer represents, warrants and agrees that it is free to enter into this Agreement and not subject to any conflicting obligations or any disability which will or might prevent Composer from, or interfere with, Composer's execution and performance of this Agreement; that it has not made and will not make any grant or assignment which will or might conflict with or impair the complete enjoyment of the rights granted to Producer hereunder; that, except for any material supplied to Composer by Producer, all material referred to in Paragraph 1 hereof will be wholly original with Composer or in the public domain throughout the world or based upon material furnished to Composer by Producer. Composer further warrants that said material will not infringe upon the copyright, literary or dramatic rights of any person.

11. NO INJUNCTIVE RELIEF: In the event of a failure or omission by Producer or any third party constituting a breach of Producer's obligations hereunder, the damage, if any, caused to Composer thereby shall be deemed not irreparable or sufficient to entitle Composer to enjoin, restrain or seek to enjoin or restrain the development, production, distribution or exploitation of the Work, the Film, or any sequels, prequels, and/or Albums or other soundtrack recordings derived therefrom, or to seek any other equitable relief. Composer's rights and/or remedies in the event of a failure or omission constituting a breach by Producer of the provisions of this Agreement shall be limited to Composer's rights to seek damages in an action at law.

> **Background: No injunction clause. This is very important. An "injunction" is a court order that could potentially halt production of the film. This clause waives the Composer's rights to injunctive relief and limits his or her remedies to suing for money damages. The filmmaker should never risk having his film enjoined (prevented from being distributed) because of a disgruntled employee.**

12. MISCELLANEOUS:

(a)   **Arbitration**. All disputes under this Agreement shall be settled pursuant to binding arbitration under the rules of the Independent Film and Television Alliance ("IFTA") before a single arbitrator in [STATE]. The prevailing party will be entitled to recover reasonable attorney fees and costs.

> **Background: The virtues of arbitration are many to the independent producer. Whatever you do, you want to stay out of court. Many people like to have mandatory mediation before going to arbitration. Mediation is the process by which the parties to a disagreement agree to talk through the problem with a neutral third party who is trained to bring people into agreement. Mediation is a good idea, but often involves some money, always involves some time delays and is something that many people would like to decide upon when a dispute arises. If it is appropriate, mediation is easy enough to institute.**

(b)   **Indemnification**: Composer shall indemnify and defend Producer from and against any and all claims and damages arising from the breach of any representation or warranty of Composer hereunder to the extent such claim or damage does not arise out of a breach by Producer hereunder. Producer shall indemnify and defend Composer from and against any and all claims and damages arising from the production, distribution, exhibition or exploitation of the Picture, or any element thereof, to the extent such claim or damage does not arise out of a breach by Composer hereunder.

(c)   **Assignment**. Composer may not assign its rights or obligations hereunder. Producer may freely assign its rights and obligations hereunder.

(d)   **Choice of Law**. This Agreement shall be governed by and construed in accordance with the laws of the State of [STATE].

(e)   **Notices**. All notices under this Agreement shall be in writing addressed to the addresses first set forth above, or at such other address as either party may designate from time to time by written notice to the other. All notices shall be served by facsimile and U.S. mail, electronic mail, recognized courier services such as Federal Express or DHL or personal delivery addressed as specified above. The date of receipt by facsimile, electronic mail or courier, as the case may be, shall be the date of service of notice.

(f)   **Employment Eligibility**. In accordance with the Immigration Reform and Control Act of 1986, any offer of employment contained herein is conditioned upon satisfactory proof of Composer's identity and United States employment eligibility. Composer must present required documentation within ten (10) days of acceptance of this offer. Failure to comply will result in termination of employment.

(g)   This agreement may be signed in counterparts. Facsimile and scanned copies shall be deemed originals for all purposes.

(h)   **Further Documents**. Composer agrees to execute, acknowledge, and deliver to Producer and to procure the execution, acknowledgment, and delivery to Producer of any additional documents or instruments which Producer may reasonably require to effectuate fully and carry out the intent and purposes of this Agreement. If Composer shall fail to execute and deliver any such documents or other instruments, within ten (10) calendar days after such documents are delivered to Composer, Producer shall be deemed to be, and Composer irrevocably appoints Producer, the true and lawful attorney-in-fact of Composer, to execute and deliver any and all such documents and other instruments in the name of Composer, which right is coupled with an interest.

> **Comment: The last sentence of the above paragraph contains a new phrase that you might not be familiar with, "a right coupled with an interest." A right coupled with an interest refers to a legal concept concerning making someone your agent, representative or attorney-in-law or attorney-in-fact. When you appoint someone as your representative and that person has an interest in the subject, you cannot cut off that representation so easily. It is not impossible, but it certainly is not as easy as when you would normally just be able to write a letter and withdraw the power to represent you.**

    (i)   This Agreement constitutes the entire agreement between the parties hereto with respect to all of the matters herein and its execution has not been induced by, nor do any of the parties hereto rely upon or regard as material, any representations or writing whatsoever not incorporated herein and made a part hereof. No amendment or modification hereto shall be valid unless set forth in a writing signed by both parties.

IN WITNESS WHEREOF the parties hereto have caused this Agreement to be duly executed and delivered as of the day and year first above written.

PRODUCER   COMPOSER

_____   _____

By:_____   SSN:_____

Its:_____

CHAPTER 4

PRINCIPAL PHOTOGRAPHY

» GETTING THROUGH THE SHOOT

Principal photography can be daunting. As well-planned as any military operation and executed under extreme pressure, principal photography tests the mettle of every producer. Shortly before principal photography commences, there will be a flurry of hiring and each person hired will need a Crew Deal Memo, which is a short form contract that covers you. The crew members receiving this memo include people like the editor, director of photography, and everyone involved in the lighting, sound, and camera departments. These crew members are typically called "below-the-line" personnel, and their contracts tend to be less heavily negotiated than "above-the-line" contracts.

There are a few key points discussed in these agreements, one of which is the guaranteed term of employment. You may decide to hire production staff "at-will," which means they can be replaced at any point, or "week-to-week," which guarantees them pay for a week regardless of whether they are terminated midweek. "Run of the show" guarantees them payment for the entire picture. Second, you must consider unions, most commonly the IATSE (International Alliance of Theatrical Stage Employees) and the Teamsters, that represent some production workers. If you hire members of these unions, you will be required to sign a collective bargaining agreement that will govern many of the deal points in your agreement.

There are also provisions that may apply to some crew members and not others, so a certain amount of custom tailoring will be required. For example, a cinematographer may bring his or her own equipment and request a provision in the contract that provides insurance in the case of equipment damage. Or you may decide that if the crew member is supplying his or her own equipment, then the contract should state that the crew member is "solely responsible for the upkeep, maintenance and safety of his or her own gear." You should check with your insurance company to determine to what extent the crew member's equipment is covered under the production company's policies. Travel, accommodations, and *per diem* expenses should also be negotiated and agreed upon in advance. Certain crew members may also be responsible for making necessary purchases for the film during production, so a "Costs and Expenses" clause may be added but should require a purchase order, and only those petty cash expenses below a certain amount (e.g., $100) and accompanied by receipts will be reimbursed.

Form 4.01: Crew Deal Memo

CREW DEAL MEMO

AGREEMENT FOR THE SERVICES OF [ARTIST'S NAME]

["Name of Film"]

THIS AGREEMENT, effective as of _____, _____ is made by and between [YOUR NAME/COMPANY] ("Producer") whose address is [PHYSICAL ADDRESS] and [ARTIST] ("Artist") whose address is [PHYSICAL ADDRESS] with respect to Artist's services on the feature-length motion picture currently entitled, "_____" (the "Picture").

> **Date:** By using an effective date right at the beginning of the contract, you eliminate disputes over when a contract was signed, which may control some of the terms. Few contracts are signed by all parties on the same day, so use any date you like as the effective date.

1. SERVICES:

    (a)   **[TYPE OF SERVICES] Services.** Artist shall render all services customarily rendered by [NAME OF SERVICES] in the motion picture industry and at all times promptly comply with Producer's reasonable instructions.

Background: This section describes the services that the crew member will perform for the film. The clause is usually drafted broadly. For example, if contracting with a cinematographer, the above contract would read "Artist shall render all services customarily rendered by cinematographers in the motion picture industry." If there are additional duties not customarily performed by such a person, then list those details in this section or attach by a separate rider. If you believe an Artist's attention must be solely focused on your project, then include that his or her services will be "exclusive through the remainder of [insert: pre-production, principal photography and/or post-production]," as you believe is necessary.

(b) **Term.** The parties acknowledge that the term of Artist's services pursuant to this Section shall commence on _____. Artist's services shall continue until the full and satisfactory completion of all services to be rendered by Artist hereunder or the earlier termination of this Agreement.

Term: This is the time period that the crew member is obligated to commence services. If the start date cannot be determined at the time the contract is executed, then provide an approximate date or a range.

2. COMPENSATION: Provided Artist is not in material breach of this Agreement, in consideration of Artist's services hereunder, Producer shall pay to Artist and Artist hereby accepts as complete consideration [WEEKLY OR DAILY AMOUNT] per [WEEK OR DAY] for up to [NUMBER OF DAYS/WEEKS].

Background: Hours paid for Idle days and Travel-only days may be negotiated at a different rate than the standard rate, unless the crew member is part of a union, where the amount is calculated according to their collective bargaining agreement. Time cards should reflect hours worked, not hours guaranteed, and should be turned in at the end of the last day of the production work. You may decide to hire production staff "at-will," which means they can be replaced at any point, or "week-to-week" which guarantees them pay for a week regardless of whether they are terminated midweek. "Run of the show" guarantees them payment for the entire picture.

3. CREDIT: Provided Artist is not in material breach of this Agreement, Artist shall receive a credit in substantially the following form:

(a)   [ARTIST TITLE]: [ARTIST NAME]

(b)   Artist's credit shall appear in the end-roll credits in the Picture.

(c)   All other aspects of credit and all other credits shall be at the sole discretion of Producer.

4. REPRESENTATIONS AND WARRANTIES:

(a)   *Freedom to Enter into Agreement*: Artist warrants that [he/she] is free to enter into this Agreement and will not do or permit any act which will interfere with or derogate from the full performance of Artist's services or Producer's exercise of the rights herein granted.

> **Background: The crew member is required to represent and warrant that he or she is not under any other obligation (contractual or otherwise) that would prevent him or her from performing the duties required under the agreement. The crew member should also warrant that any creative element which they may contribute is original. Representations and warranties are to help reduce the risk of the production company from being sued for copyright or personal rights claims as a result of a crew member using material that has not been properly cleared.**

(b)   *Artist's Material*: Artist warrants that with respect to any material supplied by Artist hereunder, to the best of [his/her] knowledge such material:

       (i)   Shall be Artist's original creation (except for material in the public domain and/or material furnished by or included at Producer's direction);

       (ii)   Does not and will not defame, infringe upon, or violate the rights of any kind, including the right of privacy, of any person or entity;

       (iii)   Is not and will not be based in whole or in part on the life of any real person except as approved in writing in advance by Producer; and

       (iv)   Is not the subject of any litigation or claim that might give rise to litigation.

5. WORK-MADE-FOR-HIRE:

(a)   Artist hereby acknowledges that all of the results and proceeds of Artist's services produced for the Picture hereunder shall constitute a "work-made-for-hire" specially commissioned by Producer and Producer or Producer's assignee shall own all such results and proceeds. Producer shall have the right to use Artist's name and likeness with respect to distribution and exploitation of the Picture. Producer may make such use of the Picture and distribution of the Picture as Producer, in its sole discretion, shall deem appropriate.

(b)   If Artist's services are not recognized as a "work-made-for-hire," Artist hereby irrevocably grants, sells and assigns to Producer, its successors and assigns, all of Artist's rights, title and interest of any kind and nature, in and to the Picture, including, without limitation, all copyrights in connection therewith and all tangible and intangible properties with respect to the Picture, in perpetuity, whether in existence now or as may come into existence in the future.

(c)   Artist waives the exercise of any "moral rights" and "droit moral" and any analogous rights however denominated now or hereafter recognized. All rights granted and agreed to be granted to Producer hereunder are irrevocable and shall vest and remain perpetually vested in Producer, its successors and assigns, whether this Agreement expires in normal course or is sooner terminated, and shall not be subject to rescission by Artist for any cause whatsoever.

> **Background: This provision is standard in all crew member, talent and artist agreements. The crew member must agree that all rights and proceeds of the artist's services on the film are treated as a "work-made-for-hire" and belong to the production company. Since "moral rights" laws, which primarily exist in Europe, may not be captured by the work-made-for-hire clause, then they are assigned to the production company.**

6. CONTINGENCIES: Producer shall have the right to terminate, suspend or delay the Term during all periods in which Artist is in breach of this Agreement; Artist is prevented from or fails, refuses or neglects to fully perform Artist's services; or the development, production or distribution of the Picture is prevented by a "force majeure" event, by the death, illness, disability or incapacity of a principal cast member, director, producer or director of photography of the Picture, or for any other reason whatsoever.

7. APPROVALS AND CONTROLS: Producer shall solely have all approvals and controls of all kinds and nature, with respect to the Picture, including, but not limited to, all decisions involving artistic taste and judgment.

8. UNIQUE SERVICES: Except as specifically provided to the contrary hereinabove, Artist's services shall be rendered exclusively to Producer, or Producer's assignee, until expiration of the Term of this Agreement, it being mutually understood and agreed that Artist's services are extraordinary, unique and not replaceable, and that there is no adequate remedy at law for any breach of this Agreement by Artist, and that Producer, in the event of breach by Artist, shall be entitled to seek equitable relief by way of injunction or otherwise.

> **Background: This clause states that the crew member's services are unique and the loss of those services cannot be fully compensated by money. This may entitle you to seek injunctive relief against a crew member, by preventing him or her from working on other films, should the crew member quit the film halfway through and harm the production.**

9. REMEDIES: Artist recognizes and confirms that in the event of a failure or omission by Producer constituting a breach of its obligations under this Agreement, whether or not material, the damage, if any, caused Artist is not irreparable or sufficient to entitle Artist to injunctive or other equitable relief. Consequently, Artist's rights and remedies shall be limited to the right, if any, to obtain damages at law and Artist shall not have any right in such event to terminate or rescind this Agreement or any of the rights granted to Producer hereunder or to enjoin or restrain the development, production, advertising, promotion, distribution, exhibition or exploitation of the Picture and/or any of Producer's rights pursuant to this Agreement.

> **Background: No injunction clause. This is very important. An "injunction" is a court order that could potentially halt production of the film. This clause waives the Artist's rights to injunctive relief and limits his or her remedies to suing for money damages. The filmmaker should never risk having his film enjoined (prevented from being distributed) because of a disgruntled employee.**

10. MISCELLANEOUS:

  (a) **Arbitration**. All disputes under this Agreement outside prior jurisdiction shall be settled pursuant to binding arbitration under the rules of the Independent Film and Television Alliance ("IFTA"). The prevailing party will be entitled to reasonable attorney fees and costs.

> **Background: The virtues of arbitration are many to the independent producer. Whatever you do, you want to stay out of court. Many people like to have mandatory mediation before going to arbitration. Mediation is the process by which the parties to a disagreement agree to talk through the problem with a neutral third party who is trained to bring people into agreement. Mediation is a good idea, but often involves some money, always involves some time delays and is something that many people would like to decide upon when a dispute arises. If it is appropriate, mediation is easy enough to institute.**

(b) **Indemnification.** Artist shall indemnify and defend Producer from and against any and all claims and damages arising from the breach of any representation or warranty of Artist hereunder to the extent such claim or damage does not arise out of a breach by Producer hereunder. Producer shall indemnify and defend Artist from and against any and all claims and damages arising from the production, distribution, exhibition or exploitation of the Picture, or any element thereof, to the extent such claim or damage does not arise out of a breach by Artist hereunder.

> **Background: This standard indemnity clause relates back to the earlier Representation and Warranty clause and obligates the crew member to indemnify the production company for any breaches of the Representations and Warranties, or other breaches of the agreement.**

(c) **Assignment.** Artist may not assign its rights or obligations hereunder. Producer may freely assign its rights and obligations hereunder.

(d) **Choice of Law.** This Agreement shall be governed by and construed in accordance with the laws of the State of [STATE].

(e) **Notices.** All notices under this Agreement shall be in writing addressed to the addresses first set forth above, or at such other address as either party may designate from time to time by written notice to the other. All notices shall be served by U.S. mail and electronic mail, recognized courier services such as Federal Express or DHL, or personal delivery addressed as specified above. The date of receipt by electronic mail or courier, as the case may be, shall be the date of service of notice.

(f) **Employment Eligibility**. In accordance with the Immigration Reform and Control Act of 1986, any offer of employment contained herein is conditioned upon satisfactory proof of Artist's identity and United States employment eligibility. Artist must present required documentation within ten (10) days of acceptance of this offer. Failure to comply will result in termination of employment.

(g) This agreement may be signed in counterparts. Facsimile and scanned copies shall be deemed originals for all purposes.

(h) **Further Documents**. Artist agrees to execute, acknowledge, and deliver to Producer and to procure the execution, acknowledgment, and delivery to Producer of any additional documents or instruments which Producer may reasonably require to effectuate fully and carry out the intent and purposes of this Agreement. If Artist shall fail to execute and deliver any such documents or other instruments, within ten (10) calendar days after such documents are delivered to Artist, Producer shall be deemed to be, and Artist irrevocably appoints Producer, the true and lawful attorney-in-fact of Artist, to execute and deliver any and all such documents and other instruments in the name of Artist, which right is coupled with an interest.

> Comment: The last sentence of the above paragraph contains a new phrase that you might not be familiar with, "a right coupled with an interest." A right coupled with an interest refers to a legal concept concerning making someone your agent, representative or attorney-in-law or attorney-in-fact. When you appoint someone as your representative and that person has an interest in the subject, you cannot cut off that representation so easily. It is not impossible, but it certainly is not as easy as when you would normally just be able to write a letter and withdraw the power to represent you.

(i) This Agreement constitutes the entire agreement between the parties hereto with respect to all of the matters herein and its execution has not been induced by, nor do any of the parties hereto rely upon or regard as material, any representations or writing whatsoever not incorporated herein and made a part hereof. No amendment or modification hereto shall be valid unless set forth in a writing signed by both parties.

IN WITNESS WHEREOF the parties hereto have caused this Agreement to be duly executed and delivered as of the day and year first above written.

PRODUCER   ARTIST

_____   _____

By: [INDIVIDUAL'S NAME]   SSN:_____

Its: [TITLE]_____

» MUSIC SUPERVISORS

Music supervisors are key to the success of your film. In addition to suggesting music to license, they often know just the right musicians to play it so you don't have to license a master. They can suggest alternatives when the license fee is too high for your budget. They have relationships with publishers. Take your time with this hire; a good music supervisor can really help your film to be as good as it can be.

Form 4.02: Music Supervisor Agreement

MUSIC SUPERVISOR AGREEMENT

THIS AGREEMENT, effective as of _____, 20__ is made by and between [YOUR NAME/ADDRESS] ("Producer") whose address is [PHYSICAL ADDRESS], and [MUSIC SUPERVISOR] ("Music Supervisor") whose address is [PHYSICAL ADDRESS], with respect to Music Supervisor's services on the feature-length motion picture currently titled "_____" (the "Picture").

> **Date: By using an effective date right at the beginning of the contract, you eliminate disputes over when a contract was signed, which may control some of the terms. Few contracts are signed by all parties on the same day, so fill in any date you like as the effective date.**

1. SERVICES: Music Supervisor shall render all services customarily rendered by music supervisors in the feature-length motion picture industry and at all times promptly comply with Producer's reasonable instructions. Music Supervisor's services shall be non-exclusive, but first priority throughout the Term (defined below). Such services shall include, but not be limited to:

(a)   Suggesting, negotiating and licensing music to be used in the Picture.

(b)   Advising Producer and Producer's legal counsel as to licensing matters for publishing, synchronization rights and master recording use rights.

(c)   Providing approvals where necessary.

(d)   Advising as to Producer's rights as to owning said publishing and/or master rights where applicable.

(e)   Advising as to the establishment and maintenance of a Producer-owned publishing company where applicable.

(f)   Administering and advising as to performance society procedures and activities, registrations for Producer's publishing company and collecting income due Producer worldwide where applicable.

(g)   Advising and assisting with all aspects of the soundtrack album for the Picture including, but not limited to, securing applicable music licenses, assisting in negotiating fee and royalty structures and assisting in negotiations with record label.

(h)   Producer shall have final approval over all agreements and all agreements shall be between Producer and the artist or publisher, as applicable.

> **Comment:** These services vary from music supervisor to music supervisor, depending on scope of work, amount of payment and the music supervisor's expertise. Just be certain that the services enumerated are accurate and that you and the music supervisor fully understand the scope of work the music supervisor will be performing.

2. TERM: The Term shall commence on the date first written above and shall continue through production, post-production and through to picture lock of the Picture and for the administration of the music placed in the Picture (as referenced in 1.a. thru 1.g. above), for a period of three (3) years from the date of first distribution of the Picture on TV, DVD, or in theatrical use subject to a forthcoming, good-faith negotiated, administration agreement between the parties. Additionally, Music Supervisor shall render services after picture lock, if required (for example, to complete the soundtrack album or if music needs to be replaced in the Picture).

3. COMPENSATION: Provided Music Supervisor satisfactorily fulfills his obligations under the Services paragraph above and is not otherwise in material breach of this Agreement, in consideration of Music Supervisor's services hereunder, Producer shall pay to Music Supervisor and Music Supervisor hereby accepts as complete consideration $_____ payable as follows: 50% upon signing of this Agreement; 50% upon delivery and approval of all music (score and third party) to be used in the Picture.

> **Comment: Compensation also varies tremendously. Make sure the price fits in your budget and that the music supervisor is going to render the services you need.**

4. CREDIT: Provided Music Supervisor secures a significant portion of the permanent music used in the final cut of the Picture and is not otherwise in material breach of this Agreement, Music Supervisor shall receive a credit in substantially the following form:

    (a)   Music Supervisor: _____

    (b)   Music Supervisor's credit shall appear in the end-roll credits.

> **Comment: Prominent music supervisors and music supervisors of films with a lot of music will be in main titles.**

    (c)   All other aspects of credit and all other credits shall be at the sole discretion of Producer.

5. FREEDOM TO ENTER INTO AGREEMENT: Music Supervisor warrants that he is free to enter into this Agreement and will not do or permit any act which will interfere with or derogate from the full performance of Music Supervisor's services or Producer's exercise of the rights herein granted.

6. WORK-MADE-FOR-HIRE:

(a)   Music Supervisor hereby acknowledges that all of the results and proceeds of Music Supervisor's services produced for the Picture hereunder shall constitute a "work-made-for-hire" specially commissioned by Producer and Producer or Producer's assignee shall own all such results and proceeds. Producer shall have the right to use Music Supervisor's name and likeness with respect to distribution and exploitation of the Picture. Producer may make such use of the Picture and distribution of the Picture as Producer, in its sole discretion, shall deem appropriate.

(b)   If Music Supervisor's services are not recognized as a "work-made-for-hire," Music Supervisor hereby irrevocably grants, sells and assigns to Producer, its successors and assigns, all of Music Supervisor's rights, title and interest of any kind and nature, in and to the Picture, including, without limitation, all copyrights in connection therewith and all tangible and intangible properties with respect to the Picture, in perpetuity, whether in existence now or as may come into existence in the future.

(c)   Music Supervisor waives the exercise of any "moral rights" and "droit moral" and any analogous rights however denominated now or hereafter recognized. All rights granted and agreed to be granted to Producer hereunder are irrevocable and shall vest and remain perpetually vested in Producer, its successors and assigns, whether this Agreement expires in normal course or is sooner terminated, and shall not be subject to rescission by Music Supervisor for any cause whatsoever.

> **Rights:** This provision is standard in all crew member, talent and artist agreements. The crew member must agree that all rights and proceeds of the artist's services on the film are treated as a "work-made-for-hire" and belong to the production company. Since "moral rights" laws, which primarily exist in Europe, may not be captured by the work-made-for-hire clause, then they are assigned to the production company.

7. CONTINGENCIES: Producer shall have the right to terminate, suspend or delay the Term during all periods in which Music Supervisor is in breach of this Agreement; Music Supervisor is prevented from or fails, refuses or neglects to fully perform Music Supervisor's services; or the development, production or distribution of the Picture is prevented by a "force majeure" event, by the death, illness, disability or incapacity of a principal cast member, director, producer or director of photography of the Picture, or for any other reason whatsoever.

8. APPROVALS AND CONTROLS: Producer shall solely have all approvals and controls of all kinds and nature, with respect to the Picture, including, but not limited to, all decisions involving artistic taste and judgment.

9. REMEDIES: Music Supervisor recognizes and confirms that in the event of a failure or omission by Producer constituting a breach of its obligations under this Agreement, whether or not material, the damage, if any, caused Music Supervisor is not irreparable or sufficient to entitle Music Supervisor to injunctive or other equitable relief. Consequently, Music Supervisor's rights and remedies shall be limited to the right, if any, to obtain damages at law and Music Supervisor shall not have any right in such event to terminate or rescind this Agreement or any of the rights granted to Producer hereunder or to enjoin or restrain the development, production, advertising, promotion, distribution, exhibition or exploitation of the Picture and/or any of Producer's rights pursuant to this Agreement.

> **Background: No injunction clause. This is very important. An "injunction" is a court order that could potentially halt production of the film. This clause waives the Music Supervisor's rights to injunctive relief and limits his or her remedies to suing for money damages. The filmmaker should never risk having his film enjoined (prevented from being distributed) because of a disgruntled employee.**

10. MISCELLANEOUS:

(a)   **Arbitration**. All disputes under this Agreement shall be settled pursuant to binding arbitration under the rules of the Independent Film and Television Alliance ("IFTA") before a single arbitrator in [STATE]. The prevailing party will be entitled to reasonable attorney fees and costs.

Background: The virtues of arbitration are many to the independent producer. Whatever you do, you want to stay out of court. Many people like to have mandatory mediation before going to arbitration. Mediation is the process by which the parties to a disagreement agree to talk through the problem with a neutral third party who is trained to bring people into agreement. Mediation is a good idea, but often involves some money, always involves some time delays and is something that many people would like to decide upon when a dispute arises. If it is appropriate, mediation is easy enough to institute.

(b)   **Indemnification**. Music Supervisor shall indemnify and defend Producer from and against any and all claims and damages arising from the breach of any representation or warranty of Lender or Director hereunder to the extent such claim or damage does not arise out of a breach by Producer hereunder. Producer shall indemnify and defend Music Supervisor from and against any and all claims and damages arising from the production, distribution, exhibition or exploitation of the Picture, or any element thereof, to the extent such claim or damage does not arise out of a breach by Music Supervisor hereunder.

(c)   **Assignment**. Music Supervisor may not assign his rights or obligations hereunder. Producer may freely assign its rights and obligations hereunder.

(d)   **Choice of Law**. This Agreement shall be governed by and construed in accordance with the laws of the State of [STATE].

(e)   **Notices**. All notices under this Agreement shall be in writing addressed to the addresses first set forth above, or at such other address as either party may designate from time to time by written notice to the other. All notices shall be served by facsimile and U.S. mail, electronic mail, recognized courier services such as Federal Express or DHL or personal delivery addressed as specified above. The date of receipt by facsimile, electronic mail or courier, as the case may be, shall be the date of service of notice.

(f)   **Employment Eligibility**. In accordance with the Immigration Reform and Control Act of 1986, any offer of employment contained herein is conditioned upon satisfactory proof of Music Supervisor's identity and United States employment eligibility. Music Supervisor must present required documentation within ten (10) days of acceptance of this offer. Failure to comply will result in termination of employment.

(g)   This agreement may be signed in counterparts. Facsimile and scanned copies shall be deemed originals for all purposes.

(h)   **Further Documents**. Music Supervisor agrees to execute, acknowledge, and deliver to Producer and to procure the execution, acknowledgment, and delivery to Producer of any additional documents or instruments which Producer may reasonably require to effectuate fully and carry out the intent and purposes of this Agreement. If Music Supervisor shall fail to execute and deliver any such documents or other instruments, within ten (10) calendar days after such documents are delivered to Music Supervisor, Producer shall be deemed to be, and Music Supervisor irrevocably appoints Producer, the true and lawful attorney-in-fact of Music Supervisor, to execute and deliver any and all such documents and other instruments in the name of Music Supervisor, which right is coupled with an interest.

> **Comment:** The last sentence of the above paragraph contains a new phrase that you might not be familiar with, "a right coupled with an interest." A right coupled with an interest refers to a legal concept concerning making someone your agent, representative or attorney-in-law or attorney-in-fact. When you appoint someone as your representative and that person has an interest in the subject, you cannot cut off that representation so easily. It is not impossible, but it certainly is not as easy as when you would normally just be able to write a letter and withdraw the power to represent you.

(i)   This Agreement constitutes the entire agreement between the parties hereto with respect to all of the matters herein and its execution has not been induced by, nor do any of the parties hereto rely upon or regard as material, any representations or writing whatsoever not incorporated herein and made a part hereof. No amendment or modification hereto shall be valid unless set forth in a writing signed by both parties.

IN WITNESS WHEREOF the parties hereto have caused this Agreement to be duly executed and delivered as of the day and year first above written.

PRODUCER   MUSIC SUPERVISOR

_____   _____

By:_____   SSN:_____

Its: Managing Member

» LOCATIONS

Now that you've scouted and picked the locations for your shoot, you want to make sure you have unhindered access and the necessary rights to shoot in those locations. If you are shooting on public property such as a public street, park or municipal building, you may also need a permit from the appropriate governmental authority, typically a permit issued by the city. If you are shooting on private property, then you will need a location release, and sometimes a shooting permit as well.

You generally do not need the permission of the owner of a building as long as all you do is photograph the building as it normally appears where it is ordinarily visible from a public place. However, if you go tramping around the building with your cameras, then you will obviously need access and more rights. Also, keep in mind that in many modern buildings, there are often separate decorative sculptures that are not architecturally part of the building. Artwork that is commissioned to decorate a building can sometimes also serve as architectural features of the building, but the problem is it is not always easy to tell the difference. Thus, you may need permission from the artist of any of the decorative art that appears in your film, including fountains and sculptures.

You should have a location agreement and necessary permits for each and every location. You don't want to show up with cameras and crew and be subject to delays. As a threshold issue, these location agreements serve as your permission to be there and do what you are doing. If you are using a distinctive location, the location agreement also serves as a release so that you can use the trademark or tradename associated with such a location, and also that you can create a new identification for the location in your film; for instance, if you were to use the capitol building in Sacramento, California and depict it as the U.S. Capitol building in your film. A location agreement should also provide you enough time to load in and set up your equipment, complete your shoot, and then remove the equipment and restore the property to its original state.

The following location agreement covers all the clearance issues and rights we have been discussing. It is a safe document for you to use. If a homeowner or landlord balks at granting one of the permissions, you can then evaluate whether you need that specific permission. Simply strike out those rights that you do not need. For instance, a landowner may say that you cannot use the real signage, or demand that you must use the real signage. If that is alright with you, just change the agreement accordingly.

Finally, be sure that you are asking the right person for the permission you need. Virtually all the location disputes we have encountered grew out of, or were complicated by, obtaining permission from the wrong person. There are three prominent possibilities when it comes to signatures on a location agreement: the owner, the tenant, or just someone who happens to be at the location such as a friend, relative, or employee. Know who you are dealing with. Always identify the person by name and relation to the property and make sure they have the right to grant you the permission you need. A building owner usually would not have authority to grant you the right to film in someone's apartment or business. Conversely, a tenant might have the right to let you into their apartment or business, but not the right to string cables into their location.

If you need to clear the use of a building's signage, you need to talk to the owner of the sign, since it is the owner who has the right to withhold or grant that permission. If the signage is of a trademark that you plan to malign in some way, you have to have permission from the owner of that trademark, in addition to permission from the owner of the sign on which the trademark is located.

Form 4.03: Location Agreement

LOCATION AGREEMENT

THIS AGREEMENT, effective as of _____, 20__, is made by and between [YOUR NAME/COMPANY] ("Producer") whose address is [PHYSICAL ADDRESS] and [GRANTOR] ("Grantor") whose address is [PHYSICAL ADDRESS] with respect to Producer's use of the location described below on the production of the feature-length motion picture currently entitled "_____" (the "Picture").

> **Date: By using an effective date right at the beginning of the contract, you eliminate disputes over when a contract was signed, which may control some of the terms. Few contracts are signed by all parties on the same day, so fill in any date you like as the effective date.**

1. FILMING LOCATION: For good and valuable consideration, receipt and sufficiency of which is acknowledged, Grantor permits Producer to use the property and the surrounding area, including any signage or identifying materials, located at _____ ("Property") in connection with the Picture for rehearsing, photographing, filming and recording scenes and sounds for the Picture.

> **Background: The grantor must provide the right to use the names and identifying signs of the location. For commercial properties, these rights may include depicting any trademarks or trade dress owned by the company that occupies that location. A name of a commercial location (e.g., store or restaurant) or a particular and distinctive way a location is decorated may function as trademarks.**

2. PRODUCER'S RIGHTS: Producer may exhibit, advertise and promote the Picture or any portion thereof whether or not the Property is identified, in any and all media which currently exist or which may exist in the future in all countries, in perpetuity.

> **Background: This provides you the right to depict the location in your film in any and all media, including promotional use (e.g., trailers) where the property may be depicted.**

3. IDENTIFICATION OF PROPERTY: Producer shall not be required to identify or depict the Property in any particular manner. Grantor acknowledges that any identification of the Property which Producer may furnish shall be at Producer's sole discretion.

> **HINT: You may have to add a sentence or two as a result of your negotiation because some landlords want recognition and others do not.**

4. TIME OF ACCESS: The permission granted hereunder is for the period that commences on or about _____ and continues until_____. The permission shall also apply to future retakes and/or added scenes, if necessary, at a time to be mutually agreed.

> **Access: This provides you with access to the location during the specified time period. You should be careful to specify not only the days and hours on which you wish to film, but also the amount of time needed for loading and setting up equipment and the time necessary to restore the property to its original state.**

5. ALTERATIONS TO LOCATION: Producer represents that any change made to the Property shall be undone to restore it to its original condition.

6. COMPENSATION:

_____ Grantor has agreed to allow Producer to use the Property at no charge to Producer.

_____ Producer shall provide Grantor with the following compensation: $_____.

> **Comment: Strike the sentence which is not applicable to your location.**

7. REPRESENTATIONS AND WARRANTIES: Grantor warrants that it has the right to enter this Agreement and to grant the rights herein.

8. RELEASE: Grantor releases and discharges Producer, its employees, agents, licensees, successors and assigns from any and all claims, demands or causes of actions that Grantor may have for libel, defamation, invasion of privacy or right of publicity, infringement of copyright or violation of any other right arising out of or relating to any of the rights granted herein.

9. MISCELLANOUS.

    (a)   **Arbitration**: All disputes under this Agreement shall be settled pursuant to binding arbitration under the rules of the Independent Film and Television Alliance ("IFTA"). The prevailing party will be entitled to reasonable attorney fees and costs.

> **Background: The virtues of arbitration are many to the independent producer. Whatever you do, you want to stay out of court. Many people like to have mandatory mediation before going to arbitration. Mediation is the process by which the parties to a disagreement agree to talk through the problem with a neutral third party who is trained to bring people into agreement. Mediation is a good idea, but often involves some money, always involves some time delays and is something that many people would like to decide upon when a dispute arises. If it is appropriate, mediation is easy enough to institute.**

(b) **Indemnification**: Producer agrees to indemnify and hold harmless Grantor from and against any and all liabilities, damages and claims of third parties arising from Producer's use of the Property (unless such liabilities, damages or claims arise from breach of Grantor's warranty as set forth above) and from any physical damage to the Property caused by Producer, or any of its representatives, employees, or agents. Grantor agrees to indemnify and hold harmless Producer from and against any and all claims relating to breach of this Agreement.

(c) **Assignment**. Grantor may not assign his rights or obligations hereunder. Producer may freely assign its rights and obligations hereunder.

(d) **Choice of Law**. This Agreement shall be governed by and construed in accordance with the laws of the State of [STATE].

(e) **Notices**. All notices under this Agreement shall be in writing addressed to the addresses first set forth above, or at such other address as either party may designate from time to time by written notice to the other. All notices shall be served by facsimile and U.S. mail, electronic mail, recognized courier services such as Federal Express or DHL or personal delivery addressed as specified above. The date of receipt by facsimile, electronic mail or courier, as the case may be, shall be the date of service of notice.

(f) This agreement may be signed in counterparts. Facsimile and scanned copies shall be deemed originals for all purposes.

(g) This Agreement constitutes the entire agreement between the parties hereto with respect to all of the matters herein and its execution has not been induced by, nor do any of the parties hereto rely upon or regard as material, any representations or writing whatsoever not incorporated herein and made a part hereof. No amendment or modification hereto shall be valid unless set forth in a writing signed by both parties.

IN WITNESS WHEREOF the parties hereto have caused this Agreement to be duly executed and delivered as of the day and year first above written.

PRODUCER   GRANTOR

_____   _____

» PROPS AND MATERIAL RELEASES

A materials release may be used for any copyrighted elements, such as photographs, props or paintings that appear in your film. Props can be anything the actors hold—not furniture, not all the things on the wall, but the things they handle: knives, magazines, letters, books, hammers, whatever might show up in their hands. Even if there is a copyright in a dagger, for instance, if it is being used for the purpose for which it is intended, you do not have to clear it. If someone creates a prop for your film, be sure that it is an original work. Creating a new work for a prop is a good thing. Copying someone else's design and calling it your own is a bad thing . . . and an expensive thing.

If a jeweled dagger of exotic design is the murder weapon and is frequently photographed and handled and discussed and helps to twist (pun intended) the plot of a film, be sure to create it yourself or clear it. If the theft of a figurine of great value forms the basis of a film's plot, and is frequently photographed and discussed by the characters in the film, create it or clear it. The more important the use of a work, the more likely the owner of a copyright is going to press forward with a claim. However, whatever you create should be original and not a knock-off. If it is an item protected by copyright, the law looks at a knock-off as a derivative work. The right to make derivative works is one of the absolute rights that the copyright holder controls. Creating one without permission is prohibited under copyright law. If the item you want to knock off is trademarked, there are problems under the Lanham Act, which is the federal anti-trust legislation. If it is someone's voice, persona, or performance that you want to knock off, there are problems involving the misappropriation of name and likeness.

The lesson is that you should create your own wonderment. Do not mimic others. It is lazy. It is frequently unlawful. And it is almost always less interesting than what you would come up with if you let your own creative juices flow. Be sure that anything you have created as a prop or piece of set decoration for your film is either a work for hire or you have a complete assignment of all the rights you need, in perpetuity, throughout the universe. In such a case, use the crew member agreement for your prop designer set out in form 4.01.

Finding the Copyright Holder

Most studios clear any item that appears in a film and is copyrighted because it is the cautious, conservative thing to do. That means you must get a signed release from the owner of the copyright. As with other areas, sometimes the hardest part of the clearance process is finding out who should give you the permission you are seeking. Most of the objects you photograph do not need to be cleared. However, if you decide to clear the object, you have to contact the person who owns the copyright.

Typically, the person who sells the painting or sculpture rarely has any rights other than the right to sell you the single item you purchased. Homeowners rarely have any copyright interest in a painting or sculpture they "own." If the artist did not sign the work, inquire as to who created it. In most instances, the creator controls the copyright to the artwork. If you cannot determine the name of the artist, find out the name of the work. You can always do a copyright search to discover the name of the artist and the address, at least as of the time of registration. If the creator has died, you will have to identify and locate the heirs. As you can see, this is often a lot more troublesome than creating your own work.

We had a client who produced a feature film shot almost entirely in an awesome house they rented in Los Angeles. The director and producer loved the house for lots of reasons, one of which was all the fabulous art on the walls and unique sculptures throughout the house. The owner signed the location release and gave them carte blanche to film. After filming was complete, a lawyer watched the film and said, "Wait a minute, did you get the rights to all of the artwork?" The filmmaker said, "Yeah, the homeowner said we could shoot whatever we wanted." Oops. That's when the filmmakers came to us. The filmmakers had to go back to the owner of the house, find out who created each piece of art and seek permission to use it in the film. Luckily this person had a good memory and the filmmakers were successful in contacting many of the artists. However, some of the pieces were purchased in the Bahamas from a local shop or at a flea market. These were much more tricky to deal with. At the end, we were able to obtain E&O coverage for the film and the filmmakers were able to exploit the film. However, had the producer thought about this ahead of time, he could have replaced or removed the artwork in which the copyright owner was unknown. This would have reduced his risk and legal fees.

For all copyrighted material that you believe you will need a release for, the following form should suffice.

Form 4.04: Materials Release

MATERIALS RELEASE

For good and valuable consideration, the receipt and sufficiency of which is hereby acknowledged, I grant to [YOUR NAME/COMPANY] ("Producer") the right to exhibit, record sound from and to photograph (the "Photography") the personal property described below (the "Materials") on the motion picture currently entitled "_____" (the "Picture").

PRODUCER'S RIGHTS: All rights to the Photography will be the exclusive property of Producer and may be used in connection with the Picture, or any

---

other production, or any advertising or publicity relating thereto, in any manner or media worldwide in perpetuity for all purposes.

REPRESENTATIONS AND WARRANTIES: I represent and warrant that I am the sole owner of the Materials; that I have the right to enter into this Release and to grant Producer the rights granted herein; that the consent of no other person or entity is required for Producer's use of the Materials; and that the Photography of the Materials, and any use thereof in connection with the distribution, exhibition and exploitation of the Picture or any other production, or any advertising or publicity relating thereto, will not in any way infringe or violate the rights of any person or entity.

RELEASE: I release and discharge Producer, its employees, agents, licensees, successors and assigns from any and all claims, demands or causes of actions that I may have for libel, defamation, invasion of privacy or right of publicity, infringement of copyright or violation of any other right arising out of or relating to any of the rights granted herein.

INDEMNIFICATION: I agree to indemnify Producer from and against any loss or damage, including reasonable attorney fees and disbursements, caused by or arising out of any breach or alleged breach of any representation made by me herein.

ARBITRATION: All disputes under this Release shall be settled pursuant to binding arbitration under the rules of the Independent Film and Television Alliance ("IFTA"). The prevailing party will be entitled to reasonable attorney fees and costs.

Description of Materials:

[LIST MATERIALS]

Comment: It is very important that this list is complete. It is OK to include items on the list and decide not to use them in your film. It is not OK to leave something out. We won't bore you with the horror stories.

Dated:_____ Signature: _____

Name (Printed): _____

Address: _____

» CROWDS AND PUBLIC FILMING

The remainder of this chapter contains forms for documentary films. This section is a good example. If you are making a live action fiction film, you hire extras for any crowd or street scenes. Take a look at *She's Gotta Have It* for a rare exception to that statement, but if you are shooting guerilla style, you still won't be using these forms.

For those people that may briefly appear in a public background shot, a signed release is generally not required. The problem is that if the shot is disparaging or invades someone's right of privacy, it could prompt a claim. Studios and broadcasters typically want releases of everyone that appears in your film to reduce the risk of lawsuits, whether they are valid claims or not. A public filming notice warns people that they are being filmed. If you put up a sign prominently at a shoot, make a video record of it for your files that shows where it was posted. An announcement at the event also helps provide some indication of where the shooting will take place within the venue.

Form 4.05: Public Filming Notice

Public Filming Notice

GENERAL PUBLIC RELEASE

THIS EVENT WILL BE RECORDED BY _____AMONG OTHERS.

THE RECORDING WILL INCLUDE SHOTS OF THE ATTENDEES.

BY ENTERING THESE PREMISES, YOU AUTHORIZE _____, ITS SUCCESSORS, AFFILIATES, SUBSIDIARIES, ASSIGNEES AND LICENSEES TO DISTRIBUTE THE RECORDINGS, INCLUDING YOUR NAME, VOICE, IMAGE AND LIKENESS VIA ANY MEDIUM NOW KNOWN OR HEREAFTER DEVELOPED, THROUGHOUT THE WORLD, FOR ANY PURPOSE WHATSOEVER IN CONNECTION WITH THE PRODUCTION CURRENTLY ENTITLED: _____.
YOU UNDERSTAND THAT ALL PHOTOGRPAHY, FILMING AND/ OR RECORDING WILL BE DONE IN RELIANCE OF THIS CONSENT GIVEN BY YOU BY ENTERING THIS AREA.

THANK YOU.

» WRITTEN RELEASES

As mentioned, it is best to have a written release for anyone that appears in your film. With a written agreement, you can specify the scope of the rights being granted to the filmmaker and you can obtain specific waivers. For example, you will most likely want the release to allow you to use the person's image in advertising and promotion of the film, such as trailers. What follows is an interview release, an individual release, and a materials release. If you are producing a documentary or film where real people are being interviewed or depicted, you will want to use an interview release.

We recommend filmmakers also capture a verbal release on film. The key is to make sure that the subjects give a full and informed release. While the camera is rolling, tell the subject of your interview that you are making a documentary film. Tell them what it is going to be about. Then explain the theatrical release. (Don't forget to tell your subject that you may sell clips from your documentary for use on news programs or in other documentaries.) This explanation takes time, but if the interview continues—as it usually will—you have recorded a valid release as indicated by the person's continued participation after your careful explanation.

Form 4.06: Interview Release

INTERVIEW RELEASE

DATE: _____

I agree to be interviewed by [YOUR COMPANY] ("you"), a company shooting a documentary motion picture tentatively entitled "_____" (the "Documentary").

If you interview me, I understand that you propose to videotape the interview and use portions thereof in the Documentary.

In consideration of your agreement to interview me, I irrevocably agree that you may use the interview in the Documentary. I further agree that you may exhibit and use the Documentary and material concerning me by any means of exhibition, which may use the interview and scenes concerning me as well as my name, voice and likeness in connection with advertising and promotion of the Documentary throughout the world, in perpetuity. This release is given without the promise of compensation.

I understand that you are not obligated to use the interview or the materials and that if you do elect to use the same, you may change, edit, add to or subtract from the interview or materials as you see fit. You agree that any portrayal of me in the Documentary will be made in good faith; however, I acknowledge that you may portray me in the manner you consider appropriate.

By signing this release, I am waiving any and all claims or demands of any nature including, but not limited to libel, defamation, invasion of privacy or right of publicity, which I may now have or may in the future have against you or against your employees, officers, directors, or agents or against any person, firm or corporation to whom you may sell, license or otherwise transfer your rights in the Documentary, the materials concerning me, or any other rights granted under this release.

> **Comment: This paragraph is the most important paragraph of this agreement. Try not to make any changes to it.**

I represent that I am of sound mind and body and have entered into this agreement knowingly and willingly.

ACCEPTED AND AGREED: IF INTERVIEWEE IS A MINOR OR INCAPACITATED IN ANY RESPECT HAVE THE PARENT OR LEGAL GUARDIAN SIGN ALSO:

_____

NAME (PLEASE PRINT)   NAME (PLEASE PRINT)

_____

ADDRESS   ADDRESS

_____

_____

TELEPHONE NUMBER   TELEPHONE NUMBER

_____

RELATIONSHIP TO INTERVIEWEE

_____

The next form of release is similar to the Interview Release. It is the preferred form where there is no formal interview.

Form 4.07: *Individual Release*

INDIVIDUAL RELEASE

I, the undersigned person, for good and valuable consideration, the receipt and sufficiency of which is hereby acknowledged, have granted permission to [YOUR NAME/COMPANY] ("you") and your successors, assignees and licensees to use my name, image and likeness as such name and/or likeness appears in photography shot in connection with the motion picture tentatively entitled "_____" ("Picture") and in connection with advertising, publicizing, exhibiting and exploiting the Picture, in whole or in part, by any and all means, media, devices, processes and technology now or hereafter known or devised in perpetuity throughout the universe. I hereby acknowledge that you have no obligation to utilize my name and/or likeness in the Picture or in any other motion picture.

Your exercise of such rights shall not violate or infringe any rights of any third party. I understand that you have been induced to proceed with the production, distribution and exploitation of the Picture in reliance upon this agreement.

> **Comment: Many individuals will not authorize the use of their likeness in your advertising without substantial extra payment. It is generally not worth the extra money, so you may have to take out that provision.**

I hereby release you, your successors, assignees and licensees from any and all claims and demands arising out of or in connection with such use, including, without limitation, any and all claims for invasion of privacy, infringement of my right of publicity, defamation (including libel and slander), false light and any other personal and/or property rights.

ACCEPTED AND AGREED: IF INTERVIEWEE IS A MINOR OR INCAPACITATED IN ANY RESPECT:

_____   _____

INTERVIEWEE'S SIGNATURE   PARENT/LEGAL GUARDIAN'S SIGNATURE

_____   _____

NAME (PLEASE PRINT)   NAME (PLEASE PRINT)

_____   _____

ADDRESS   ADDRESS

_____   _____

CITY/STATE/ZIP   CITY/STATE/ZIP

_____   _____

TELEPHONE NUMBER   TELEPHONE NUMBER

5

DISTRIBUTION

So, you've done it. You shot your film, completed post-production, your family and friends love it, and now you're ready for the world to see it . . . what to do now? At the time we're writing this book, distribution is undergoing a major transition. There are new, cost-effective ways of getting your film before a broad audience that weren't possible just a few years ago. Some may say it's a difficult time, but it's also a very exciting time for independent filmmakers.

If your film was financed solely through private equity, you now own 100 percent of the rights of the completed film and can exploit it however you choose. If you raised funds through pre-sales, many of the foreign territories may already be sold, so keep that in mind while reading this chapter. If a distributor or television outlet provided production financing, you probably had to give up all or most of your ownership, though you should have retained a nice participation in the profits. You may also have retained foreign rights and the right to sell DVDs from your website (more on that later).

We're hopeful that you're reading this section before you've finished your film, because we'd hate for you to be in the position where the first time you are thinking about distribution of your film is when it's ready to be distributed. Ideally, you should start thinking about marketing and distributing your film from day one. Thinking about ways to build your core audience early on can be very helpful in the long run. There are countless ways to do this and each filmmaker will go about it differently, but here are a few ideas:

- build your website during development and keep your core audience updated on things like casting decisions and other attachments;
- create a teaser trailer and update or change it as production continues;

- build your email lists;
- survey your core audience on topics related to your film;
- create interactive games to keep your audience interested;
- keep your audience updated on new subject developments, if your film is a documentary—this is a great way to get people interested in your project before you have a film to show them.

Regardless of what steps you take to market your film, the bottom line is that you must think about distribution strategy and costs at the inception of your project so you are not hit with unexpected expenses and obstacles once you've completed your film. Jon Reiss, filmmaker and author of the book *Think Outside the Box Office*—a great book about indie film distribution—advises that when raising money, you should have a 50/50 model: 50 percent for production, and 50 percent for marketing and distribution. We think that's brilliant.

There are entire books written about distribution and marketing. We find Jon Reiss's book, as well as Stacey Parks's *Insider's Guide to Film Distribution*, to be particularly well-written and informative. We'll leave the strategy to the experts here and we'll stay focused on the legalities of distribution and the agreements you need. We start with defining the roles of those people who will help sell your film.

» PRODUCER'S REPRESENTATIVE

A Producer's Rep is an agent who represents your film and helps sell it either to a foreign sales agent, a domestic distributor or a studio, or some combination of those. The relationship between you and a Producer's Rep is very similar to the relationship between an actor and his talent agent—a talent agent works to get his clients jobs in the entertainment industry and if that happens, he helps negotiate the key deal points and gets a commission. A Producer's Rep works to sell your film and if that happens, he helps negotiate the key deal points and gets a commission. He brings to the table connections and contacts with buyers who might be interested in your film.

A Producer's Rep most often comes on board once your film has been accepted to a major film festival. This is especially true for first-time filmmakers; a more established filmmaker might have formed a relationship with a Producer's Rep earlier on or, even more likely, won't need a rep because he has already built relationships with distributors and sales agents. The Rep will talk to potential buyers, get them to your screening, help negotiate acquisition/licensing deals, and assist with festival strategy, if applicable. If the film's not in a festival, the Rep will arrange buyer's screenings, send out screeners to interested parties and engage in other efforts to sell your film. If the Producer's Rep finds a buyer for your film, he will help negotiate the material terms of the agreement, but it will be up to the filmmaker or his lawyer to negotiate the fine points of the deal.

A deal with a Producer's Rep is relatively very short; most often the term will be one year, two at most. Producer's reps typically charge a 15 percent fee based on income you receive from the sale or license of your film. The Producer's Rep's initial financial investment in your film is little to none, and in fact many require that you pay a fee for their services on top of the commission they receive in connection with sales they make. Some Producer's Reps ask that the filmmaker cover the costs to attend the festival or market. This used to be a red flag indicating an unscrupulous rep, but not anymore. We are seeing more and more agreements in which the Rep is requiring some type of upfront fee to cover their expenses. Sometimes you can make that fee recoupable against commissions earned. At the end of the day, it's a judgment call as to whether you trust the particular person or company, and whether you want to do business with them.

» FOREIGN SALES AGENT

A Foreign Sales Agent is a middleman between you and the ultimate distributor(s) of your film in various countries around the world. They do not actually get your film to an audience, but have contacts with the foreign buyers and will take care of collecting revenue earned from around the world. A foreign sales agent will sell to each territory, deliver the film, collect revenues, and account to you as an essential member of your team. When you enter into an agreement with a Sales Agent, you will "deliver" the film to the Sales Agent and the Sales Agent will then handle the negotiation of agreements with various foreign distributors, usually for all rights in the territory. Your Sales Agent will most likely pay for marketing and other costs and may give you an advance against future revenue. Often, the Sales Agent is the party to the contract with the distributor, not you. You give, and are entrusting, the Sales Agent with the authority to sell your film and depending on the deal, the filmmaker may have very little say in how the film is sold. Although the term of a Sales Agent agreement varies greatly from deal to deal, it is almost always for a long term—anywhere from seven to 25 years is relatively common. Because of this high level of commitment and risk, the fee paid to a sales agent is higher, typically between 20–35 percent.

Sales Agents sell films all year round, but the big sales efforts take place at film markets. There are markets all year long, but the three biggest markets are American Film Market (AFM), which takes place in Santa Monica in November; European Film Market, which takes place in Berlin in February, and Marche du Cannes which occurs at the same time as the Cannes Film Festival in May. If you've never been to a film market and you have an opportunity to go, you should. The American Film Market takes over an entire hotel in Santa Monica. Each sales agent takes up a room or two, removes the furniture, and converts it into a sales office. Movie posters are hung displaying the films for sale, flat screens in the room are playing trailers, the lobbies are filled with racks of trade magazines and packed with industry personnel. It's pretty interesting to see how it all works.

The foreign marketplace is much tougher than it was several years ago. Buyers are acquiring less and are therefore much more selective. Advances are smaller. Pre-sales discussed in Chapter 2 are becoming more difficult. However, it is still an important market and potentially very profitable. Studios count on 50 percent of their gross from foreign countries. Independents may see as little as 10 percent from foreign sales if the film is considered "too American," up to much more than 50 percent for films that may never receive a decent domestic deal. You can't navigate the foreign market alone—you have to have a foreign sales agent who has the right contacts abroad to make sales, keep accounting records and collect money.

Even if you decide to self-distribute your film (do-it-yourself, or DIY, distribution), you want to get a Foreign Sales Agent for your film if you hope to have any kind of traditional distribution outside of the U.S.

» DOMESTIC DISTRIBUTOR

A distributor actually gets your film in front of an audience. It is the company that puts your film in theaters or on TV or for sale on iTunes or Netflix. These are the guys who ultimately do the marketing and publicity for your film and have a whole lot to do with who will end up seeing your film. Examples of distributors are a broadcaster or network (e.g., HBO or NBC), a studio (e.g., Sony or Magnolia) or a company that services your film, such as Roadside Attractions (Service Deals are discussed later in this section). The economics of a distribution deal vary depending on the distributor and your film. A distribution deal is typically for a minimum of seven years.

None of these deals is automatically better than any other one. You must look at the distributor, the type of distribution and what makes sense for your film. Every film is different and deals are structured in a myriad of ways.

» DO YOU NEED A PRODUCER'S REP, FOREIGN SALES AGENT, OR A DISTRIBUTOR?

That depends. What is available to you? If you have a reputable Producer's Rep who loves your film and wants to help you sell it, that's fantastic, and we'd say team up with that person. If you don't, that's okay too. That doesn't mean no distributors will see your film. If your film is as good as you think it is, you will get into festivals and people will know.

If Sony Classics is interested in acquiring all rights to yours film, and you are interested in making that deal, you won't need a Producer's Rep; your lawyer can negotiate the deal. Also keep in mind that the fewer agents you are working with, the fewer commissions you have to pay, which means more money directly to you. Not to say that their fees aren't worth it—they are, but only if their services are needed. Look at your particular situation and what you need. Don't worry so much about standards and what other filmmakers do or don't do.

» HOW TO CHOOSE WITH WHOM TO WORK?

This is the ongoing question for most filmmakers. The best way to start is to talk to other filmmakers. Go to the Rep's, Sales Agent's or Distributor's website and call the filmmakers on the roster. Ask if they're happy with the job that company is doing. Did the agent or distributor do what they committed to do in the contract? Did they issue timely statements and payments? Was the filmmaker kept abreast of what efforts were being made on behalf of the film? Notice that money (an advance) is not among the key questions. Your initial decision should be to find someone whose reputation for honesty and fair dealing is beyond question. Check them out carefully.

Be cautious when you hear complaints such as, "we never received any money." Ask probing questions to find out if the Sales Agent didn't even try to sell the film (not good), it was sold but not enough to cover costs (usually the Sales Agent lost money too), or no one bought the film despite the Sales Agent's efforts (usually the film's fault). Also, look at the other films that company represents. This will tell you a lot about the types of films that interest that company and whether your film is something they will be passionate about. Also ask yourself whether you like the other films on the list—are they films you want your film to be associated with? These are fundamentally important questions.

As you inquire as to a company's reputation, you will receive lots of advice about money. You'll hear things like, "so-and-so received an advance of $1.2 million and you're getting a bad deal if it's anything less than that." Always question this advice carefully. First of all, Americans love to puff a bit when it comes to money; you're going to hear exaggerated secondhand quotes. Secondly, you should know that the market for independent films fluctuates just like the stock market and the commodities market. Also, when you hear that so-and-so was paid $1.2 million for her film, you want to be sure that you are selling the same bundle of rights and that the film is similar in terms of its genre and money-making potential. As an extreme example, if your film is a small horror flick with no named talent, you will not get the same advance as the film with an ensemble cast of A-listers. If you are only selling, for example, domestic television rights, the payment will be a lot lower than if you are selling all rights. Additionally, sometimes those numbers are in part contingent on performance of the film at the box office or even an option price for the filmmaker's next film.

» ALL-RIGHTS DEALS VS. SPLIT RIGHTS DEALS

You might be hearing a lot of talk about these "split rights deals," "DIY distribution," or "hybrid deals." What exactly are these? For starters you should know that splitting your rights gives you more control over your film and an opportunity to receive revenue from several different sources.

Not too long ago an independent filmmaker would make a film with the hopes of selling that film to one of the major studios. The studio paid the filmmaker a large advance that more than covered the budget, and the studio assumed all rights and obligations with respect to marketing and promotion of the film. The filmmaker didn't have to put up any additional money and the filmmaker was happy—sometimes. Now that advances are no longer what they used to be, these big studio deals don't always make economic sense. We had a client who produced a documentary with a budget of approximately $650,000. A studio wanted to buy it, all rights, worldwide, for a $150,000 advance. Looking at the contract, it was clear that he would receive nothing else but that advance, unless the film was a major, major hit. He passed on the deal and was right to do so.

Also, studios are not always the best place for your film. Some films don't require multi-million dollar publicity and advertising campaigns or large theatrical releases. Some filmmakers can easily tap into their core audience and create a successful release for their film truly independently, and that's what a split rights deal allows you to do.

Now a filmmaker has options. Let's get into some specific detail.

All-Rights Deal

An all-rights deal is a deal in which the filmmaker sells all of the rights to distribute his film to one company—theatrical, television, Internet, new media, foreign and educational. This can be great for a filmmaker, especially if there is a large advance. If you're selling to a studio, the biggest upside is the potential to reach a mass audience through resources that few individuals have. The marketing support pretty much can't be matched. The second biggest upside is that selling all rights allows a filmmaker to move on to his next project, while a company that specializes (or should specialize) in distribution handles the marketing and distribution of the film—and pays for it.

However, the downsides for an indie filmmaker are many. First, the cost. Distributors spend a lot of money, and all of that money is recouped by the sales of your film. More often than not, that money is cross-collateralized. Cross-collateralization means that the money spent in connection with the distribution of your film, regardless how spent, will be paid back to the distributor (recouped) from all revenue earned, regardless how earned. For example, if a studio does a theatrical release for you and spends $1 million, but only sees $100,000 from box office revenue, the other $900,000 will be recouped from all other sales such as DVD, foreign, and digital sales. Just like a financing deal with a studio, the likelihood of seeing any back-end is slim to none, so make sure your advance is large. The problem with this advice is that the days of those high six and seven figure advances that used to be reported in the trades rarely happen anymore.

The second downside is exploitation. The studio you sell to might be interested in theatrical and DVD releases, but has no plans to sell internationally or to exploit the potentially valuable subsidiary rights. For instance, perhaps the distributor does not have the expertise or interest to exploit educational rights. If you are going to sell all the rights to one place, be sure you inquire about what the distributor's plans are for each of the rights. They require different skill sets and different contacts. If the distributor is just going to hire a foreign sales agent, you should do that yourself and save a bundle in the process on unnecessary fees from the studios. Perhaps you have a documentary that museums and universities might be interested in showing. Does the distributor intend to sell to museums and universities? If not, reserve those rights. They could be valuable.

The third downside is loss of control. The distributor buying the rights will most likely retain all rights related to the exploitation of the film. All marketing and advertising decisions will be made by someone other than yourself. Even whether or not there is a theatrical release will be decided by someone else. This actually might be music to your ears—yes, please, someone make those decisions for me! But read about split rights before deciding; you have many options and avenues to sell your film.

If you are going to enter into an all-rights deal, make sure the distributor is right for you and your film. Do all you can to ensure that your film will be exploited in a way that will make you happy and proud. If there are rights that you want to hold back, ask! The distributor might just say okay.

> HINT: Especially important to keep are the rights to sell to individuals from your website and the right to make so-called "back-of-the-room sales" at screenings, conferences and seminars.

Split Rights Deal

A split rights deal or DIY distribution is just that—the filmmaker sells different rights to different companies and often exploits some rights himself. For example, you may release the film theatrically with a booker, and then sell DVD rights to one company, educational to another and foreign to another. Splitting rights and selling them to companies that really specialize in one form of distribution is a great way to maximize the exposure of your film and ensure that all of your rights are well exploited. It's also a lot more work than selling all the rights to one company.

You may also have to spend a significant amount of money upfront if you are truly "doing it yourself" as the marketing, publicity, and advertising costs that are typically paid for by the distributor are now your responsibility. That being said, with the methods of exploitation rapidly changing and it becoming easier and easier for an individual to reach larger and larger audiences through the Internet—blogging, Facebook, Twitter, etc., etc.—you might be better off keeping some of your rights and avoiding the high cost of teaming up with a studio.

Many filmmakers have become discouraged with the state of film distribution as it currently exists. Films that are well-made and well-received are given offers from companies that simply do not make financial sense. Advances don't come close to covering the filmmaker's debt and the terms of the agreement are designed so that the filmmaker is unlikely to see anything after that small advance. It's been said that nine out of 10 filmmakers are dissatisfied in some respect with their distributor. In response to this frustration, filmmakers have taken things into their own hands, literally. An individual can put his film online through companies like iTunes, Netflix, and Amazon and make it available by video-on-demand for very little cost. There is not always a need to manufacture DVDs, which can be costly. You should understand emerging technologies so you can be innovative and use what's available to your advantage.

Here's a list of your distribution rights:

U.S. Distribution
- Theatrical
- Semi-theatrical—film societies, museums (paid admission)
- Non-theatrical
- VOD (video-on-demand)
- Television
- Retail DVD
- Direct DVD (from website, back of the room sales)
- Educational
- Digital/Online

Foreign
- Television
- Other (DVD, digital)

These rights can be sold individually or retained by the filmmaker. By splitting up your rights you are maximizing the profit potential of your film by avoiding cross-collateralization and ensuring that each right sold is actually exploited. Additionally, you are able to control the sales strategy and promotion of your film, and best, you will see money much more quickly than with an all-rights deal—you will most likely have fewer expenses to recoup and a more straightforward accounting system.

As a note of caution, when doing it yourself, it is very important to ensure that one deal does not preclude you from making other deals. For example, you might enter into a DVD deal in which the agreement states you cannot exploit the film by any other means for one year. Make sure this doesn't conflict with any of your other agreements, and if it does, change it. Holdback periods, periods in which the distributor requires that you not exploit the film by other means, are common, but you do not want them to unnecessarily burden your film.

If you're interested in DIY distribution and need some help getting started, read Peter Broderick's article, "Declaration of Independence: The Ten Principles of Hybrid Distribution" (www.peterbroderick.com). Peter is an independent film consultant and a wonderful resource. He strongly believes that split rights arrangements are the way to go for indie filmmakers and helps his clients shape their distribution strategy.

CASE STUDY: Valentino: The Last Emperor

Let's take a break and enjoy a successful DIY story.

First time producer-director Matt Tyrnauer put up hundreds of thousands of dollars of his own money (well, Capital One's money) to make the film *Valentino: The Last Emperor*. Matt knew there was a movie in Valentino's story and literally put all he had at risk to make that film. He did good. The film premiered at Cannes in 2009 to rave reviews. But—surprise, surprise—Matt was unhappy with the distribution offers he received, so he and his partners actually formed their own distribution company, Acolyte Films, to release the film. Matt then got very lucky. Ivan Reitman (director of *Ghostbusters* and producer of *Animal House* and *Up in the Air*, among others) saw *Valentino* in Toronto, loved it and asked for a print to show his neighbors. Matt, of course, gladly accommodated this request. Now, if I were to show the film to my neighbors, the only thing that would happen is a few extra DVD copies would be illegally burned onto someone's computer. However, Ivan has different neighbors than I do, and one of those neighbors happens to be Oprah Winfrey. Oprah just loved it. In fact, she loved it so much that she devoted half of one of her shows to the film, and we all know what happens when something is "Oprah-fied"—the film took off. *Valentino* had an international theatrical run that lasted over six months and grossed nearly $2 million domestically and approximately $500,000 overseas. DVD sales have been successful as well.

» DIGITAL RIGHTS

There's a lot of talk about what to do with digital rights. At the time this book was written, there was still not an established industry standard regarding the economics of these sales, and people were still trying to figure out how to monetize digital rights. Because of this, many people advise that you freeze or retain these rights. That may not be the right answer, especially because digital distribution is such a great way to reach a broad audience quickly and you don't want to miss out on that opportunity. However, you need to protect yourself to ensure that you receive a fair payment or royalty if these rights are monetized. In other words, these rights should be negotiated separately from other rights.

If you are considering selling these rights, here are some basic guidelines:

1. Ensure that measures are taken to protect your film, such as geofiltering capabilities (i.e., the ability to prevent access outside the licensed territory) and anti-piracy protections.
2. Require that the distributor have accounting and reporting mechanisms that enable the distributor to trace each stream or download.
3. If you are selling rights to different companies, make sure that the windows of exploitation do not conflict with one another. "Windows" is a term of art that refers to the time period in which exploitation of a particular media occurs, such as the theatrical window or the television window. A typical window schedule for a film would be theatrical first, then paid video-on-demand, then DVD sales, followed by DVD rentals and then television (realizing there are other means of exploitation).
4. Because there are no actual goods being created (like a DVD), the cost to the distributor is much lower and so is the financial risk. There is no packaging, shipping or duplication. There is no need to order hundreds or thousands of copies before a distributor knows if even one will sell. Accordingly, your revenue share should be higher. The economics are so different that digital rights should not be bundled with other rights.

There are three emerging revenue models for digital distribution: PayPerView (iTunes), Subscription (Netflix—Watch Instantly) and Advertiser Supported (YouTube, Hulu). Understanding how your film will be exploited will help you maximize your revenue streams. If you know your film will be shown on an Advertiser Supported website, you will want to structure your deal so that you share in advertising revenue. Of course, with this model, your royalty on sales will be zero.

The Independent Film & Television Alliance (IFTA) publishes a regularly updated New Media Guide, which is available to its members. This guide explains in detail what these rights are, discusses emerging licensing issues and trends, and reviews other important information related to new media rights. IFTA has also created "Internet and Wireless Rights" deal terms. These can be found in the New Media Guide. I highly recommend reading this—it's a great resource for indie filmmakers.

» DIGITAL RIGHTS DISTRIBUTOR / AGGREGATOR

There are several distributors who specialize in digital rights. Companies like iTunes and other digital distribution outlets only accept content from aggregators. Aggregators are companies that acquire content from several filmmakers and then sell the content as a package to the digital outlets. Aggregators take a percentage of sales for this service. Cinetic Rights Management, Distribber, and Brainstorm Media are just a few aggregators that specialize in digital distribution.

» THEATRICAL RELEASES

BOOKERS

Limited theatrical releases have become viable for the indie filmmaker, even without a theatrical distribution deal in place. Let's say you can't find a distributor to do a theatrical release, but you really believe that a theatrical release is crucial for your film. You want the reviews and may even want to qualify for an Oscar. You are in luck.

A "booker" is an independent entity that helps put your film in theaters by actually booking the theater for you. The booker has the direct connection to the theaters and will deal with the logistics such as timing and precise location. A booker typically does not do any marketing or promotion for your film and accordingly, the cost is relatively small. You can get your film into the theaters in NY and LA starting at around $30,000. Companies such as Vitagraph book independent films in theaters.

If you want people to actually show up at your screening, you will also need a separate marketing plan and a publicist to help get the word out.

SERVICING DEAL

A servicing deal is a bit more involved. You pay an upfront fee and often a percentage of box office returns to get the film into theaters. With a servicing deal, the company actually promotes the film, prepares marketing materials and helps make your theatrical run a success, but you pay the costs.

There are different levels of service deals. They range from being a true servicing deal for a theatrical release only, to helping formulate and execute entire distribution strategies. For example, Roadside Attractions is a full-service distributor that charges a fee to cover its distribution expenses. (Roadside does pick up films in which they don't charge a fee; the determination is simply a risk analysis.) Full-service means just that: they provide a full-range distribution strategy and execute it, including marketing and publicity, theatrical release (if appropriate), video deals, VOD, etc. Roadside has output deals with various companies that will exploit these other rights.

Other companies that specialize in service deals are Freestyle Releasing, Paladin, Emerging Pictures, Variance and The Brakefield Company. Most of these companies will help you as much or as little as you choose. So if you want them to only do a theatrical release, they will do that, but if you want them to help sell other rights to your film or be involved with the overall marketing strategy, they'll do that as well.

Landmark Theaters has a program called "Truly Indie." Truly Indie is a "four-wall deal"—a theater rental system. The Truly Indie fee at the time of printing is approximately $10,000 per city with a minimum of five cities. Landmark provides the screenings and some limited publicity for this fee.

Self-distribution of a theatrical release will cost you somewhere between $30,000 to as high as millions for a national release with marketing, publicity and advertising. The filmmaker will typically see about 40 percent of the box office revenue after paying the theaters, for publicity, etc. The upside to these servicing deals is that you retain all the rights to your film; the obvious downside is the financial risk.

CASE STUDY: One Six Right

Brian Terwilliger loved aviation. He had been working in the film industry for a few years and he was ready to make his first film. He decided to make a movie about aviation as seen through the eyes of a small airport—the unsung hero of aviation. He knew that most aviation enthusiasts were loyal, passionate, wealthy and committed to the industry. He knew there was a group of people that would be very interested in being involved in the film he envisioned, as there were no other films like this on the market. Brian, perhaps by luck, but perhaps because he is a really smart guy, made this dream come true. I don't think he knew this as he was making his film—but talking with him afterward, it certainly seems like he made many, if not all, the right moves. Here's his story:

In 2001, Brian started telling potential investors about his vision. He spent two years looking for funding with no success. Through this process it became clear to him that he could talk all day about his project and get people excited, but he needed to create something visual so his potential investors could really see Brian's vision and the film he was capable of making. He put together a teaser by scrounging up $7,000, and finding a team who believed in the project and was willing to work for deferred payments. Just six weeks after he began using his teaser to raise funds, he raised 100 percent of the money he needed to make the film.

LESSON NO. 1: YOU CAN TALK ABOUT YOUR IDEA ALL DAY AND NIGHT, BUT NOTHING SELLS IT BETTER THAN AN ACTUAL VISUAL PRESENTATION.

Although Brian used state-of-the-art cameras and editing equipment to make his film, hired an amazing composer, and put together an experienced and talented crew, the budget of Brian's film remained relatively low. Because of his ties with the aviation industry and community, Brian was able to save a lot of money on the production. He delivered a very high-quality documentary, *One Six Right*, for a fraction of what the actual cash budget would have been without his connections and relationships.

LESSON NO. 2: GO WITH WHAT YOU KNOW. NOT ONLY IS IT BETTER TO TELL A STORY THAT YOU ARE PASSIONATE ABOUT, BUT YOU MAY BE ABLE TO SAVE A LOT OF MONEY!

Brian began thinking about distribution before he started filming. His goal was to broadcast on Discovery Wings, a television network dedicated to aviation. Because of that, he found out what their delivery requirements were and made the film that exceeded those specifications. It's almost like going to college—when a kid has his sights set on going to UCLA, he knows what GPA and SAT scores are necessary and what extra-curricular activities admissions officers look favorably upon. This is what Brian did: he set his sights on a particular distribution outlet and made his film so it would be ready to deliver, which made his product that much more attractive. The fact that Discovery Wings was cancelled and Brian never had his broadcast premiere there is not important. He had his sights high and created a product that exceeded this network's specifications. This ensured that he'd have a product that not only Discovery Wings would accept, but other broadcasters as well. In fact, Brian shot the film in HD-CAM (which was not being done in 2003), and when Discovery HD Theater premiered his movie in 2006, they did so in part because the film met that station's requirements—a station that did not exist when he began filming. Again, it's like applying to college: UCLA's requirements aren't much different than other similarly prestigious schools.

LESSON NO. 3: DECIDE WHAT YOUR IDEAL DISTRIBUTION OUTLET WILL BE EARLY ON AND CREATE YOUR FILM TO MEET OR EXCEED THEIR SPECIFICATIONS.

In October 2004, Brian finished his final edit—known as a "locked picture." He scheduled a theatrical premiere but at the last minute, he cancelled it. Brian realized that he still had elements of the film that he needed to add or change; the picture was not ready yet. Brian raised more money and worked on the film for another six months.

LESSON NO. 4: IF YOUR FILM IS NOT THE FILM YOU SET OUT TO MAKE, DON'T STOP WORKING ON IT. CREATE THE PRODUCT YOU INTENDED TO MAKE.

On June 25, 2005, Brian rented the Pacific Theater in Hollywood and finally had his theatrical premiere. This was Brian's shot to get distributors to see his film on the big screen, and to see the film alongside the crowd it was made for—the audience Brian knew would love it. He invited everyone interested in aviation and anyone who might be interested in distributing the film. He had a red carpet and big after-party. The theater was packed with more than 1,000 people. Prominent people in aviation showed up, celebrities showed up. Everyone loved the film. Brian was psyched . . . until he discovered that there was not one buyer or one reviewer in the house. This amazing screening, although a lot of fun, did not get Brian what he needed—distribution. Brian even hired a publicist to help generate buzz and get the right people to the screening, but unfortunately, the publicist was not the right fit and was not able to get the right people to that premiere.

LESSON NO. 5: HIRE THE RIGHT PUBLICIST. THERE'S A LOT OF COMPETITION OUT THERE AND PUBLICISTS THAT SPECIALIZE IN INDEPENDENT FILM OR DOCUMENTARIES CAN BE VERY, VERY HELPFUL IN THIS AREA.

In the month following the premiere, Brian received some very meager offers for distribution; he knew he could have more success distributing the film himself than accepting one of these deals. Brian wasn't looking to self-distribute, but his goals were to use this film as a platform to make more films and to pay his investors back. He needed to establish credibility. He needed to get his film before as many eyeballs as possible. In order to do that, he had to keep working and distribute the film himself. (You'll hear this from most producers who DIY. They don't choose the DIY method—it chooses them.)

According to Brian, this next phase in the filmmaking process was the toughest part by far. Creating the DVD extras, artwork and packaging was more work than he anticipated. He had made a first-class movie with a high-level composer, prominent interview subjects, state-of-the-art equipment. He wanted the distributed product to have that same high quality. He did most of this work himself. The final product was a 73-minute film with 25 minutes of special features.

DVD Release

When August came around, Brian was ready to press DVDs. This cost was upward of $100,000 to make approximately 70,000 units, plus 10,000 CD soundtracks (for which he also created the packaging). He financed this portion through loans.

I asked Brian how he decided how many units to make. Brian's website was up and active with a significant amount of traffic. He developed a DVD reservation application and by simply asking the visitors of his site to provide their names, email addresses and the number of DVDs they would like to "reserve," he knew there were at least 12,000 potential buyers out there. These reservations were not a commitment to buy, but simply offered Brian a good measure for how many DVDs he could sell. Based on this information, he ordered 30,000 copies for the first run. He found a fulfillment center and started selling DVDs on his website.

According to Brian's experience, if you plan to sell DVDs directly from your website, you might want to think twice. Due to the extremely high volume of sales, Brian and his crew became a customer service center by default. The fulfillment center shipped packages, but if a shipment was late or a package didn't have the right number of DVDs, Brian received the call. This was a 24-hour job. It only took Brian a few weeks to team up with an aviation organization that had the infrastructure to take on this customer service burden. Eventually, he partnered with Amazon to sell the DVDs. Amazon takes a 55 percent fee and Brian believes it's worth every penny. Of course, include a link on your website to a place where the DVD can be purchased, but send those sales to a company that is set up to deal with customer service.

LESSON NO. 6: IF YOU EXPECT HIGH VOLUME SALES, PARTNER WITH AMAZON OR ANOTHER COMPANY THAT CAN HANDLE THE CUSTOMER SERVICE AND LIABILITY ISSUES THAT GO ALONG WITH SHIPPING PRODUCTS.

The initial price of the DVD was $28.95. You might think this is a high price for a DVD, and it is, but it was also carefully calculated based on Brian's research: This was the highest price he could charge his audience, as there was nothing else like this film in the market. Brian sold more than 45,000 units in the first year of release.

LESSON NO. 7. COLLECT STATISTICAL INFORMATION. DO SURVEYS. GAUGE THE INTEREST IN YOUR FILM. BRIAN WISHES HE WOULD HAVE COLLECTED ZIP CODES OF THOSE INTERESTED BUYERS AS THAT WOULD HAVE HELPED HIM DECIDE WHERE HIS FULFILLMENT CENTER SHOULD BE, AMONG OTHER THINGS.

Television Release

Now that *One Six Right* had made a name for itself, Discovery heard about it and reached out to Brian. Brian negotiated this deal himself. He was successful in doubling the opening offer and was able to obtain a non-exclusive deal. (This is impressive, but not typical: We would not recommend trying this without a lawyer.) The film premiered on Christmas Day in 2006.

Brian did not want to enter into any exclusive deals. His goal was to get his film out to the public through as many outlets as possible, and he wanted the right to sell the film to other networks if he chose. Discovery had a six-month holdback period, but after that six months, Brian was free to make another television deal.

Brian had his sights set on PBS. He saw the corporate sponsorship sale as a great opportunity to make a significant amount of money. As you may or may not know, PBS has a 60-second sponsor "pod" at the beginning and end of each program. The filmmaker is responsible for securing those sponsorships and gets to keep any revenues received. PBS viewers are typically highly educated, affluent decision makers and accordingly, PBS is held in high regard by sponsors. Brian was confident he could secure four sponsors (15 seconds each) for the broadcast. He did so and made his investors quite a bit of money.

Other Distribution

One Six Right is available on iTunes, Netflix, Amazon and more. It is shown in museums, in-flight, cruises, prisons and other non-theatrical venues. Brian also sells clips of his film as stock footage. When we spoke with Brian, he was negotiating deals with Xbox and PlayStation. Brian's goals with this film were volume and exposure. He did this by entering into as many non-exclusive deals as possible. In fact, none of his agreements were exclusive.

Brian has paid all of the people who worked for deferred salaries and has paid his investors back in full, all of whom have seen substantial profits from the exploitation of this film, which continues. This is a rare statistic. If more people were willing to work as hard as Brian, the statistic just might become more common.

How did Brian do this? Perseverance, he says, and hard work . . . he believed in his product and went all in.

» ONE-NIGHT EVENTS

If your film has a unique angle and would do well paired with a live event (e.g., concert, panel discussion, sporting event), another type of theatrical release that you should consider is a one-night event, or a few one-night events. These work especially well for documentaries that have a niche audience. Companies like Area 23a, Fathom, and Roadside have experience orchestrating these one night events with filmmakers.

National CineMedia (NCM) is the company that originally started orchestrating one-night events (albeit not with films, but with other entertainment like concerts), utilizing satellite technology to broadcast an event across the country at a relatively low fee. NCM operates the largest digital in-theater network in North America through agreements with AMC, Cinemark (Century Theaters) and Regal, the three largest theater operators in the U.S., as well as several other theaters. NCM can distribute live and pre-recorded concerts, sporting events and other entertainment programming content to theatres across their digital network to approximately 400 theaters via satellite. NCM's intent with this program was to utilize their national chain theaters on less busy nights, Monday through Thursday.

Documentary filmmakers were quick to see the benefit of these one-night events as a way to reach their niche audience in a new and interesting way. They could now show their film in hundreds of theaters without having to spend the money to create and ship prints all over the country. The financial structure of this is much the same as any other theatrical release—the movie theater retains its usual 50 percent + of the box office and the distributor also takes their agreed-upon cut. It also provides an added benefit to your audience by creating a unique live experience.

Now, don't be misled, this certainly isn't an alternative to a theatrical release— it won't qualify your film for an Oscar and it probably won't generate the same type of reviews that a typical theatrical release would. Additionally, some art house theaters don't like these events because they arguably eat up the core audience who would have otherwise seen the film at that theater. Nevertheless, it's a great, unique option for the right types of films. As you'll see in the case study below, some filmmakers have successfully used this one-night event idea to launch the theatrical release.

CASE STUDY: I.O.U.S.A

In 2008, the film I.O.U.S.A., a powerful documentary that examines the rapidly growing national debt and its consequences for the United States and its citizens, had its premiere at Sundance. When the film was scheduled to be released theatrically by Roadside Attractions in August of that year, it wanted to figure out a great way to kick-start the theatrical run. Roadside came up with the idea of doing a one-night event during which the screening would be followed by a live discussion about the issues raised in the film. Roadside teamed up with NCM and Fathom Events (the division of NCM that produces these events) and came up with the idea of having a town hall meeting immediately after the screening. The producers put together a round table discussion for this meeting, which was moderated by Becky Quick and featured Warren Buffett, Dave Walker (the primary subject of the film) and several other prominent financial experts. People were able to submit questions via email prior to the event, and the audience members at the theater where the event took place (in Omaha) were able to ask questions during the "meeting." This made for a very interesting discussion immediately after the film and was broadcast live to all the theaters showing the film.

I.O.U.S.A. was a particularly good fit for a one-night event because the subject matter was incredibly timely, they had an aggressive media partner who was able to provide advertising and publicity for the event (CNBC), and the owners of the film (The Peter G. Peterson Foundation) had the wherewithal to put this high-profile town hall meeting together with Warren Buffett.

The publicity for this event was pretty amazing. NCM ran a 30-second commercial (cost-free to Roadside and the film) for an entire month leading up to the event in all of their theaters (almost 15,000 screens nationwide). This commercial exposed the film to not only documentary lovers and art house theater movie-goers, the typical audience for this type of film, but to audiences of films like *The Dark Knight* and other blockbusters. It was in NCM's best interest to publicize the screening because they not only keep some of the ticket sale revenue, but the theaters keep all the concession sales for the event. In other words, NCM wanted the theaters packed, and the cost to create this 30-second spot was well-worth it. In addition to this, the film's media partner, CNBC, contributed a significant amount of advertising time by running commercials and information for the event on their ticker during Becky Quick's show, *Squawk Box*.

To keep the numbers associated with this event in perspective, keep in mind that on a typical Thursday night in America the average movie theater sells less than 10 percent of its tickets. The Thursday night that *I.O.U.S.A.* played, the participating theaters sold half of all tickets available. The projections for the event were that the film would screen in approximately 150 theaters and they'd sell about 15,000 tickets. In fact, the film was broadcast to over 350 screens and they sold 45,000 tickets. The gross ticket sales were over a half million dollars from this event, which cost the *I.O.U.S.A.* folks about $150,000 to put together. The publicity it generated gave the 10-city theatrical release, which began the next day, a great boost, which helped future ticket sales.

By now you might have noticed that the examples of successful DIY distribution and one-night events have a common thread: they are focused on documentaries. There's a good reason for that. Documentaries are very well-suited for this type of distribution because they almost always have a core niche audience. The outreach and ability to create events around documentaries is often easier than with features. This is not to say that features can't be exploited this way; to the contrary, with a bit of creativity and a lot of hard work, a feature filmmaker could certainly DIY. But with documentaries, the filmmaker knows that there's a very specific main audience for the film, and knows exactly how that audience will want to see the film; that makes DIY distribution more easily achievable.

» SPLIT RIGHTS WRAP UP

I'm hopeful that this chapter has shown you that there are many ways to exploit your film aside from the traditional all-rights deal. And there are distributors who specialize in just about every type of exploitation—DVD, digital, non-theatrical, television and educational rights. DIY distribution can be hard work and can cost a substantial amount of money, but there are people out there to help you formulate a split rights distribution strategy that works for you and your budget. The companies mentioned in the Servicing section are just a few. There's also a non-profit organization called The Film Collaborative (www.thefilmcollaborative.com) that is dedicated to distribution of independent films. They offer a full range of affordable distribution, educational and marketing services to independent filmmakers. It's a wonderful resource if you are DIY-ing it. Also, consultants like Peter Broderick can assist in helping with your strategy.

» NEGOTIATING TIPS

Your distributor will provide you with the form of agreement which you will need to negotiate. Each distributor's form is different from the next, so instead of providing you with a sample distribution agreement, we will go through the most important provisions that show up in all distribution agreements and provide some negotiating tips:

1. TERM—The goal from the producer's perspective is to make this as short as possible under the circumstances. This is primarily because so many filmmakers are unhappy with their distributors. You want to make sure that the company charged with selling your film is doing a good job, and if they're not, you want a way out.
   a. *Producer's Rep*: The standard term for a Producer's Rep agreement is three months to two years. Big range, we know. The most typical term

for these agreements is one year. If you don't have a prior relationship with the Rep, you want to make sure that the relationship is for this particular picture only. Many times the Rep will try to add language attaching them to any sequels or other works based on the film.

b. *Foreign Sales Agent*: A Foreign Sales Agent will take your film for a longer period of time, generally somewhere between seven and 25 years. This longer term is justified because the Sales Agent's job is different than a Rep's. As discussed earlier in the chapter, the Sales Agent actually enters into agreements with distributors, takes responsibility for delivering your film, collects revenue and accounts to you. You want them to continue to do this for as long as your film is making money. Again, if this is a new relationship, try to make the term as short as possible.

c. *Distributor*: The Distributor will take your film for no less than seven years (typical for a TV sale) and up to perpetuity (which is common among studios).

If the Sales Agent or Distributor insists on term that you're not comfortable with, put benchmarks in the agreement which allow you to get the rights back after a certain number of years if the distributor has not met certain sales goals. These sales goals should be based on the budget of your film. For example, if the budget of your film is $1 million, you want to see that money back after two to three years from the exploitation of the film. So if you've entered into an all rights deal with a Distributor for 25 years, add language to the agreement stating that if the distributor does not pay you $1 million from sales made during the first three years of the agreement, all rights revert back to the filmmaker. You won't always get this, but you should always try.

We often see automatic renewals in these agreements. We are not fans of these. If the relationship is going well and both parties want to continue working together, they will. You don't want to be stuck in a relationship that is not working. Also, if you can terminate the agreement upon notice, the notice period should be as short as possible—if the notice period is six months prior to expiration of the term, it's quite likely that this date comes and goes without you realizing it and then all of a sudden, the agreement has continued for five more years without you even knowing it. Luckily, most of us have some type of electronic calendar in which we can calendar dates which are really far away, so if you have an automatic renewal capability, make sure to calendar that date with enough notice to cancel the agreement if you want to.

2. DEFINITION OF MEDIA—Read this carefully as the contract defines how the distributor can exploit your film. "Media" may be as broad as all rights to as narrow as educational rights only. The key is to make sure you fully understand what rights you are granting. Only grant rights that: 1) you have; and 2) you believe the distributor is going to exploit. Retain all others.

3. TERRITORY—Make sure this is accurate. Some deals are worldwide, some are domestic only, others are all foreign, and others are a limited number of domestic rights. If you are granting digital rights make sure there is language in the agreement about "geo-restrictions"—the technology that restricts a film from being transmitted outside the allowed area. There should also be language about "footprints." Typically, this applies to satellites and the fact that they cannot transmit programs in a way that exactly matches a country's borders. Often times the satellite feed bleeds into neighboring countries. This is fine so long as it is a legitimate footprint issue and not an attempt to exploit rights that are not granted to the distributor.

4. ADVANCE—An advance is money received typically upon delivery of your film and in advance of the distributor (or you) earning any revenue. Distributors can recoup advances against your royalty or back-end participation. It's always nice to get an advance, and if you are selling rights to a studio, you definitely need one because the chance of you seeing any back-end participation is unlikely. If you are granting only limited rights, such as educational rights, to a small distributor, an advance is desirable but not quite as important because you will most likely see some revenue (relatively quickly) assuming your film is moderately successful.

5. FEES—There are three typical types of fee structures:

   a. *Royalty deal*—The filmmaker receives a percentage of "gross" receipts. The word "gross" is in quotes because typically, the distributor will deduct some costs (i.e., any delivery costs and marketing costs) prior to paying you the "gross" royalty. Royalty deals are most commonly seen in connection with DVD sales. The royalty ranges from approximately 20 percent to 35 percent.

   b. *Revenue split*—All revenue earned by the distributor after expenses are recouped is split with the filmmaker. We like to see this split 50/50, although it is sometimes 60/40 or even 70/30 in favor of the distributor. These types of deals are commonly seen in connection with new media sales (e.g., downloads, mobile and the like).

   c. *Fee paid to distributor*—Distributor will take a percentage from gross sales (typically between 20 to 35 percent), recoup its expenses, and the remainder, if any, will be paid to the filmmaker. This deal is often seen with Producer's Reps, Foreign Sales Agents and other all-rights type deals. It is important that this fee be inclusive of any sub-distributor fees (except for the Rep's fee, which will almost always be on top of any other fees). Often, distributors team up with other entities to exploit different rights. Each entity takes a fee. You don't want to be in a position where you are paying 25 percent to your sales agent, 10 percent to the guy who makes the TV sale, and another 20 percent to the guy who's selling your film overseas. The highest total percentage you should pay is 40 percent—and that's pretty high. The other thing to negotiate is different fees for different rights. For example, a U.S. television deal should involve a smaller commission, something like 10 or 15 percent; it's an easier sale as there are only a handful of outlets, and more importantly, there is usually not another distributor or agent in the picture, so the entire fee goes to your rep or agent. In, say, a foreign sale where there is often another party involved, the fee will be split, which justifies a higher fee.

6. EXCLUSIVITY—Most deals will, at a minimum, start out being exclusive, and some distributors will only take rights if they can have them exclusively for the entire term. Exclusivity is okay so long as you are not prohibited from selling the rights that the distributor has not acquired. Or if, for example, it's a television deal, exclusivity is okay so long as the agreement is only exclusive for the first six months or the time period that the broadcaster intends to air your program. Digital rights are more commonly not exclusive, so you can sell your film on iTunes and Amazon and Netflix.

Regardless of whether your deal is exclusive, you should always retain direct DVD Sales. It's great to be able to sell your film from your website and so-called "back-of-the-room sales," such as at educational screenings, conferences and seminars, whether or not you are present. This is cash that comes directly to you, immediately, with no deductions. If you do plan to sell from your website, make sure you team up with a good, centrally located fulfillment center like Cinram (used by some of the bigger studios) or The Regan Group, and that you have the capabilities to handle customer service issues (if you don't remember what happened to Brian, read the *One Six Right* case study again).

7. APPROVALS—Producer Reps typically retain no approvals—you approve or disapprove the deal(s) that they bring to you. However, Sales Agents and Distributors do retain approval rights over most or all aspects of distribution. If you are really reluctant to hand these approvals over, you should think twice about whether you want this person/company to distribute your film. That being said, there are several things you should have in your agreement to ensure that you are kept in the loop regarding decisions being made about your film:

a. Schedule of Minimums: You should definitely have one of these in your Sales Agent agreement. A Schedule of Minimums is a list of territories with the minimum price the Sales Agent may sell your film for in each territory. If the Sales Agent wants to sell your film for less than the agreed upon amount, he must get your approval first. This is really helpful because it prevents a distributor from selling your film for 50 cents bundled together with 12 other titles (exaggeration, but you get my point). This is also referred to as a Take/Ask list. Here's an example:

TERRITORY	ASK PRICES	TAKE PRICES
AFRICA	$ _____	$ _____
AUSTRALIA	$ _____	$ _____
AUSTRIA	$ _____	$ _____
BALTICS	$ _____	$ _____
BELGIUM	$ _____	$ _____
BRAZIL	$ _____	$ _____
CANADA	$ _____	$ _____
CIS	$ _____	$ _____
CHINA	$ _____	$ _____
DENMARK	$ _____	$ _____
E. EUROPE	$ _____	$ _____
FINLAND	$ _____	$ _____
FR. CANADA	$ _____	$ _____
FRANCE	$ _____	$ _____
GERMANY	$ _____	$ _____
HUNGARY	$ _____	$ _____
HONG KONG	$ _____	$ _____
INDIA	$ _____	$ _____
INDONESIA	$ _____	$ _____
ISRAEL	$ _____	$ _____
ITALY	$ _____	$ _____
JAPAN	$ _____	$ _____
KOREA	$ _____	$ _____
LATIN AM.	$ _____	$ _____
MIDDLE EAST	$ _____	$ _____
MALAYSIA	$ _____	$ _____
NEW ZEALAND	$ _____	$ _____
NETHERLANDS	$ _____	$ _____
NORWAY	$ _____	$ _____
PHILIPPINES	$ _____	$ _____
POLAND	$ _____	$ _____
PORTUGAL	$ _____	$ _____
RUSSIA	$ _____	$ _____
SINGAPORE	$ _____	$ _____
SOUTH AFRICA	$ _____	$ _____
SPAIN	$ _____	$ _____
SWEDEN	$ _____	$ _____
SWITZERLAND	$ _____	$ _____
TAIWAN	$ _____	$ _____
THAILAND	$ _____	$ _____
TURKEY	$ _____	$ _____
UK	$ _____	$ _____
U.S.	$ _____	$ _____
TOTAL	**$ _____**	**$ _____**

The prices aren't filled in because they fluctuate so much depending on many factors, including the nature of your film (documentary, drama, comedy) and the cast.

b. Bundled/Packaged Sales: You also want to have a right to approve bundled and packaged sales. A bundled sale is when the distributor sells several films in a package to one buyer. If your film is bundled it's often tough to determine what share of that bundle you should get. A lot of times the split is equally among all the filmmakers, but what if your film is the lead item and the reason the buyers are willing to take the other, potentially less valuable films? Or vice versa? You need not answer that question now; it simply illustrates the point that the value of your film will vary relative to other films and you should try to get approval rights over bundling and packaging of your film.

c. Artwork: With respect to artwork, advertising and promotional materials, you want to have at least a right of meaningful consultation. The word "meaningful" is important. Although it's certainly subject to interpretation, that word at least ensures that you will be involved in a real discussion about the artwork, rather than a notification after it has already been created. The distributor will almost always retain final say, but at least you get to put your two cents in if you want to. Also, if you have pre-existing materials, you might want the distributor to use those—this will save on costs and hopefully ensure that your marketing materials look like you intended them to look. Don't forget, these guys are supposed to be experts in this field, so if you don't trust their judgment perhaps they're the wrong distributors.

d. Term: You might also be able to get the distributor to give you a right to approve sales that are effective for longer than a certain term; most importantly, a sale with a term that is longer than the term you have with your distributor or agent. This is beneficial to you because when the term expires you'll want to know what rights are available to exploit and whether there are existing contracts.

e. Residuals: With smaller films you also want to make sure that a sale that triggers guild residuals or an upgrade (e.g., DVD or television sale) is worth it. Residual payments are triggered for actors, writers and directors, who are members of the relevant guild (SAG, WGA, DGA), when the film is exploited beyond the original intended distribution. For example, DVD sales trigger residual payments, as does a TV sale of a program that was originally made as a theatrical motion picture. Upgrades are typically triggered if you produce a low-budget film and the final budget ends up exceeding the maximum budget for that agreement. There are other ways upgrades can be triggered, so just be sure you consult with your union rep about this so you fully understand all the consequences. Be sure to ask yourself: Will I be able to pay those residuals or upgrade payments if the sale is made? Will those fees exceed the potential income?

f.   Writing: On a general note about approvals, always make sure that approvals are in writing. This is good protection for you as well as the distributor as it avoids any confusion or disagreement later on about what was actually approved. Say the distributor is going to a film market and asks you for approval to cover expenses. You say sure, but tell him that you don't want to pay more than $5,000 in expenses. The distributor bills you for $7,000 in expenses and claims that he doesn't recall you ever limiting the amount they could spend. If this was in writing, even a simple email, there would be no dispute.

g.   Signed Agreements: Make sure your rep or distributor is obligated to provide you with copies of final agreements, immediately upon execution. This will ensure that you stay abreast of what deals have been entered into, what monies should be coming in and how well your agent or distributor is doing with your film.

8.   EXPENSES—Expenses incurred by Reps, Sales Agents and Distributors can be tricky and sometimes confusing. To protect yourself against unwarranted spending, you want as much language in the agreement as you can to help control the amount of money spent on your film. A simple marketing expense clause may look something like, "Distributor will pay all costs related to the publicity and marketing of the Film." Okay, wait. You want the distributor to put up some money to promote your film, but you don't want it to be out of whack with your budget, nor do you want the distributor to spend so much that you never see a dime. You want to make sure that the amount of money spent on marketing is proportionate with your film's budget and the type of film itself.

Film market expenses can also be a tricky area to monitor. You want to make sure that you are paying your fair share of expenses incurred by your Sales Agent to attend film markets. This is difficult even for the Agent to determine. You'll find that Agents do their best to split the cost proportionately among the films they bring to the market. Often they will split the bulk of the expense with their new films and allocate a smaller portion, as appropriate, to their older films.

Here are some suggestions for how to control expenses:

a.   Put a cap on the total amount of money spent. If the budget of your film is $500,000, you probably don't want them spending more than $25,000 or so without getting your approval.

b.   Try to get approvals over all expenses greater than a certain amount, such as $2,000.

c.   Use a flat fee. More and more companies have started starting using this model. Initially this was a red flag. Getting used to the shift of our client getting paid for the rights to exploit his film to a model where they are now paying a fee (out of revenues earned, but still), was a bit difficult. We've come around and now we think it actually works pretty well; neither party has to concern themselves with accounting and how much is being spent. Often you'll see a company charge a

$50,000 fee for marketing and publicity. This fee is paid out of revenues earned in connection with the film. When we negotiate a deal like this, we like to either spread the flat fee over time, or, at a minimum, ensure that the filmmaker gets something from each sale, so the distributor doesn't recoup the entire fee from the first sales.

  d. The more approval rights you have in this area, the better.

9. CHANGES—Ideally, you do not want the distributor to make any changes to your film. That being said, companies often have to make changes to comply with broadcast requirements or legal issues. This is okay, but make sure that the distributor is prohibited from making creative or substantive changes without your prior written approval. You might also have ideas about what should be cut in the event a shorter version needs to be made. If this is the case, make sure you negotiate a right to make those changes. Also check the language about changes to the title. For foreign sales, the title may have to change, which may be fine, but you want to, at a minimum, have a right of meaningful consultation.

10. GUILD RESIDUALS—The producer is always responsible for paying all residuals incurred from the exploitation of the film. Guild residuals are based on gross sales. So if your distributor enters into a DVD sale for $10,000, you will owe residuals based on that $10,000 sale, regardless of whether you see one penny from that sale or not. This obligation can be very burdensome for an indie filmmaker who does not have a reserve to pay these residuals when they become due. Sometimes a distributor will "assume" these rights and pay them on behalf of the producer by way of a residual Assumption Agreement. However, beware: if the distributor assumes this obligation and then defaults (i.e., does not pay the residuals), you, the producer, are still liable for this payment. You are not off the hook simply because the distributor said they would pay. Your best bet is to have a reserve so you can pay these residuals when they become due.

11. INSURANCE—Distributors will require that you maintain an Errors and Omissions (E&O) insurance policy for a minimum of three years from the first release date. The three year period is because the statute of limitations (the amount of time one has to file a lawsuit) on claims that would be covered by your E&O policy is also three years. After that three-year period, third parties should not be able to successfully file a claim against you. (I say "should not" rather than "cannot" because the person filing the claim might have a reason to extend this statute of limitations if he reasonably did not know about the film's existence until sometime after its release date; e.g., the release was very limited.) Distributors typically require that your policy have limits of $1 million per occurrence (claim) and $3 million in the aggregate, meaning that the insurance company will shell out no more than $3 million in connection with all claims during the term of the policy. Distributors often ask for the deductible to be no more than $10,000; however, a $25,000 deductible is much more common and affordable. You

can often get the distributor to raise the maximum deductible to $25,000. The producer is responsible for paying the deductible, so it seems that the distributor shouldn't really care—but they do, especially if they don't think you have the resources to cover it. If the distributor's form agreement has limits that are higher than those stated previously, ask why. If you don't have a high-risk film, it's excessive to have higher limits.

12. ACCOUNTING—An accounting is a statement that lists all revenue earned and expenses spent. Ensure that you receive accountings, along with payments if there are any, on a quarterly basis for at least two years after the initial release. The accountings can then go to semi-annually or annually after that. The thinking is that most activity will occur during the first two years of distribution and after that the level of activity will drop. Accounting statements should be detailed, with all expenses clearly outlined and all revenue earned by the distributor recorded.

13. AUDITS—Make sure you have a right to audit the company's books and records on an annual basis. The statute of limitations is four years on any accounting irregularity, but companies routinely limit your right to audit their books to a one or two year period from the date of the disputed accounting statement. We don't like this, but it's often hard to get a distributor to agree to allow you to audit books for more than a two-year period. Because of this, you must make sure you diligently review your statements and ensure their accuracy in a very timely manner. If you don't receive statements in a timely manner, hound the company to get them. You do not want to lose your right to contest a statement.

14. INDEMNIFICATION—You will always have to indemnify the distributor—cover the cost of any claim arising based on a breach of the agreement. This is not unreasonable. If you are representing that you own the film, it's original and does not infringe on anyone else's rights, the distributor should be able to rely on those statements. However, indemnification should go both ways. If the distributor breaches and gets you caught in the middle of a dispute, it should be liable as well. Additionally, make sure that the distributor is obligated to indemnify you for claims arising from the distribution, exploitation and advertising related to the film.

15. ARBITRATION—We like to include arbitration language in our agreements. By adding this language the parties agree to resolve disputes by binding arbitration and accordingly, waive their rights to a jury trial. We do this because arbitrations are faster, less expensive and less time consuming than going to court. Also, an individual can represent himself during arbitration (although we don't recommend that!) and arbitrations are held in private. And if keeping things confidential is important, arbitration is definitely the way to go.

These negotiating tips cover many of the major points that will be addressed in a Rep, Agent or Distribution agreement. Of course, every agreement looks different and some companies are more flexible than others when it comes to this negotiation. You need to weigh all of the factors together and determine if the deal is right for you. If you're not comfortable with the manner in which the negotiations are being conducted or the company's unwillingness to move on certain points, think about whether this is the right company for you. This is a long-term relationship, very similar to a personal relationship. You're giving this company your baby and you need to trust them.

A key thing to remember when negotiating your distribution agreement is that regardless what your agreement says, the relationship you have with the actual people who will be working on your film is of paramount importance. What we hope happens is that you spend a bunch of time negotiating a contract, it gets put in a drawer and neither party ever has to look at it because things are going so well. At the end of the day, if the distributor is dishonest, it doesn't matter what the agreement says, that company will have no problems breaching it. If you don't trust your distributor or if you don't communicate well with them, it's unlikely that the relationship will be successful. If the relationship is open and honest and the communication is easy, your chances of success are much higher.

Good luck distributing your film!

6

DELIVERY

This is so important. Many filmmakers just sign on the dotted line without paying close attention to the delivery schedule. This is a big mistake. If you're getting an advance, payment typically triggers upon delivery of the film. Often the term of the agreement doesn't begin until delivery is complete. If you can't comply with all the delivery requirements, you risk being in breach of the agreement before sales even start. But, you may ask, what exactly is "delivery"?

Delivery is providing the agent or distributor with all the elements of the film, technical and paper, which are necessary to actually get the film in front of an audience. This includes everything from a 35mm print (used for a traditional theatrical release) to the agreements with your crew. Every company has a slightly different set of delivery requirements and each company will provide you with a list of required deliverables, which will be attached to the distribution agreement. The delivery schedule will dictate what needs to be "delivered" in order to successfully deliver the film. Often these lists are full of materials that are not necessary, are expensive, and truthfully, are sometimes not even needed by the Distributor. Go through the list carefully and remove all items that you do not have (and can't easily obtain). If the delivery schedule asks for a 35mm print, but there is not going to be a theatrical release, this very expensive item should be removed for the list of required items. Bottom line on this point is simply to make sure that you can deliver everything listed on the schedule and if you can't, get it omitted, or figure out how to make it work!

In short, it's very important to review the list of deliverables carefully and ensure that you can actually deliver what's being asked of you.

Now, technical delivery is up to you. As great as we lawyers are, some of us don't know what an NTSC Digibeta is or how you shot your film or whether you have all of the necessary sound elements. When you negotiate the delivery schedule with the distribution company, make sure the person you're negotiating with understands what each delivery item is and most importantly, how much it costs!

Your lawyer will assist with the paper delivery requirements. However, you will save a lot of fees and anguish if you are familiar with the terms and what is required before you actually have to deliver the film. Below are some of the standard (paper) items asked for:

» CHAIN OF TITLE

All too often, I get asked the following question: "The insurance company needs the chain of title, can you get that to me?" Chain of title is not one thing or one document, but rather it is the group of documents that show who owns the film. Think of a title for your car. Your title will show all the owners in chronological order, from what periods each owner owned the car and other information that might be helpful in assessing whether you want to buy the car. The chain of title for a film is the same thing. The purchaser just wants to make sure that you actually own what you are selling or licensing. The most important chain of title documents relate to any underlying rights and writer agreements. It's also important that your director agreement and all crew agreements are in place. It needs to be clear that all services rendered in connection with the film were either work-for-hire or assigned to the production company. Sometimes you (or your lawyer) will create a flow chart of sorts that demonstrates you own the film—it will essentially be a summary of all the agreements showing that all rights flow to you or your company.

For example, let's say you made a film based on a book called *Donaldson and Callif to the Rescue*. It's a great drama/thriller about two high-powered attorneys trying to save the world one film at a time. You option the book from the author, hire a writer to write the script and then you produce the movie. The chain would look like this:

> Book (Optioned to filmmaker) _Script (WFH for filmmaker) _Book (option exercised by filmmaker so he owns all rights) _ Film (all elements owned by filmmaker demonstrated by all agreements that indicate WFH)

» E&O INSURANCE

E&O insurance is the shorthand name for "errors and omissions insurance." Errors and omissions insurance is similar to that purchased by doctors, lawyers, and accountants to compensate others for damage caused by negligent mistakes. If you accidentally infringe a copyright, slander a trademark, invade someone's privacy, violate someone's right of publicity, or otherwise stub your toe on any of the many obstacles that can happen during filmmaking, E&O is the insurance policy that applies. It's the insurance policy that covers intellectual property and personal rights-related claims. E&O policies typically cost between $3,000 to $12,000 depending on the expected distribution of your film. Theatrical release is most expensive because insurers believe (and typically they are right) if your film is in the theaters, there is more exposure because of increased viewers. They also consider whether the film is "risky" or controversial in nature.

Your E&O carrier will require that along with your application, you submit several reports that ensure you have the rights to exploit your film. Among those reports are the following:

Title Report

A title report lists all the films, books, songs, and plays that bear the same or similar titles, together with press mentions of those titles. Before anyone distributes your film, whether through a theatrical release or television or DVD sale, you must have cleared your title. It is a relatively easy process. You simply send your title along with the appropriate fee to a company that creates these reports. Any one of them will prepare a report on the title you want to use and similar titles that have been used in the past for films, plays, songs, books, websites and other works. The cost ranges from approximately $350 to $1,500, depending on how quickly you need the report and whether or not you also want a legal opinion with your report. Here are a few recommendations:

Dennis Angel (New York), (914) 472–0820
requests@dangelesq.com
www.dangelesq.com
A firm that specializes in providing copyright information to the entertainment industry.

Thomson Compumark (Washington, DC), (800) 356–8630
(Boston, MA), (617) 479–1600
www.thomson-thomson.com
Thomson Compumark is the leader in trademark and copyright services.

Clearance Unlimited (Los Angeles) (818) 988–5599
www.suzyvaughan.com
A full service clearance company.

Here's the beginning portion of a title report:

Title Report—CROSSINGS

We have conducted a search of the records of the Copyright Office, Thomson CompuMark's proprietary databases, and other entertainment databases and sources with regard to the proposed use of the title CROSSINGS for a documentary film.

This title was searched using the following strategy:

CROSSIN(')(G)(S)

The following references were found:

Motion Pictures

CROSSINGS: Hong Kong and U.S. motion picture in 102 minutes running time, produced by Riverdrive Productions in 1994, directed by Evans Chan, starring Anita Yuen, Lidzay Chan, and Simon Yam, registered for copyright in the name of Riverdrive Productions, Ltd., as published May 7, 1994, and described as a drama. Currently listed as available in a variety of video formats through Facets Multimedia, Inc.

CROSSINGS: Motion picture short in approximately 10 minutes running time, produced by Lee Bridgers/Musiak between 1988–90, in the series entitled "Variations on a Theme," and described as a film about a deer that has been killed by a car and which lies on asphalt as cars zoom past. We do not find that this work is currently being distributed to television, nor is it available in video format under this title.

Television

CROSSINGS: Miniseries consisting of three episodes in a total of 360 minutes running time, a.k.a. DANIELLE STEELE'S CROSSINGS, produced by Aaron Spelling Productions in 1986, directed by Karen Arthur, starring Jane Seymour, Lee Horsley, and Cheryl Ladd, registered for copyright in the name of Spelling Ventures Organization by Aaron Spelling Productions, Inc., a successor & [sic] interest to Spelling Ventures Organization, as published September 23, 1986, and described as a story set during WWII of an affair between a steel magnate and the wife of a French ambassador, based on a novel by Danielle Steel. This miniseries premiered over ABC on February 23, 1986. Currently listed as available for television distribution worldwide with exclusions through Warner Bros. International Television Inc.

CROSSINGS: Episode in the series entitled "Alias," registered for copyright in the name of Touchstone Television an a.d.o. Disney Enterprises, Inc., as published January 8, 2004.

Games/ Multi-Media

No references found.

Radio

No references found.

The title report is sent to your E&O carrier and if the underwriter has any concerns about the title, they will ask that your clearance attorney prepare a letter stating that use of the title is permissible. Our firm routinely issues opinion letters for our clients and insurance companies. If the title may be used, the letter is very simple—it looks something like this:

Dear [NAME]:

You have forwarded to our firm for an opinion, a title report prepared by Thomson CompuMark dated _____ on [NAME OF PROJECT] for use in connection with your film. The Thomson CompuMark report included a search of the Copyright Office, Thomson CompuMark's proprietary databases, and other entertainment databases and sources.

In forming my opinion, I received and reviewed the following items:

1. Thomson CompuMark Title Research Report dated _____;

2. Thomson CompuMark Analyst Review—USPTO Report dated _____;

3. Thomson CompuMark Analyst Review—Internet Domain Name Report dated _____; and

4. Thomson CompuMark Reported Owner Index dated _____.

> Based upon my review and analysis of the _____ Thomson CompuMark report, I am of the opinion that [NAME OF PROJECT] is available for use as the title of your film.

» SCRIPT CLEARANCE REPORT

There are a number of companies that are in the business of script clearance. Script clearance is really a misnomer since no permissions are gained. Rather, these businesses and individuals provide the very useful service of flagging all the potential clearance problems—no matter how remote—contained in the script.

The script clearance report identifies copyright and trademark issues, but actually it is particularly helpful with matters that seem to have nothing to do with copyright. For instance, the script clearance service checks phone books in the locale where your film is supposed to be set to see if you are inadvertently using the name of a real person or a real business. They also check the area for real phone numbers. If a car's license plate number is readable on screen, they can check with the state's Department of Motor Vehicles to be sure that it doesn't belong to anybody.

A script clearance service provides a report that sets forth everything that could possibly need to be cleared. However, the report merely points out which items might have to be cleared—leaving the responsibility of deciding what to clear or change, what to leave, and when to accept the risk or obtain permissions to you or your attorney. The report alone does not protect your production company should a subsequent lawsuit be levied against it. It merely alerts you to possible problems.

If your film is based on a true story or uses actual names or public figures or you think the subject matter might lend itself to certain clearance issues, it's a good idea to get a script clearance report before you start filming. That way you can avoid any clearance obstacles early on and avoid the cost of reshooting or editing.

Many individuals and businesses are available to write script clearance reports. Here are a few places to go:

Hollywood Script Research
448 W. Maple Street
Glendale, CA 91204
(818) 553–3633
www.hollywoodscriptresearch.com
info@hollywoodscriptresearch.com

Act One Script Clearance, Inc.
230 North Maryland Ave., Ste. 206
Glendale, CA 91206
(818) 240–2416
www.scriptresearch.com
info@actonescript.com

Mosquito Productions
7721 Twining Way
Canoga Park, CA 91304
(818) 676–0220

Below is a brief excerpt from a typical script clearance report. You can see from the report that it just lists the potential problems. A script clearance report for a feature film generally runs 10 to 20 pages and costs about $1,500. It can be completed in a couple of weeks, unless you want to pay more for a rush job.

CAST	COMMENT
Pep Pep p.4	Presume to be nickname use only.
Steve Chisker p.7	We find no listing for a prominent person with this name in the U.S. We find no residential listing for this name in the U.S. We find no conflict.

PAGE	COMMENT
1	(Music: Dramatic, creepy)—Advise check music clearance.
1	EXT. WOODS—Possible location agreement. Presume any names to be visible for signage will be checked through Research.
1	humming a tune—Advise check music clearance.
1	INT. DIGITAL WORLD—Advise do not identify any copyrighted or protected material, or any data pertaining to actual persons, firms or organizations.
1	Rap music plays—Advise check music clearance.
1	All the dads sing—As above.

2	INT. PLAY ROOM—Advise do not identify any copyrighted or protected material, or any data pertaining to actual persons, firms or organizations.
2	I JAMMER—We find one trademark listing for this name: (abandoned, federal, toys, namely battery operated dolls, figures, animals, creatures, structures or objects, which react to external or internal sources of sound, or to electronic signals corresponding to sound, to generate movement, sound, light, or combinations of the above, by Thinking Technology Inc.). We find no business listing for a product/brand with this name in the U.S. Advise check with legal counsel.
2	We see a large, cumbersome cube with lights and buttons—Advise avoid proprietary design.
2	intermittent rhythmic tones—Advise check music clearance.
2	E Bumpin—We find no federal or state trademark listing for this name. We find no business listing for a product/brand with this name in the U.S. We find no conflict.
3	trying to watch TV—Advise do not identify any actual television station, network or cable/satellite source by name, call sign, frequency, channel number, logo, etc. Permission advised for copyrighted or protected program material identifiable on screen or soundtrack.
3	INT. ANOTHER KIDS PLAYROOM—Advise do not identify any copyrighted or protected material, or any data pertaining to actual persons, firms or organizations.
3	watch an analog monitor—Advise avoid commercial identification.
3	Oh HUNGEE—We find no federal or state trademark listing for this name. We find no business listing for a product/brand with this name in the U.S. We find no conflict.
3	INT. BASEMENT—Advise do not identify any copyrighted or protected material, or any data pertaining to actual persons, firms or organizations.

| 3 | We see pictures of Casey Tatum—Presume to be created especially for production and will not reflect any copyrighted or protected material, or any data pertaining to actual persons, firms or organizations. Possible permission from any living photo subject identifiable on screen who is not a cast member. |

» COPYRIGHT REPORT

A Copyright Report is a report that provides available information relating to the ownership of your film. This report includes a search of possible copyright registrations and recorded documents from the U.S. Copyright Office. Your insurer will require this because they want to make sure that there is no one else out there who can claim ownership over your film. Typically, the same companies that issue title reports also issue copyright reports.

» REGISTERING COPYRIGHT OF YOUR COMPLETED FILM

Your distributor will require that you register your film with the Copyright Office. You can now do this online at www.copyright.gov through the Copyright Office's eCO portal. The form is simple and the cost relatively inexpensive ($35 at the time of printing).

Keep in mind that you'll probably need to file two hard copies of your completed film with the Copyright Office unless you upload an electronic version (see "Submitting Copies of Your Work" below). This means that you need to send them copies of the film on DVD upon completing the online registration process. Here's a guide to get you through the online registration process:

The eCO Portal

Go to the Copyright Office's website and click on to the link "Register Online," then click on the link that directs you to the eCO (Electronic Copyright Office) portal. If you've already created an account with eCO, enter your account details; if you haven't, click on the link to sign up. Once you're in the portal, click on "Register a New Claim" to begin the registration process. At this point, you can either continue and click on "Start Registration" or read more about the three major steps required to register your work. Luckily, you can save your application at any time throughout the process by clicking the "Save for Later" button and pick up where you left off next time you log in.

Most of the steps are pretty self-explanatory and if you have any questions, there are step-by-step directions on the site. However, we think it will be helpful to highlight some of the areas that often present problems or questions for our clients:

Title of the Film

This seems simple enough, right? Well, usually it is. Trouble sometimes comes up when you're registering a series of works. If that's the case, you'll also want to create a record of the "Series Title" under which this individual film is being registered. For example, if you're registering individual works within your documentary series entitled "The History of Gangster Movies," the series name would be listed as the "Series Title," and the individual program—the work you're currently registering (let's say it's "The 1990s and Beyond")—would be the "Title of Work Being Registered." You can create multiple entries in this section to fit your specific situation (and the Copyright Office provides you a good list of examples on their "Help" page), but you must have an entry for "Title of Work Being Registered."

Publication

You need to indicate to the Copyright Office whether your film has been published. If you made copies of your film for the purpose of distribution to the public, including screenings for potential buyers, then your film has been published. If all you did was have a cast and crew screening, then the film has not been published. On the next page of the form, enter the year of completion of the film. The application also asks you for a preregistration number. If you're just now registering your completed film for the first time, you will not have a preregistration number. Preregistration allows you to register your film before it's been published. The benefit is that you can sue for infringement of your copyright before your work has been published and, if successful in such an infringement action, you will be eligible to receive statutory damages and attorneys' fees. Preregistration might be helpful if you think it's likely that your uncompleted film might be infringed before you release it, but it is *not* a substitute for regular registration and is only available for certain types of works, which happens to include films.

Author/Copyright Claimant

This section is probably the most confusing part of the registration process. Weird, right? The reason it gets confusing is because the author is typically a corporate entity, which seems pretty counterintuitive. Also, because the author is a corporate entity, so many of the boxes don't apply, so it just feels like you're doing something wrong. The eCO instructions are quite helpful here.

In brief, the author is the person or organization who created the work and the copyright claimant is the person or organization who now owns the copyright. If you have formed an LLC or corporation for the purpose of creating the film, you will want to list that LLC or corporation as both the author and the copyright claimant and you'll indicate that the film is a "work-for-hire." You'll also want to claim the "entire motion picture," even if there are elements in the film that you don't own, such as third-party music. This is addressed in the next section. If the copyright owner is someone or an entity other than the author, you must include a "transfer statement" indicating how that other person or entity came to own the copyright (usually by written agreement like an assignment).

Limitations of Claim—Inclusions / Exclusions

This part of the process asks you to indicate areas of the work that are either not yours or are already registered. If you have a film that is based on a previously registered script, you should select "Script/Screenplay" under "Material Exclusions" and select "Production as a motion picture" under "Material Inclusions." Or let's say you've made a documentary film with a great deal of third party materials that were either licensed, used pursuant to fair use, or in the public domain. In this case, you'll want to select any exclusions that apply—for instance, "Preexisting footage" and "Preexisting photographs"—and under "New Materials" select "Editing," "New narration," and "All other cinematographic material." If you previously registered the film but have added new material, select the boxes for whatever new material has been added, or write in your own explanation.

Reviewing Your Submission

Make sure you review your submission where it prompts you to do so! You can't go back and make any changes after you've officially submitted your application. After reviewing the submission, enter your billing information.

Submitting Copies of Your Work

If you haven't yet published your film or have only published it online, you *could* upload an electronic version of your film through the eCO portal if you can compress the file enough to meet the portal's standards. However, the Copyright Office requires that you provide them with the "best edition" of your film. This might mean that you send an actual film print (if you shot in film), but it is also acceptable (although less preferable according to the Copyright Office) to send DVDs. The eCO portal will allow you to generate a shipping slip if you're going to send hard copies of your film. You should send hard copies of your film to the address on the slip as soon as possible after making completing your submission to expedite the process.

And that's it! If you register online, you'll get a notice stating that registration will be complete within nine months, but it generally won't take that long (however, it will take approximately six months or so). If you have any questions about the registration process you can contact the following numbers at the Copyright Office:

> For technical inquiries:
> Copyright Technology Office
> (202) 707–3002 / ctoinfo@loc.gov
> For registration-related inquiries:
> Copyright Public Information Office
> (202) 707–3000 / copyinfo@loc.gov

» COMPLETING DELIVERY

In addition to your E&O policy and all of the reports required by your insurance carrier, you will also be expected to deliver a completed film (the technical aspect) and all the agreements showing that you have the right to sell it. The distributor will also require a list of any restrictions on publicity, use of talents' name and likeness, all credit obligations and more, all of which are contained in the agreements with the people who work on the film. For example, your lead actress might only want to be in publicity materials if others in the cast are also in those materials. Or you may need to get approval from your leading guy before you can use any photographs with his image. It is a good idea to keep a running list of these obligations during production and as the contracts are signed. Waiting until the end to compile all of this information can be difficult and time consuming.

To get you familiarized with delivery requirements, we've included a very comprehensive delivery schedule below. This will give you an idea of the items a distributor will request. As you can see by reviewing this schedule, you must be careful to remove any unnecessary items or you could be looking at tens of thousands if not hundreds of thousands of dollars in expenses. And don't be afraid to ask to remove items. We view this schedule as a wish list and we've found that distributors are very amenable to adjusting this schedule to what is actually needed, rather than simply wanted. In fact, this process is so common that distributors do not bother to tailor the list of deliverables until after the filmmaker has had a look at it.

SCHEDULE OF DELIVERY ITEMS REQUIRED

LAB ACCESS: Lab access must be provided by Licensor to Sales Agent throughout the active term of this Agreement for both the *Feature* and *Release Trailer* in each of the formats listed below. These elements are in addition to those to be delivered to Sales Agent in the following sections of this schedule:

1. Original Negative

2. Original Soundtrack Source

3. 35mm Interpositive or Digital Intermediate

4. 35mm Internegative

5. 35mm Stereo Optical Soundtrack Negative

6. 35mm Final Answer Print from Negative

7. 35mm Check Print from Negative

8. 35mm Textless Sections Interpositive

9. Reel-By-Reel Fully-Filled M&E

10. MASTER FILE: a 2K or High Definition Uncompressed AVI File Sequence, delivered on a Firewire hard drive

11. PROJECT FILE: Final Cut Pro or AVID file (including all sound files)

12. PAL 25fps 4x3 Full Frame masters on Digital Betacam (DBC)

13. 23.98fps or 25fps HIGH DEFINITION (HD) master on a HD-CAM SR tapes

THE ITEMS THAT FOLLOW ARE TO BE DELIVERED TO SALES AGENT

FILM ITEMS: All elements listed below must be provided for both the *Feature* and *Release Trailer*. These elements are in addition to the prints being kept at the lab and may be used on loan to distributors:

1. 35mm Internegative

2. 35mm Stereo Optical Soundtrack Negative

3. 35mm Textless Sections Interpositive

4. 35mm Release Print

VIDEO ITEMS: Masters must be provided for both the *Feature* and *Release Trailer* by Licensor to Sales Agent for all items listed below:

1. PAL 25fps and NTSC 29.97fps 4x3 Full Frame masters on Digital Betacams (DBC).

2. PAL 25fps and NTSC 29.97fps 16x9 Full Height Anamorphic masters on DBC

3. 23.98fps and 25fps HIGH DEFINITION (HD) 16 X 9 Full Frame masters on a HD-CAM SR

4. MPEG-2 files in both PAL (720x576 pixels / min 5000/448 kbps) and NTSC (720x480 pixels / min 5000/448 kbps)

5. HI-DEF Quicktime files

6. CLOSED CAPTION files time-coded to agree with both the NTSC and PAL Digibeta masters in .CAP format

7. BONUS FEATURES on a DVD video disk in both NTSC and PAL

SOUND ITEMS: Continuous audio elements must be provided by Licensor to Sales Agent per below:

1. 29.97fps and 25fps sets of PCM or AIFF digital audio files

2. Sets of 5.1 digital audio files, either PCM or AIFF

ANCILLARY ITEMS: The following items must be provided by Licensor to Sales Agent:

1. Contractual Credit Block

2. Synopsis

3. Production notes

4. Layered Key Art

5. High-Definition Frame-grabs

6. Digital production photographs

7. Lab Access Letter (see sample below)

8. Quality Control ("QC") Reports with an "approved" grade must be delivered for all high definition masters

9. Errors and Omissions policy maintained by Licensor for five (5) years

10. Complete chain of title comprising the following:

    a. copies of copyright registration certificate filed with the U.S. Copyright office with respect to the screenplay and the motion picture;

    b. copies of a Copyright Report (including opinion) and a Title Report (including opinion);

    c. a complete statement of all screen and advertising credit obligations;

    d. a statement of any restrictions as to the dubbing of the voice of any player, including dubbing dialogue in a language other than the language in which the Show was recorded;

    e. copies of all licenses, including, but not limited to: fully-executed master use and synchronization /performance music licenses; contracts; assignments and/or other written permissions from the proper parties in interest permitting the use of any musical, literary, dramatic and other material of whatever nature used in the production of the Show;

    f. copies of all agreements or other documents relating to the engagement of personnel in connection with the Show including those for individual producer(s), the director, all artists, music composer(s) and conductor(s), technicians and administrative staff;

    g.   Final shooting script

    h.   Chain of Title Opinion

11.   Certificate of Origin

12.   The dialogue continuity script

13.   Music cue sheet

Once you have completed delivery, your distributor will need to make copies of your film for the theatrical release, foreign markets, and DVD distribution. In order to do this, the distributor needs your permission to do so. The letter of permission is called a lab access letter. A typical example follows.

LABORATORY ACCESS LETTER

[DATE]

[NAME OF LAB]

[ADDRESS]

Re: "_____" (the "Picture")

To Whom It May Concern:

1.   *PICTURE/TERM/TERRITORY*: The undersigned, [FILMMAKER] hereby notifies you that it has transferred all right, title and interest in and to the Picture (including, without limitation all film and sound elements currently in your possession) to _____ ("Distributor"), and further that Distributor has the unfettered right to manufacture, market, distribute, exhibit and otherwise exploit the Picture for a Distribution term in perpetuity, (the "Term") for the territory of the Universe (the

"Territory"), subject to the terms of the Distribution Agreement dated as of _____, 20__ between the parties, whose terms are of no concern to you.

2.   *MATERIALS*: Laboratory confirms that the material as set forth on the attached Annex I (the "Material") is satisfactory for the manufacture of first-class technical quality prints, video masters, network broadcast quality standard masters and duplicate pre-print material. During the entire period of said license, the Material shall remain in Laboratory's possession and under Laboratory's control at its facility located at the above address and shall not be removed from the facility located at the above address without the express written consent of Distributor. Upon notice in writing from Distributor to the Laboratory of its intention to remove any of the Material on Annex I, the Material shall be sent as designated by Distributor.

3.   *DISTRIBUTOR'S ORDERS*: This will authorize, direct and instruct Laboratory to fill all orders of Distributor or Distributor's Designees at any time during the Term for duplicate material or positive prints of the Picture as Distributor or Distributor's Designees shall request at the sole cost and expense of Distributor or Distributor's Designees.

> **HINT: It is very important for you to be sure the lab can't come after you for a bill that is owed by the distributor. Also, be sure your agreement with the lab (which you sign when you first start doing business with them) does not allow the lab to hold your materials hostage should your distributor default.**

4.   *NO CLAIM*: Notwithstanding any claim or lien which Laboratory may now or hereafter assert against Stressbox, Inc. or others with respect to the Picture or any of the Material, Laboratory agrees that it shall not, by asserting or enforcing any claim or lien, refuse to accept or perform any requests placed by Distributor or Distributor's Designees as hereby provided.

5.   *IRREVOCABILITY*: The instructions, authorizations and directions herein contained in favor of Distributor are being relied on by Distributor and are coupled with an interest and may not be revoked, rescinded or in any way modified without the written consent of Distributor.

6.   *FACILITY ACKNOWLEDGMENT*: By signing in the space provided below, Laboratory agrees that it will fill all orders from Distributor or Distributor's Designees, as the case may be, in accordance with the authority granted herein

without regard to any liability or obligation of Licensor or any third party and Laboratory agrees to be bound by the foregoing instructions and directions.

By signing in the spaces provided below, the signatories agree to all of the terms and conditions herein set forth.

Very truly yours,

By: _____

Title: _____

Date: _____

ACKNOWLEDGED AND AGREED TO:

[NAME OF LAB]   [DISTRIBUTOR]

By: _____   By: _____

Title: _____   Title: _____

Date: _____   Date: _____

Well, that's it. Congratulations on making it through! You're probably saying what a lifesaver this book was to you, and that you couldn't have made your film without it by your side. (Ah, we're touched.) We just hope that your production team benefited from this and that you now have a cleared film with agreements that will last.

Index

A

accounting paragraph, 13, 25, 32, 35, 98, 112
actors agreement, 105–115
advance, 173
advertisement credits, 108
all-rights deal, 158–159
American Federation of Television and Radio Artists, 82–83
ampersand, 42
and, ampersand vs, 42
answer print, 89
"applicable," in options, 5
approvals, 174
arbitration, 12, 24, 35, 44, 55, 72, 97, 104, 112, 121, 131, 138, 143, 179
articles of organization, 61
assignment, 38
at-will, 125, 127
audit provision, 44
author, optioning and, 3, 28

B

"back-end points," 108
bank financing, 79
basing film on existing property, 2–15
"below-the-line" personnel, 123
bonuses, 8, 32, 90
booker, for theatrical release, 163

box office bonuses, 90
business entity formation, 60–77
business plan, 74

C

capitalization, 65
casting director, 100–104
casting services agreement, 101–104
chain-of-title issues, 82, 182
characters, optioning and, 6
collaboration agreement, 39–45
comic books, 6
composers, 115–123
conditions precedent, 87
consideration, 38
contingent compensation, 7, 32, 50, 56, 108
Coogan Account, 115
copyright claimant, 190–191
copyright law, 1
copyright registration, 189–192
copyright report, 189
copyrights, of props and materials, 145–147
creative control, 92
credits, 67
    advertisement, 108
    director, 91
    music supervisor, 135

credits *(continued)*
　　names and, 40
　　optioning and, 32–33
crew deal memo, 125–133
crew selection, 81
crowds, 148

D

default, writer, 53
delivery
　　chain of title and, 182
　　completion of, 192–198
　　overview of, 187–188
　　schedule, 192–196
description of property, optioning and, 28
digital rights, 161–162
digital rights distributor, 162–163
director, 84–85
director's agreement, 85–100
director's credit, 91
distributor fee, 173
doing business as, 59
domestic distributor, 156
droit moral clause, 94

E

eCO portal, 189–190
effective date, of contract, 16, 27, 39, 46,
　　85, 101, 106, 116, 126, 133, 141
E&O insurance, 182–186
exclusivity, 48, 174
existing property, basing film on, 2–15
expenses, distribution, 177–178
extension of option, 4, 29

F

favored nations, 92
festivals, 91
fictitious names, 59–60
financing, 78–79
first negotiation right, optioning and, 10
fixed compensation, 89
foreign sales agent, 155–156
forms
　　Actor Services Agreement, 106–114
　　Casting Services Agreement,
　　　101–104
　　Collaboration Agreement, 39–45
　　Composer Agreement, 116–123
　　Crew Deal Memo, 126–133
　　Director's Agreement, 85–100

Individual Release, 151–152
Interview Release, 149–150
Life Story Rights Agreement, 16–26
Location Agreement, 141–144
Materials Release, 146–147
Music Supervisor Agreement,
　　133–140
Operating Agreement, 61–77
Option and Purchase Agreement,
　　2–15
Public Filming Notice, 148
Writer Agreement, 46–58
free options, 3, 28

G

guild residuals, 178

H

Hulu, 162

I

idle days, 127
indemnification clause, 131
individual release, 151–152
inducement clause, 100
injunction, 55
insurance, 111, 178–179, 182–186
International Alliance of Theatrical Stage
　　Employees, 125
investment premium, 66
investor credit, 67
investors, 78–79
I.O.U.S.A., 169–170
iTunes, 162

L

lab access letter, 196–198
last refusal right, optioning and, 10
law, copyright, 1
liability insurance, 111
life story, basing on, 15–26
limited liability company (LLC), 60
loan-outs, 85
locations, 138–144

M

marketing, 58
material releases, 145–147
materials list, 147
media definition, 172
Minimum Basic Agreement (MBA), 47

minors, contracts with, 115
moral rights, 94, 120
music, 116–123
music supervisors, 133–140

N

names, credits and, 40
National CineMedia, 169–170
negotiation tips, in distribution, 171–180
Netflix, 162
no injunction clause, 44, 121, 130, 137
    actor's agreement and, 111
    director's agreement and, 97
    life story rights agreement
        and, 24
    optioning and, 12
    script optioning and, 34
"non-applicable," in options, 5
no-obligation-to-produce
  clause, 97

O

"off the top," 43
one-night events, 168–169
One Six Right, 164–168
operating agreement, 61–77
option and purchase agreement, 2–15
oral contracts, 82

P

passion, optioning and, 3
"pay-or-play" clause, 107
premieres, 91
pre-sales, 78–79
price, optioning and, 7
producer's representative, 154–155
production insurance, 111
progress requirements, 30
props, 145–147
pro rata, 66
protection, copyright and, 1
publication, copyright and, 190
publication rights, optioning and, 10
public filming, 148
publicity restrictions, 94, 109
purchase price, optioning and, 31

R

Reitman, Ivan, 161
releases, 149–152
renewal of option, 5

representation and warrant, 128
reserved rights, optioning and, 10
residuals, 84
reuse fees, 84
revenue split, 173
"right coupled with an interest," 26, 37,
    41, 57, 99, 114, 123
royalties, music, 117
royalty deal, 173
"run of the show," 125, 127

S

salary, actor, 107
Screen Actors Guild, 82–83, 105
script clearance report, 186–189
script optioning, 27–37
script writing, 39–45
sequels
    life story rights agreement and, 22
    optioning and, 6
service agreements, 81–82
services clause, 127
servicing deal, 163–164
sole writing credit, 50
soundtrack, 116–123
source-material credit, 9
split-rights deal, 159–161

T

talent insurance, 111
tax incentives, 78
term clause, 127
term negotiations, 171–172
territory, 173
Terwilliger, Brian, 164–168
theatrical releases, 163–168
time of access, location and, 142
title report, 183–186
trademarks, locations and, 142
travel compensation, 127
Tyrnauer, Matt, 161

U

union, 82–83

V

Valentino: The Last Emperor, 161

W

waiver, in life story rights agreement, 21
"week-to-week," 125, 127

Winfrey, Oprah, 161
Work for Hire, 52
work-for-hire clause, 82, 94, 110, 120, 129, 136
working conditions, 83–84
writer agreement, 46–58
writer's credit, 51
Writers Guild of America, 1, 33

writing
 hiring someone for, 46–58
 of script, 39–45
written releases, 149–152

Y

YouTube, 162

About the Authors

Over thirty years ago, entertainment attorney Michael C. Donaldson founded his Beverly Hills-based law firm with the purpose of lending a voice to independent filmmakers. In 2008, entertainment attorney Lisa A. Callif became a named partner. Donaldson + Callif specializes in representing independent filmmakers in all aspects of filmmaking including financing, production, and distribution. Additionally, Donaldson + Callif is now known as the industry's go-to firm for fair use and other clearance-related issues. Their mission is to help filmmakers tell their stories, their way.

In addition to representing such world-class filmmakers as Oliver Stone, Davis Guggenheim, and Lawrence Bender, Donaldson + Callif represent an array of Sundance-chosen films, Oscar and Independent Spirit Awards-nominated films, and such stalwart organizations as Film Independent and the Writers Guild Foundation.

Donaldson + Callif also works hard in the pro bono arena and is renowned in the industry for winning a ruling with the United States Copyright Office providing documentary filmmakers with an exemption from the Digital Millennium Copyright Act provisions that criminalize the act of ripping material from DVDs, for noninfringing use in their films. Donaldson + Callif filed a brief for the independent film community to protect the Reporters' Privilege by supporting filmmaker Joe Berlinger in his battle with Chevron in connection with his film *Crude*. And Donaldson + Callif arranged independent filmmaker support for the amicus brief filed in the Supreme Court's *United States v. Stevens*, the result of which was a ruling in favor of free-speech protections guaranteed by the First Amendment to the United States Constitution.

» MICHAEL DONALDSON

When Michael Donaldson was President of the International Documentary Association, he organized a coalition to successfully fight the migration of credits from the cable television screen to the Internet. He has organized Amicus Briefs in three different, successful federal cases on behalf of individual filmmakers who were under attack and helped draft the Orphan Works bill. In 2007 and 2008, Michael negotiated the first riders to E&O Insurance policies that explicitly covered material used by filmmakers pursuant to the fair use doctrine of the U.S. Copyright Act. Michael also helped author the *Statement of Best Practices in Fair Use by Documentary Filmmakers*, a similar Statement for Online Videos, and yet another for Dance Archives. He serves on the advisory committee of the Stanford Fair Use Project. All of these tasks were performed on a pro bono basis.

Michael has authored five other books, which collectively have garnered three national book awards, have been translated into 11 languages, and have sold over a quarter million copies. In addition to his thriving law practice and writing career, Michael maintains a steady schedule of international teaching and speaking. His *Clearance and Copyright* is used in over 50 film schools around the country.

Michael is an award-winning photographer, is a world-wide hiker, and won gold medals in the 1996 and 1998 Senior Olympics in gymnastics. He lives in Santa Monica with his partner, Tim Kittleson.

OTHER BOOKS BY MICHAEL DONALDSON
Introduction to Conversations with Michael Landon
Do-it-yourself Copyright and Trademarks
Negotiating for Dummies, 2d Edition
Clearance and Copyright, 3d Edition
Fearless Negotiating
Thriving in the Work Place (Contributor)
Movies: The Ultimate Insider's Guide (Contributor)

»LISA CALLIF

Lisa Callif is an entertainment attorney whose primary focus is on representing independent filmmakers in all aspects of their moviemaking. As part of her practice, Lisa does a significant amount of clearance work for documentaries, including rendering fair use opinion letters, which permit her clients to use limited amounts of unlicensed material in their films under the fair use doctrine as codified in U.S. Copyright Law.

After graduating summa cum laude from New York University with a BS in Communications, Lisa worked extensively in the music industry in New York and Los Angeles before enrolling in the Southwestern University School of Law. At Southwestern, Lisa received her J.D., made the Dean's List, participated on the moot court team—where she placed first in both writing and oral advocacy in a national competition—and was a Lead Articles Editor on Southwestern's *Law Review*. Additionally while in law school, Lisa wrote an article about online distribution of motion pictures, which was published by Hastings' *Communications and Entertainment Law Journal*. After law school, Lisa spent four years at Proskauer Rose in the Litigation Department where she practiced general civil litigation, including entertainment matters.

Lisa is currently an adjunct professor at Southwestern University School of Law and a frequent speaker on panels sponsored by Film Independent, American Pavilion and UCLA.

She lives in Los Angeles with her husband, Dustin, and their son, Diggy.